Jesse L. Lasky, Jr., the son of the famous
California film pioneer, was born on Broadway,
grew up with Hollywood, was educated in
Princeton and Dijon, France, and served for three
and a half years in the Pacific during the Second
World War under General MacArthur. At
seventeen he achieved success as a poet, and then
went on to write four novels, over fifty film
scripts in the film capitals of the world, including
being a screenwriter on eight Cecil B. De Mille
epics such as *The Ten Commandments* and *Samson
and Delilah*. More recently he has written the
amusing and affectionate memoir *Whatever
Happened to Hollywood?*

Pat Silver was born in Seattle, Washington and
studied Theatre Arts at University of Washington,
Stanford University and Reed College. As Barbara
Hayden, she attended acting classes with Marilyn
Monroe at 20th Century-Fox, toured with a
Shakespearian company, and co-wrote/produced/
directed and acted in *Mabel's Fables*, which
received an Emmy nomination. She has co-
authored seven films and over one hundred TV
scripts, including two for the award-winning
Explorer series for the BBC.

The Laskys have made their home in London since
1962.

JESSE LASKY, JR. and PAT SILVER

Love Scene

**The story of Laurence Olivier
and Vivien Leigh**

SPHERE BOOKS LIMITED
30/32 Gray's Inn Road, London WC1X 8JL

First published in Great Britain by
Angus & Robertson (UK) Ltd, 1978
Copyright © Jesse L. Lasky, Jr. and Pat Silver 1978
Published by Sphere Books Ltd, 1980

Set in Monotype Garamond

Printed in Great Britain by
William Collins Sons & Co Ltd
Glasgow

To Felix Barker, author of *The Oliviers*
published in 1953,
with grateful thanks for his help,
and to David Fairweather
for his constant guidance.

Acknowledgements

Among the many who helped by sharing their personal recollections, we wish to thank: Sunny Alexander (Lash); Irving Asher; Renée Asherson; Edward Ashley; Sir Michael Balcon; Felix Barker; Paul Bretow; George H. Brown; Charles Castle; George Cukor; Bumble Dawson; Basil Dean; Kay and Roy Dotrice; Commander John Dykes (formerly Fleet Air Arm); the Honourable Honor Earl; Douglas Fairbanks, Jr; David Fairweather; Trader Faulkner; José Ferrer; Lee Garmes; Greer Garson; Stanley Hall; Radie Harris; Olivia de Havilland; Richard Huggett; Robert Jorgensen; Wright King; Kay Kyser; Toni Landi; Mervyn Le Roy; Wolf Mankowitz; John (Jack) Merivale; Lady Alexandra Metcalf; Steven Pallos; Aage Sørensen; and Al Weingand. We also thank a number of others, who ask that their names should not be mentioned, and those who helped with the research in Hollywood, New York, and London: Betty Lasley, Bernice Stone, and Marek Kanievska.

Contents

Preface

Love Scene draws on many sources of unpublished and published material from books, magazines and newspapers, and personal interviews with friends, co-workers, and associates of Olivier and Leigh.

Dialogue has not been invented – but is recorded as recalled by those who heard it.

This book has been formed out of admiration and gratitude for the gifts and the art of Laurence Olivier and Vivien Leigh – together, and separately – during the quarter of a century that their lives touched. In the world of theatre and film, such immortals illuminate the journey of lesser folk. There can be no portrait without shadows, no endurance without pain. But, finally, the giver is measured by the gift.

J.L.L. and P.S

Time is a cruel taskmaster; it flays with a whip of years. At last, it steals the thunder of the heart. Memories outlive everything, coloured and shaped by the mind's eye of each beholder. In this is the magic – and the mystery.

Actors and actresses are the least likely to be seen in any true light even by themselves. They are the multi-layered projections of a hundred concepts. Each role adds another mask. Sometimes it sticks to the face. The actor struggles to tear it free, replace it with another, but always some layer of the one beneath remains, imprints a texture of feelings; and always the roles keep changing. Another illusion, as though a painter had overpainted – over and over – but always something of the underpainting shows through. Gradually true identity is blurred in the minds of his audience, and in his own mind. He becomes the reflection of many images. And even his closest friends, who burn the incense of affection before the icon, can scarcely see the man.

I *First curtain calls*

When Laurence Olivier and Vivien Leigh went to Denmark to play in the Old Vic production of *Hamlet* at Elsinore in the summer of 1937, he was thirty and she twenty-three, and they were in love.

They were also married to two other people. To add to their dilemma, their marriages could not be called unhappy, their mates inconsiderate or unloving, and each had a young child, Olivier's scarcely a month old.

It had all begun like this: the actress had first seen the actor posturing joyously in the 1934 production of *Theatre Royal* (called *The Royal Family* on Broadway). This splendidly entertaining satire was based on the lifestyle of America's leading theatrical family, the Barrymores, with Olivier portraying John. His own bounding vitality blended with every flamboyant moustache twitch of Barrymore-recalled, for he had met 'the great profile' in Hollywood. Olivier charmed the critics into rave notices and won the unqualified admiration of every woman in the audience – including a fledgling actress newly married to a successful young lawyer, Leigh Holman. She had been to see him three times as the dashing Tony Cavendish – and was to see him fourteen times as Hamlet. To her, he brought a breath of vitality which made her know – she was to tell a friend years later – that the theatre was the world to which she must belong.

Olivier was already a star. He had played over forty roles on the stage and enough films to know that he hated the movies. He was considered a thinking actor, one for whom his profession already had a profound respect. But that didn't diminish his romantic image, burnished by his role as Victor Prynne in the 1930–1 productions of *Private Lives*, which he played in London and New York.

Olivier got his first glimpse of Vivien Leigh the following year, in a play called *The Mask of Virtue*. The play's greatest virtue seems to have been Vivien herself. Those who saw her never forgot the impact of exquisite fragility and vivacity. She filled the stage with a beauty that stunned the mind.

The two did not meet until some time later. She was dining with a theatre friend, John Buckmaster, at the Savoy Grill in London. Olivier and his wife, the actress Jill Esmond, were at a nearby table. Buckmaster, son of Gladys Cooper, knew everyone in the theatre, it seemed. To the career-minded Vivien it was all very intriguing that her idol returned Buckmaster's wave. Over a lobster Newburg and a glass of Les Forêts '34 they discussed the fact that Olivier had shaved his Tony Cavendish moustache.

'What an odd little thing Larry looks without it,' observed Buckmaster disparagingly.

'Not in the least, Johnny!' Vivien protested. She wore the hint of a French hat perched low on her forehead, and all eyes in the room were on her and she knew it and was glad. She could feel Olivier's glance and of course she found him madly attractive. 'With or without a moustache,' she insisted to Buckmaster.

Awaiting their taxis in the Savoy lobby, it was all easy friendliness in the theatrical tradition of everyone half knowing everyone anyway; the jolly-go-lightly world of the stage where virtual strangers are instant 'darlings' and everyone exudes extravagant promises of lunch or to see each other or to ring each other up. Invitations were exchanged. Perhaps she and Mr Holman would come and visit Dower House? At Burchett's Green, near Maidenhead, where he and Jill were living at the moment.

Buckmaster observed the meeting between Larry and Vivien as one who had engineered a minor amusing conversation piece. Not worth dining out on, but perhaps a drink at the Ivy.

Laurence Olivier had made his entrance on the stage of the world in 1907 – the year the Plaza Hotel was built in New York, and Elinor Glyn was banned in Boston. On the morning of 22 May, Agnes Crookenden Olivier presented her third child to her husband. Gerard Kerr Olivier, High Anglican churchman, named his son for his earliest known ancestor, a sixteenth-century French Huguenot, Laurent Olivier.

Gerard, now in his late thirties, had outgrown the agnostic rebellions of his college days, and had left a position of schoolmaster with a comfortable income because he had 'heard the call'. He had taken Holy Orders and almost inevitable poverty as a way of life. For two centuries there had always been an Olivier in the church. Laurence grew up in penury, flavoured with fire and brimstone, ritual and dramatic eloquence, for Gerard's sermons were vividly dramatic. He had a taste for singing and theatricals, and attacked his Low Church parishioners with such zealous dedication that the bishop received complaints of popery. Father Olivier, as the clergyman preferred to be called, had taken to wearing cassock and black shovel hat, and to burning incense. He was promptly sacked.

Agnes and her small brood found life with Gerard not only threadbare but peripatetic. The vicissitudes of parish-hopping led from a red-brick semi-detached in Dorking (where they could envy the affluence of their chimney-sweep neighbour) to the slums of Notting Hill in London. Again Gerard was cast adrift, but finally came to anchor as assistant at St Saviour's in London's Pimlico district.

By now, the son of this pious Ulysses had learned to entertain himself, since he had little chance of making friends. Draped in an eiderdown, young Larry emulated his father, conducting his own services in 'Laurence's shrine'. Noting his son's flair for drama, Gerard built him

3

a play stage when he was seven.

Larry's Uncle Sydney had escaped the family vocation to become Governor of Jamaica and Lord Olivier. More important to his stagestruck nephew, he had known George Bernard Shaw. When the lad asked if Uncle Sydney went often to the theatre, the answer was a thundering no! 'I prefer the cinema. Makes less tax on the intelligence!'

The boy's formal education began at the Francis Holland Church of England School for Girls. But perhaps he would never have become an actor at all if he had not moved on to All Saints School, Margaret Street, London. At this formidable citadel of education and Christian participation in the arts, Geoffrey Heald ruled the Choir School productions, which always drew an impressive theatrical audience. Larry got his first rave notice there at ten, in a production of *Julius Caesar*.

'My dear man, your son *is* Brutus!' the great Forbes-Robertson told Gerard. And Ellen Terry announced, 'The boy who plays Brutus is *already* a great actor!'

On being told the remark, young Master Olivier enquired, 'Who is Ellen Terry?'

Ellen Terry, now an Olivier fan if he was not yet hers, saw his final performance at All Saints as Katharina in *The Taming of the Shrew*. On this occasion she remarked that she had never seen Kate played better by a woman, except for Ada Rehan. Sybil Thorndike, watching this performance, thought him 'the best Katharina I ever saw'. She was to remember him later and offer him a helping hand into repertory, the training ground for British actors. He also appeared as Maria in *Twelfth Night*.

The curtain was lowered on his childhood by the tragic death of Agnes when Larry was thirteen. With his mother gone, the heart seemed to have gone out of their home. The heart, but not the poverty. Even at sixteen, Larry was forced to share his father's bathwater to save on heating. That year, brother Dickie left for India to work on a rubber plantation. Larry's greatest dream was to follow Dickie and become a tea planter.

When he voiced this desire to Gerard, the elder Olivier was visited by a flash of prophecy: 'You're talking nonsense,' he proclaimed. 'You're going to be an actor!'

Before she met Laurence Olivier, Vivien's climb to fame had scarcely reached filmdom's foothills. She and Leigh Holman enjoyed a happy marriage, and if his pretty wife wanted a career, he had no objections. He admired her for staying on at the Royal Academy of Dramatic Art almost to the moment their daughter Suzanne was born. And even the child caused little disruption, with Leigh able to provide nurse and maid in their cosy Queen Anne house at No. 6 Little Stanhope Street.

Of course, her pursuit of a career had grated at times. Little annoyances, like letting the chance of 'crowd work' in a film interrupt a yachting holiday. Some of his yachting companions had found it curious, to say the least, when Leigh turned up alone. But on his return an elated Vivien gave him the news: she'd pushed her way out of the crowd at a guinea (at that time roughly five dollars) a day and into a speaking part. In *Things Are Looking Up* (1934), things were, though she admitted it was no more than a single line. But she told him how the director, Albert De Courville, thought her face photogenic. Worth a good thirty shillings (about $7.50) a day on the screen. Not for the world would Leigh have complained about the constant invasion of their lives by her career until the time when she might decide to give it up of her own accord.

Still, he had not taken it seriously until a cocktail-party contact with a young theatrical agent, John Gliddon, who happened to be a friend of a friend. Gliddon took the fledgling actress under exclusive management, and liked everything about her but her name, which was at that time Vivien Hartley. To her horror and amusement, he even suggested calling her April Morn. She had laughed at Gliddon from beneath a great circular hat that flattered a face requiring no flattery. She told him she was rather attached to Vivian, since it had always been attached to her.

5

She suggested perhaps using her married name, Holman, but to him it sounded more suitable for a mustard. He saw her more as a symphony of spring, he announced with half-closed eyes. In the end they settled on her husband's first name, and as such Vivian Leigh was christened by John Gliddon. (The spelling would be changed later.) Perhaps in that way she would always carry a part of her marriage with her. And perhaps their names would appear together in lights.

She had known almost from the beginning that she had it in her to succeed. But if she did not reach the top she had no intention of languishing on the slopes or joining those queues of fading actresses she had seen haunting auditions.

Entrances and exits . . . Vivien's first entrance had been in India, footstool of an empire where polished British boots rested so profitably and so comfortably – Kipling's India of tea, elephants, maharajas, cobras, dust, polo, parasols, and fakirs. When the summer months lowered the heat like a coffin lid on the teeming population, the Hartley family took to the hills. Ernest Hartley, her father, was an English exchange broker in Calcutta. Vivien was born on 5 November 1913, in a bungalow outside Darjeeling, with Everest looming like a great white ghost above the horizon. Not a bad year for an entrance, really. There were war mutterings in Europe, of course. But something else was born that same year: Hollywood's first feature-length film, *The Squaw Man*, produced by my father, Jesse L. Lasky. It was to be the beginning of an industry that would vitally affect the lives of Laurence Olivier and Vivien Mary Hartley Holman Leigh.

Vivian Leigh. So much for a name. It was the face that Gliddon was betting on. It turned heads at the Ivy, distracted directors from their potted shrimp at the Moulin d'Or. And Gliddon knew how to move his new client around all the right people. It was a practice as old as show business – parading the glossy horseflesh before the race to elicit bets. In restaurants or studio commissaries, at first nights or theatrical parties. Introductions always by chance, never seeming premeditated or opportunistic. The art of agentry, practised by an artful pro.

'May I present Miss Leigh? Perhaps you saw her recent film for Gainsborough?' (Forget the fact that it was only one line!) 'As the Americans say, she's going places. Where? Up for a lead, actually, at British and Dominions. Of course she'd be glad to come in and discuss the part . . .'

It worked. Nothing stupendous at first, but a part. A lead, even though it was in a miserable potboiler, called *The Village Square*, one of those 'quota' films that shored up the British industry against the Hollywood dollar invasion. Vivien had been given the lead in it – one week at five guineas a day. This was followed by another of the same ilk. And then, because an actor in the first film remembered her, she was offered a part in a tryout of a play at Kew. If *The Green Sash* failed to make theatrical history, it brought Vivien's first important press notice from Charles Morgan in *The Times*: 'Her acting had precision and lightness, if the material lacked substance.'

And before the end of the one-week run, in 1935, Gliddon had a call from Associated Talking Pictures at Ealing. It moved Vivien into higher echelons and gave her a chance to play comedy with the popular Gracie Fields in *Look Up and Laugh*.

On more than one occasion, the seasoned Gracie helped the neophyte actress to bear up under the terrible tongue-lashings of British film tycoon, Basil Dean, which had been known to shake even such unflappable stalwarts as Laurence Olivier. But when the time came to pick up Miss Leigh's option, Dean had a look at his property in the hard glare of the projection room. Vivien Leigh was out.

Leigh Holman was full of consolation. Vivien consoled herself that renewal at Ealing Studios would only have meant one low-budget comedy after another in parts that would never bring her any real distinction. And the Holmans hardly needed the meagre addition to the family income. Leigh Holman was doing very well, while Vivien's salary scarcely paid for the nanny. John Gliddon was quick to agree that it was for the best. Basil Dean had a reputation for having a bark which really was as bad as his bite. This was one of his few theatrical errors.

Shortly afterwards, Vivien had a phone call from Gliddon. He had managed to arrange an audition with Sidney Carroll, the West End manager, who was casting a new play that was going into the Ambassadors Theatre. She was to be in the producer's office at ten the following morning.

After her first reading on a bare stage, Sidney Carroll called her over and said, 'First rehearsal is next Tuesday at the Phoenix.'

There was no one more surprised than Vivien.

January, 1936. Laurence Olivier, rising popular star of the London stage and screen, had been appearing in the New Theatre production of *Romeo and Juliet*, alternating the roles of Romeo and Mercutio with John Gielgud – a fascinating challenge, since Gielgud, doubtless the most praised Shakespearian actor at the time possessed a style totally different from Olivier's.

Gielgud's first concern was the poetry, which resulted in a lyrical, almost singing performance. Olivier's interest was already pointed towards a cerebral yet extremely physical characterisation. He achieved a convincing realism: his Verona youth swaggered through a hot, dusty Italian summer, torrid enough to give the audience a prickly-heat rash. Ralph Richardson, his good friend and constant counsellor, had contributed useful hints about the playing of Mercutio, gleaned from his own tour with Katharine Cornell and Maurice Evans in the States.

Most critics were shocked by Olivier's 'irreverence' to the Bard. A 'ranting and roaring Romeo', one complained. Another affirmed his blank verse 'the blankest I ever heard'. He played it as though he were 'riding a motor bike'.

Shaken by these attacks, Olivier offered his resignation to producer Bronson Albery. It was promptly rejected.

Olivier's concept was ahead of its time, but none the less it did find admiration and support from a few notable quarters. The drama critic on *The Observer* daringly observed: 'I do not think I ever wish to see this play again, lest my memory of Olivier be dimmed.' Richardson had said to Gielgud, 'He just stands against the balcony with such an extraordinary pose that this animal magnetism and vitality and passion come right over.'

Gielgud later generously recalled, 'I was very busy enunciating all the poetry very beautifully but I was very cold aesthetically compared with him.' Margaret Webster wrote: 'Very dear Larry, never mind the critics – what do they know about it? I found your Romeo full of passion, sincerity, and beauty.'

But the highest praise of all came from a director at the Old Vic, who courted the young actor with 'This is fan mail! I have been deeply thrilled and moved . . . Your performance had such terrific vitality – speed, intelligence, and gusto, and muscularity – and you got a lyric quality pictorially if not musically.' The letter was signed Tyrone Guthrie, and the part he was to play in Larry's life turned out to be Cupid, although he did not know it.

The actor was certain of one thing: he didn't want to waste any more time in films. But he had been made an offer he couldn't refuse. Although he disapproved heartily of Shakespeare on the screen, he couldn't say no to the chance of working with the great Austrian actress Elisabeth Bergner. Her husband, Paul Czinner, was to produce and direct *As You Like It*.

'No one can play with Bergner without learning something from her. It's a big chance for me to play with her,' he told his friend Ralph Richardson.

Richardson's comment was laconic, as always. Olivier would have the 'artistic satisfaction' of six hundred pounds (then about three thousand dollars) a week.

Though Olivier had been excited at the prospect of working with Miss Bergner, he barely saw her. His shooting schedule brought him to the set at dawn, where he also had two professional wrestlers training him for Orlando's bout. Bergner customarily arrived in the afternoon. Czinner absorbed this inconvenience by shooting Orlando's close-ups reacting to an invisible Rosalind. Felix Barker quotes the unruffled director as suggesting to Olivier that he had 'better look from side to side because Miss Bergner will probably be walking all around you when she speaks'.

Olivier was incensed. The screen, the silver screen that blew up one's faults to giant size, chopped a performance into tidbits. Just when you're soaring, somebody yells 'Cut!' The whims of directors and panderings to stars! No, however lucrative the movies might be, he'd have as little as possible to do with them ever again.

But fate, of course, had other plans, and fate had a Hungarian name – Sándor László Kellner, who was to change great lives and influence mighty people as Alexander Korda. In him were blended the tycoon-conquistador and the sensitive artist, the promoter's deadly charisma and the dreamer's vulnerability. One cannot over-estimate the importance of Korda in the lives of Olivier and Leigh. He was the spirit who brought about the magic of their professional association and personal attachment; they were never closer to anyone than to this genial genius.

By 1936, Korda was fully established in his own private Babylon, Denham Studios, which he had built with British investment and Hungarian charm. He had begun building Denham in the summer of 1935. It boasted the best-equipped studios in Europe, with buildings covering twenty-eight of its one hundred and sixty-five acres, and included a mile and a half of river, gardens, woodlands, and meadows, which could adapt to almost any exterior filming. There were seven large sound stages, four of them air-conditioned. Here could be re-created anything the imagination could conceive, and Korda was a man of unlimited imagination. His foreign legion of talent might concentrate as many as twenty different nationalities on a single film, resulting in some of the finest 'British' movies ever made.

Hollywood was impressed, and Korda played host to

visiting moguls. On the evening of 15 May 1935, he dined at the Savoy Grill with Joseph Schenck, of Fox, Murray Silverstone, head of United Artists in Britain, and the English film man Monty Banks (born Mario Bianchi, Italian comic-turned-director).

Korda no longer wore his Middle-European brush moustache; his oval face was set off with thin-rimmed glasses, framed by thick dark hair and prominent ears. He had already adopted the emblems of filmdom puissance and affluence, the wide-lapelled double-breasted blue flannel suit with neatly-folded pocket handkerchief covering three cigars. Later the producers planned to attend the opening night of *The Mask of Virtue*.

Since the birth of sound movies, British theatre had become a happy hunting ground for new talent, so of course the Americans wanted to go.

By the time they took their seats, the play was well into the first act. For the rest of the performance they scarcely stirred. That the play was less than distinguished didn't matter. Nothing did from the moment they saw Vivien Leigh, who projected that mysterious theatrical magnetism known as 'presence'. A black bow banded her slender throat above a wide white lace collar. No single feature detracted from the whole, the perfection of that Dresden-china face.

The final curtain triggered wild applause and even shouts of 'Bravo!' for an unknown actress in her first leading role. Schenck looked at Korda, Korda looked at Banks, Banks looked at Silverstone, Silverstone looked back at Schenck.

Schenck had to admit the kid had something.

'A face,' deprecated Korda.

Silverstone allowed blandly that he might find something for her since they didn't want her.

'Who said I didn't want her?' Korda protested.

Walking up the aisle by now, through an audience that seemed reluctant to go home, Korda considered that maybe he could use her with Laughton in *Cyrano*. Who'd notice if she couldn't act? Besides, he was not about to allow these

Americans to take anything away from him, even if he didn't want it. But had there been any possibility of double-crossing their Anglo-Hungarian host, the others would cheerfully have done so. These giants had not come to power by Boy Scout deeds and gentlemen's honour.

Vivien's dresser opened the door to reveal the diminutive actress – still in black velvet costume, dark hair in tight ringlets – against a backdrop of a profusion of delphinium and white stock amidst the roses. Two rows of telegrams studded the mirror, including one from Holman. In a sense it was his first night, too. He stood in the background of Vivien's dressing-room and her career. Leigh Holman belonged to an England that still remembered when gentlemen and officers married actresses at the risk of their own careers.

The film men entered, wreathed in self-importance and cigar smoke. Korda introduced the others and himself. They may have expected a flutter of truckling deference, but the young actress faced them with a poise that combined vulnerability with a slightly imperious quality.

Korda was first at the post with his offer of a contract, reminding her that his London Films was second to none.

'In England,' allowed Schenck, with a fleshy crocodile smile.

Korda invited the actress to his office in the morning. She replied that, although flattered by his interest, she'd have to discuss it with her agent, John Gliddon. And, of course, her husband, who happened to be a lawyer. She further made it clear that in no case would she be interested in a long-term contract that would keep her away from the stage. She sensibly avoided mentioning that she had just been dropped by Korda's rival, Basil Dean.

No lamb to the slaughter, this innocent. The wise men looked at each other and sipped champagne. They couldn't help noticing that Vivien's beauty had even more impact close up.

Sidney Carroll, the producer and theatrical critic, burst

into the dressing-room to congratulate his protégée. (It was he who had convinced her to change the spelling of her name to Vivien, which he had announced was 'indisputably more feminine'.) His gambler's instinct in casting Vivien for the role of Henriette had paid off. Now he was full of praises – for her and for himself – and confident that she would be flooded with offers.

Vivien introduced him to her first offer. 'But perhaps after Mr Korda reads the reviews, he'll change his mind.' She smiled.

'Like Mr Carroll, I don't need reviews to know my mind,' replied Korda.

But if Korda should change his mind, Schenck suggested hastily, Miss Leigh could always reach him through Fox. 'Second to none in Hollywood!'

Such praises did not unbalance Vivien. Leigh, the Hartleys, and a few chosen friends celebrated with her, dining at the Savoy and dancing at the Florida. She refused to go home until she had read what the pundits had to say.

Dawn was silver-plating the City when she and Leigh took a taxi to Fleet Street. When they drove homeward, the taxi was loaded with morning papers fresh off the press and filled with the kind of notices that she could only hope Korda would see. Her performance seemed to have wiped out all other news that May morning:

NEW STAR TO WIN ALL LONDON
VIVIEN LEIGH SHINES IN NEW PLAY

There were plenty more of the same. But one critic, the illustrious James Agate, described her neck as a tulip, adding that 'some tulips have too long stems'. (Many years later, Vivien was to recall it as 'a remark that had me worrying about my neck for years when I should have been worrying about my acting'.)

It was no surprise to Vivien that the *Daily Telegraph* review was a rave. Sidney Carroll had written it himself. He proclaimed his discovery the sort of raw material from which would emerge the Bernhardts and the Duses of the future: 'It would seem grossly unfair that any one person should be blessed with all these merits I have enumerated, but it sometimes happens and when it does, fame comes in a night, and small wonder . . .' Carroll went on to congratulate himself for having given Miss Leigh the chance without seeing any press notices, photos, or relying on anything but his own judgement – plus a knowledge of palmistry. (In fact, he had actually read Vivien's palm and told her that her line of destiny was absolutely unique.)

They were coming true, all the things Vivien had imagined. And though she might doubt that Leigh possessed the precise qualities of a stage-door husband, she firmly believed at this moment that he and eighteen-month-old Suzanne would always come first in her life.

There was no extra sleep for Vivien the next morning. She knew that, despite all the praise, she still had a lot to overcome. It stuck in her mind that the director, Maxwell Wray, had not been happy with her during rehearsals. He had complained to Carroll and she had overheard much of it. Her voice was too light, her mannerisms maddening. Carroll, a shade overdefensive, flatly vetoed Wray's request to replace her, and had taken her off between rehearsals to coach her himself.

But on opening night Maxwell Wray had been the first back to her dressing-room, almost weeping in admiration. On stage, she had succeeded in overcoming his objections. Her hands (which she always considered too large) were kept busy at a harpsichord or fluttering in economic gestures, or clasped demurely. No fuzzy movements. No wasted motion. He freely admitted that he had seriously underestimated her capacity to learn. And she had learned: grace, repose, how to project her voice – although its improvement would take years of dedication. But Vivien Leigh would make certain that no one ever underestimated her again.

'You wouldn't believe it, Mr Korda. This morning I found

a stack of cables and telegrams a foot high. Absolutely everyone is after Vivien. Phone calls from Hollywood. Why, they're breaking down my door to sign her up!' John Gliddon faced the film-maker across Korda's spacious desk in his pale grey office.

Korda would have mentally pardoned such exaggeration. All film business was conducted in hyperbole, the normal language of Wardour Street, Burbank, or Culver City. 'Stupendous' meant acceptable, 'sensational' meant fair, 'rolling in the aisles' meant you're lucky to get a laugh, and 'breaking down a door' indicated mild interest.

Korda pointed out that Miss Leigh had seemed quite receptive to his offer in her dressing-room.

Gliddon pointed out that he hadn't actually made an offer. The showman waved a hand in gesture of unbridled generosity. So now he would make it: £750 (about $3,750) a year.

Gliddon forced a laugh. 'You have a sense of humour, sir.' He was careful not to take a position from which retreat would be impossible.

The £750 would represent only the first year, Korda assured him. If he picked up her option, the price would go up. Gliddon drew breath and countered. As keen as Vivien was to work with Korda, a man she admired more than any in the business, she could earn more than that in a month.

'I don't bargain, Mr Gliddon,' announced Korda crisply.

Gliddon let slip that the first two phone calls had been from Fox and United Artists.

'Schenck and Silverstone!' Korda exploded.

The agent demurred that he had not mentioned names. He kept to himself Vivien's description of the dressing-room visitation. To further convince the producer, Gliddon brought forth a sheaf of reviews. The gesture was no more than ritual. Each man knew that the other had read every review or they wouldn't be here talking. Gliddon suggested that a reasonable starting figure would be in the area of

£1,500, adding that he might have a difficult time persuading his client to accept such a sum after her rave notices. His attitude was that he was actually fighting for Korda.

Benevolently, Korda suggested a five-year contract.

Gliddon pointed out that Vivien wouldn't want to give up the stage for so long.

Korda raised his offer – £1,200, then about $6,000, up to £1,600 on options.

Gliddon countered – £1,300. with options to £18,000, and he would try to make her see the light. For that, Korda suggested, she should see the burning bush. But their hands met across the desk and they had a deal.

Korda watched the agent leave. If Vivien Leigh lived up to his expectations, he knew he had a bargain. And if she didn't – well, at least he had beaten Silverstone and Schenck.

The legal department of London Films drew up a standard contract: £1,300, with options for five years. The publicity department of London Films released the news: Alexander Korda had just signed Miss Vivien Leigh for £50,000!

Reading this figure in *Variety*, Schenck and Silverstone would have automatically cut it in half.

In May of 1936, Laurence Olivier had returned to his first love, the theatre, this time in the dual role of actor-manager in collaboration with Ralph Richardson. They were in partnership with the author of the play (the cheapest way to deal with authors). J. B. Priestley's *Bees on the Boat Deck* gave Olivier the chance to show off his customary athletic zest, swinging through the rigging like Douglas Fairbanks in *The Black Pirate*.

The summer had been unusually sunny for England, and matinée theatre business was suffering accordingly. On one particularly deserted matinée, Richardson noted that Olivier seemed to be playing to one box in the void, where Vivien Leigh could easily be spotted sitting with Ivor Novello.

Vivien and Novello paid their respects backstage, and

Larry invited Vivien to lunch.

It was their first meeting alone, though she and Leigh Holman had spent a weekend at Dower House with the Oliviers. But now it seemed suddenly important to know each other better. Perhaps it would have ended with lunch had not the failure of *Bees* forced Olivier to accept another film for Korda. What he could not foresee was that his luncheon guest would soon be kissing him before the cameras.

2 *Love theme, softly played*

'Mr Korda is unable to talk, Miss Leigh.' . . . 'Mr Korda is inaccessible.' . . .

'Mr Korda is in meetings with United Artists all week.' . . .

Vivien was properly indignant. Korda was paying her hundreds of pounds and she couldn't even get him on the telephone. The actress had repaired to the wailing wall of her agent's office in St John's Wood to shed a few tears of frustration. Gliddon assured her that Korda was every bit as busy as his secretaries always insisted. But Vivien was not to be consoled. Once the producer had her safely tucked away under that exclusive contract, he seemed to have forgotten she ever existed. Yet London Films had made five pictures without even testing her for one. Her eye caught a familiar publicity postcard stuck under the glass top of Gliddon's desk. When *Mask* had transferred to the St James's Theatre, Sidney Carroll had papered London with postcards of Vivien in a soft cream satin gypsy blouse, hair neatly curled, hands gracefully curved in her lap, eyes soulful. It was captioned: 'The Fame-in-a-Night Girl.' Fame in a night – oblivion in a year. Like some rare bloom the show didn't survive transplanting and closed in a fortnight.

Pacing Gliddon's office like a caged tigress, Vivien insisted she'd been better off before signing with Korda the invisible. Gliddon had news for her.

'Good news and bad. Which shall it be first?'

'The good. No, the bad,' she said.

'The bad is that Leslie Howard wants you to play Ophelia to his Hamlet on Broadway.'

She jumped up, instantly enthusiastic. 'You call that bad news?'

He nodded. 'Bad because Korda won't let you.'

Her white-gloved hand protested to heaven. Her contract clearly stated that she could play in the theatre! He reminded her that Korda had first call on her services. And he'd decided to test her for the role of the heroine, Roxane, in *Cyrano de Bergerac*, with Charles Laughton. This was certainly good news.

Gliddon broke it to her gently. It was only a test. And they wanted her to dye her hair blonde for it. He knew she considered her hair crinkly, and longed for straight hair.

Vivien exploded at the thought of bleach. If Korda wanted a blonde, let him hire Harlow!

It was not Korda who had decided Roxane should be blonde, Gliddon said. That was Laughton's idea.

Hadn't he ever heard of wigs? she enquired grandly. She would not do the test if she had to dye her hair and that was the end of it.

Gliddon sighed. He was familiar with this trace of imperiousness in his lovely client. Now she was telling him to cable Leslie Howard and say she would accept *Hamlet*. This, of course, he could not do. Besides, he insisted, she was being offered a chance for a really important part in a truly big film with a great star and she was letting it wash away for a bottle of bleach.

'It's my hair, and you can advise Cyrano to keep his nose out of it,' she announced.

The wig won out, as it would for almost every role Vivien was to play from then on, even though in the thirties wigs were all but unmentionable. Everyone was pleased with Vivien's test, and the role of Roxane might have projected her to stardom years ahead of *Gone With the Wind* if Laughton's putty nose had not jammed up the works.

'This project cannot breathe without the right nose, Alex,' Laughton complained to Korda. 'Cyrano *is* a nose. Everything hangs on it.'

What worried Laughton most was that the nose must look natural, part of his face. None of them had yet struck him as being '*le nez juste*'. Korda was getting bored with the problem, and as a final panacea to his star he imported a very short, bearded, Viennese plastic surgeon who appeared in his office, flanked by a sculptor and a make-up artist. The assignment was explained and the team retired to prepare designs. While Korda fumed, weeks dragged by – weeks of research and experiment, as one model after another was considered and discarded. At length the surgeon announced he was ready to present his master-piece.

For the momentous occasion, Korda invited the pro-duction designer, cameraman, art director, and publicity chief, and offered a round of cigars. The surgeon whisked a cloth off a huge silver tray. All leaned closer. Silence. There lay an eight-inch tubular object fashioned of putty.

'Well?' asked Laughton.

'Charles,' the producer replied, 'I think it looks like a big pink prick!'

What might have been the greatest of all Cyranos never reached the screen. Perhaps the public were the losers. For years afterwards, the back lot of Denham was littered with putty noses of every shape and description. They were occasionally referred to as the 'cocks of the walk'.

When Vivien learned of the cancellation of *Cyrano*, she fired off a frantic cable to Leslie Howard accepting the New York *Hamlet*. He cabled back that regrettably he had been unable to wait and had been forced to cast someone else.

After seven months, the gallop to stardom had landed her in the ditch. Not that Korda's contract had actually promised stardom. It had only promised certain terms of payment for which she was to perform certain obligations, the legality of which could be explained to her by her lawyer husband. The most important obligation was to do nothing until she heard from Korda – in effect, to be paid not to work! It was enough to bring on a flow of the profanity Vivien was learning to use – but even when she used a four-letter word it came out like moonlight and roses.

She and Leigh drove into the country to spend a quiet New Year's weekend together at the ancient Lygon Arms in Broadway, the heart of the Cotswolds. It had been Leigh's idea – to have her all to himself, for a change. They could reassess their lives together and lay plans for the future.

She glanced out the car window towards a bleak December landscape, deflowered by winter, snow-bleached, bare as the landscape of her heart. Leigh drove carefully, almost meticulously; he was a man who did everything well – nothing foolishly or poorly considered. Oh, she was lucky to have Leigh.

Her flow of profanity now had been provoked by thoughts of Korda. Her eyes, which could change colour like a storm-swept sky, darkened to deep violet. The two of them had been discussing the chance of her doing a play for Ivor Novello, *The Happy Hypocrite*; it was a part she would adore playing. But Korda had insisted he might need her in the spring, without saying what for. Maddening, filthy luck! She had a good mind to do it anyway, whether or not it violated her contract.

They arrived in ancient Broadway just as the snow began to clog the windscreen-wipers. When they had settled into their cosy room at the inn and ordered tea and cakes sent up, the Korda discussion continued. Even if he had a film for her, she wouldn't in the least mind filming by day and playing in the theatre at night. She scrawled a hasty note to Gliddon, telling him just that, and adding, 'It will be a wonderful experience and just what I want.' It didn't in the least worry her that she must combine these two careers with being mother and wife.

Vivien's world was being drawn more and more deeply into the orbit of Alex Korda. And Korda controlled a veritable universe. His charm and his influence on all his stars, including Olivier and Leigh, was almost as boundless as his power. Corpulent Charles Laughton once described him as 'a Hungarian who entered the film world armed with little more than his accent. I shouldn't want to be caught in a revolving door with him, but I'll make a film with him any day.' But now the ethnic jokes were over – Korda had become a naturalised British subject.

To produce his next epic, *Fire Over England*, Korda had chosen Erich Pommer, as German as Hohenzollern. Pommer had joined the swelling stream of talented refugees stoking the film foundries of England and Hollywood. Just the man to guide a film epic about England's greatest queen. And Korda had chosen an American director, William K. Howard, who had recently finished *The Power and the Glory* for my father.

But epics cost money, and Korda had been worried that his projected saga of Queen Bess might lack American box-office appeal. What Korda felt he needed was a visually powerful love-interest subplot – a girl who could create the proper romantic image playing opposite Laurence Olivier, who had agreed to take the part of Michael Ingoldsby, a swashbuckling officer in the Elizabethan navy.

Clemence Dane and Sergei Nolbandov were adapting the A. E. W. Mason novel, and nobody was happy, including them. The reality of the casting problem had been haunting Korda for weeks. Then he remembered the girl he'd put under contract the year before. Her agent had been bugging him to find something for her. And she had been pestering him to do a play, to which he had finally agreed. Perhaps, he thought, he'd better have another look at his property in the Ivor Novello play, whatever it was called. Oh, yes, *The Happy Hypocrite*.

'You recall that Hungarian gentleman who signed your prison sentence?'

'Are you going to spoil my lunch, John?' Vivien was toying with a salad at the studio commissary.

Why, Gliddon asked, did she think he had invited her to

lunch at Denham? Korda, he announced, had pardoned her. *Fire Over England* had finally managed to get script approval. Flora Robson was to play Queen Bess and Vivien had been set for the part of Cynthia, the Queen's lady-in-waiting.

The agent paused expectantly, but the actress said nothing. He went on to add that Cynthia was the romantic lead. Couldn't she even manage a tinge of effervescence?

But Vivien was not enthusiastic. Sidney Carroll had another play for her and, as John knew, her first love would always be the theatre.

Gliddon sighed. She had just laid Anne Boleyn to rest in an open-air Regent's Park production of *Henry VIII* for Sidney. Even her kindest critic said her voice was on the slight side for outdoor acting. And that, following the unhappy *Happy Hypocrite*, which laid a melon-sized egg! Gliddon felt his client should be grateful for Korda's largesse. Besides, Cynthia was a bloody good part.

However, her curiosity was piqued enough to ask who would be playing opposite her.

'You know him, actually. Very dashing. Larry Olivier.'

Did Gliddon note a slight twinge of excitement? Digging into his steak-and-kidney pie, he added that Korda thought they'd make fantastic lovers, and the film needed romantic interest to add a sugarplum to the historic pudding.

'Tell Mr Korda that I'll do the part,' she said rather grandly.

He didn't point out that contractually she had no choice, and the following week Vivien was back at Denham for costume fittings. Olivier was also in for fittings, and they crossed paths. The dark, magnetic eyes focused upon her. Vivien remarked that it would be very nice to be acting together.

'We shall probably end up by fighting. People always get sick of each other when making a film,' he replied.

Things happen in two ways in the world of theatre and films. There are the parts you want, scheme, and fight to get. And there are the opportunities that present themselves unexpectedly. Few actors have charted a self-made course. More often, chance, luck and timing are the arbiters. Sometimes the part you didn't want changes your future – or the one you wanted most matters least in the end. Olivier had been seduced into accepting this role by the temptress money. For the next fourteen weeks, Vivien became Olivier's temptress, on screen and off.

Commander Oswald Frewen noted in his diary, Monday, 31 August 1936: 'Returning to the Vivling's, and she came in with Laurence Olivier and an influenzal throat and chill . . .'* The ageing Commander, a first cousin of Sir Winston Churchill, was a loyal friend of the Holmans.

Leigh wouldn't have been concerned. The association with Larry could only be interpreted as congenial friendship, which would doubtless cool with the end of filming. The actor and actress would have been bubbling over with flamboyant accounts of the day's happenings and Leigh would be laughing his head off at instant impersonations of the people involved in whatever succession of nonsense had taken place without him.

At first, *Fire Over England* seemed merely to be the usual Tower of Babel collective indigenous to Korda enterprises: an American director and a German producer, to whom had been added the Chinese cameraman James Wong Howe, a White Russian costume designer, an Italian make-up man, and Canadian Raymond Massey playing the Spanish Philip. Among the few Englishmen was George H. Brown, serving as assisting director.

A film company is something more than the producer's calculated stratagem. It is a spawning ground of intense personal relationships. People who scarcely know each other, who wouldn't think of touching hands across a table, find themselves playing scenes of passionate emotions, being thrust daily into the most intimate physical and mental contact. Sometimes, as Olivier had observed, they begin to hate each other.

Actor Leslie Banks, playing the role of Leicester, was not

* Alan Dent, *Vivien Leigh: A Bouquet.*

the only person on that set who noticed the growing attachment between Olivier and Leigh. But screen lovers quite often develop brief crushes that come off with the make-up, wigs, and costumes. If they didn't, actors would be divorcing after every picture. Vivien and Larry were in each other's arms in front of the camera, sharing the emotional attitudes of their roles. They would rehearse in some quiet corner, or in her dressing-room. Nobody thought much of it at first. Nor apparently did they.

They fell into the habit of lunching alone, which is not usual in the crowded studio commissary. Compared to a Hollywood film factory, Denham was small, personal, excitingly creative. It offered quiet walks along its gentle river amid landscaped vistas. Larry and Vivien were thrown together in a hazy world merging fantasy and life.

One night she stayed to watch them film the burning of the Armada. A section of galleon deck had been constructed amid a forest of masts and rigging on the back lot. Somehow the word had got around and the area was now fringed with vicarious pyromaniacs waiting to see *Fire Over England* go up in flames. Flora Robson had stayed on, too.

After several takes, Bill Howard squinted through a finder, correcting details. Satisfied at last, he called 'Action!'

The actor's dark figure separated itself from the moon-streaked shadow on the wooden deck. A torch blazed aloft from his hand. He bounded across planks presoaked in petrol to ignite instantly, paused, glanced about, and hurled the firebrand in a blazing arc. ust ahead of the licking tongues of flame, he darted to the rail. With a mighty spring the actor vaulted headfirst into the 'sea' below (actually a concealed high-wire net stretched above the field). He bounced out of the net off camera, spray-drenched from the hoses now trained on the fire.

'Cut!' shouted Howard. 'Great, Larry!'

'Insane,' growled Erich Pommer. 'Why does that lunatic

always have to do his own stunts?'

'Try to talk him out of it,' George Brown said, laughing, and carried a coat to throw over the actor's shoulders. He was soaked through and shivering from the bite of dying winter in the air.

'Ah, grown a moustache, have you, Brownie? Might try one myself again, after this film,' the actor said.

'A touch of the Ronnie Colmans?' Brown suggested.

'For Christ's sake, Larry, from now on I insist you are using a double,' Pommer pleaded.

Flora Robson backed up Olivier: 'Larry would feel a fraud to be praised for a scene he didn't do himself.'

'All film acting is a fraud,' growled Pommer.

Vivien joined them, bringing steaming coffee. Their fingers touched around the warmth of the cup.

'Your hands are the freezingest, Larry,' she said. It was one of her pet solecisms.

Rumour had it that a butt of real mead had been secreted in the prop box. Someone went to ferret it out. Vivien and Larry walked away hand in hand.

Looking after them, Howard observed, 'Alex is very happy with those two in the rushes.'

The bulky little Chinese genius Jimmy Howe came over. He spoke to Howard in a low voice, forming a box with his thumbs touching, fingers up straight, the way cameramen do when they're discussing a shot. The director nodded, then called the actor back.

'We've got to do it again, Larry. This time let's make Erich happy and let the stunt man earn his money.'

Olivier threw off his coat, hoisting himself up to the section of deck against all protest.

'I should have had that fellow with me in 1916,' muttered Pommer. 'The Kaiser would have been in Buckingham Palace.'

Again the crew positioned hoses ready to extinguish the flames. With each take, the wooden deck was getting more dangerously dry, the fire more difficult to douse. Howard peered through his finder like a sharpshooter squinting along a rifle barrel. Jimmy Howe adjusted his focus. Too many takes devoured time and budget.

George Brown bellowed for silence at last. The actor took his position on the deck. Vivien watched with Flora Robson and Vivian Griffith, the hairdresser; she seemed nervous as the crew prepared for the take.

The clapper-board man stepped in to reveal his number to the camera. 'Take four,' he announced.

'Action!' said Bill Howard, chewing an empty pipe.

For the fourth time that night, Olivier bounded down the deck. Reaching his mark, he stopped and looked around in the simulated moonlight. As he let his firebrand fly this time, a clot of flame separated itself to land dangerously close. The deck flared to a blaze around his legs. He hurled himself through towards the rail as Howard shouted for the hoses. But the stream of water seemed to increase the flames. Larry sprang to clear the railing and his foot slipped. He sprawled across, falling headfirst into the net. Shaken but unhurt, the actor came over.

'Ingoldsby *en brochette*,' George Brown quipped, expressing the relief all felt.

'That wraps it for tonight,' Howard announced.

But Olivier was concerned that the shot had looked bad and wanted to try it again.

'Not tonight you don't, Master Ingoldsby. Nor never! From now on you are using a double and no arguments!' Doubles with broken necks Pommer could replace. It was, all agreed, a spectacular feat; but any encore would be an anticlimax.

The crowd began to drift away to their cars. Olivier would take his bruises home. Jill would be waiting. Lovely, competent, devoted Jill, about to give birth to their first child – a fact that hovered between Larry and Vivien like an invisible barrier.

One day, during one of those interminable waits between takes, Vivien was seated beside Larry, a crossword puzzle in her lap. She was wearing a dress with a stand-up lace collar that framed her long neck, bow earrings, and a

27

baroque pearl necklace. Her dress had a black panel coming to a point at the waist with a huge rose worked up the front of it to bloom at her bosom. Her face was angelic above it.

Olivier was committing to memory more ringing words than the screenwriters had provided him for *Fire*. For Tyrone Guthrie, who had not forgotten the actor's Romeo, had just persuaded him to play Hamlet for the Old Vic. The challenge of the role weighed heavily. Everyone was convinced he could play it except Larry himself.

Tamara Desni flounced past them, cornering Howard. She was playing the part of Elena, daughter of the Spanish admiral, who vied for the affection of Ingoldsby in the complex plot. Now she fed the director her most beguiling smile; she'd given up wasting it on Olivier, who seemed always too occupied with Vivien.

'This next scene, Mr Howard,' she cooed. 'How do I play it?'

'As though you're trying to get the guy in the hay, Miss Desni.'

'But . . . my motivation?'

'Glands, sweetheart,' the American threw over his shoulder as he stepped away for a word with the Virgin Queen. Outside Flora Robson's dressing-room, old Morton Selten, playing Burleigh, beamed up from his canvas-backed chair, his teacup held in two hands. Almost eighty years old, but never complaining.

'Are you well today, Mr Selten?'

'Splendid, thank you, Mr Howard.' The old man had worked with Henry Irving, Ellen Terry – all the greats.

Howard stepped into Flora's dressing-room, came in behind her and the make-up man staring at her mirrored reflection. Her age progression was becoming a serious challenge. Forehead now higher, white mask thicker, wrinkles more pronounced.

'The new rubber base – a great improvement, don't you think?' asked the make-up man.

Howard nodded, satisfied. He kissed her and walked

out, blessing his luck. No matter how much he hated the script, he loved these English troupers.

For Vivien and Larry, the end of filming would bring the end of a casual, natural time together that required neither arrangement nor conspiracy – a time of laughing together over private jokes without arousing gossip. From now on, any social contact should include Jill or Leigh.

Before going into *Hamlet* at the Old Vic, Olivier took a short holiday with Jill. They went to the Hotel Quisisana in Capri for a spot of sun and the world's bluest water. Vivien, too, took a break from work. Unfortunately Leigh couldn't get away, so she travelled with Commander Frewen as chaperon. Frewen made another note in his diary on 29 October 1936, of their arrival at this same hotel in Capri:

'Larry, the other side of the Hall, cried in a loud voice, "Vivien!" and Viv, my side of the Hall, cried loudly, "Darling!" and Jill uttered further love-cries, as all three met in the middle of what I could only describe as a joint passionate embrace, the while I smiled agedly and with benignity! They then "broke away" and both Larry and Viv at the same moment made an advance on me and introduced Jill . . . I was given a room on one side of the Oliviers and Viv on the other, so we were three in line and all on a communal basis – nobody ever knocked to enter and we all used all three rooms at will, and Viv confided to me that she thought it was "all right" and that we were not unwelcome . . . (It was a great surprise, not because I *need* have been surprised at Viv behaving like that, or her friends, but just because it is rather outside my earlier experience of "The Young".)' He failed to note, though, whether their arrival at the same hotel had been entirely accidental.

Once their holiday was over, Korda in his infinite wisdom saw fit to throw his two stars together again – not for their sakes, but for his. *The First and the Last* appeared to have all the right ingredients: a John Galsworthy book, a Graham Greene screenplay, and Basil

Dean as director. But they failed to serve up the right dish. The film turned out a non-starter, though it did keep the romance simmering. Enough so that Frewen noted on 4 March 1937: 'Vivling and I supped at the Moulin d'Or with Larry and Jill, and though we returned by 1.20 we sat up talking till 2.30 together.' The following day's entry bears a footnote: 'I begged her not to run away with Larry "anyway for a year", and she was gentle and said it was "good advice". So it was, but she didn't take it.'

Olivier's filming schedule had to be worked around his Old Vic production of *Hamlet*. He would rush from the studio to the theatre for evening performances, and wouldn't film on matinée days. Not an unusual schedule for a busy actor.

With filming coming to an end, though, Vivien knew she would be seeing less of Larry. Then one morning in May, while sorting through the post, Vivien's eye caught an envelope bearing the seal of the Old Vic Company. She opened it to read: 'The Danish Authorities would very much like it if you could play Ophelia, and we, too, would be delighted.'

3 *Lovers at Elsinore*

'The geography of Shakespeare's plays is ultra-romantic,' once observed G. B. Shaw. And Elsinore, the setting for *Hamlet*, may have appeared so in the sixteenth century. By 1937, however, the sleepy Danish town was mainly a launching site for ferries to Sweden.

The Dutch baroque architecture of the present Kronborg Castle, added during the seventeenth and eighteenth centuries, was more Hans Christian Andersen than the Bard's stark, lonely towers and ghost-stalked battlements. But there had always been a fortified castle at Elsinore, and always additions to it. The most recent, a heraldic gate, commemorated Christian X whose Silver Jubilee was to be celebrated in 1937 by an unprecedented theatrical event.

London's Old Vic Company was to bring the first troupe of English players to perform at the original Kronborg Castle since Will Kemp, the Elizabethan clown, had led a company of the Earl of Leicester's men to Denmark in 1585.

How would the Danes take to this second English production almost four hundred years later? Would it be worth the enormous effort and expense of moving cast, crew, props, costumes, lighting? The logistics were staggering. This had been Lilian Baylis's immediate reaction when the idea was first presented to her Old Vic Company by Robert Jorgensen of the Danish Tourist Office. At the time, Olivier was already playing Hamlet under Tyrone Guthrie's direction at the Old Vic as part of the full season's repertory, which included *Twelfth Night*, *Henry V*, and *Macbeth*.

'More an institution than a person,' was G. B. Shaw's description of Lilian Baylis. By 1937, her stolid, homely, bespectacled features had become familiar as the manager of the Old Vic and Sadler's Wells. She had produced every work in Shakespeare's First Folio, plus *Pericles*. She had also produced a deep veneration in the hearts of Olivier and every member of her company.

In contrast, her director, Tyrone Guthrie, looked much like a character out of a Noël Coward play – svelte, polished, attractive, with slicked-back hair and thin moustache. He had begun his stage career in repertory at the Playhouse, Oxford, in 1924. For two years he was producer at the Festival Theatre, Cambridge. Then to escape the academic sanctuaries he moved into radio, producing plays in Canada. Guthrie returned to London as producer of a series of plays at the Westminster Theatre. For the 1933–4 season, Guthrie was recruited to the Old Vic where his brilliant staging of *Twelfth Night*, *The Cherry Orchard*, *Henry VIII*, *Measure for Measure*, *Macbeth*, and now *Hamlet* had earned him an international reputation.

When Lilian Baylis invited Guthrie and Olivier to meet Robert Jorgensen, the Dane had been serving as press representative for several London theatres. It had been his idea to present the play at Kronborg Castle. But the Old Vic was so broke that Jorgensen had to put up £240 out of his own pocket to fund his dream. With Olivier and Guthrie, he chartered a plane between performances to fly to Denmark and reconnoitre the castle. They had to know if it could provide a practical setting, how large a stage would have to be built, whether the acoustics were acceptable, and so on.

Their first reaction was dubious. From the balcony of the Marienlyst Hotel, the castle in its sentry position above the harbour appeared like a monarch's birthday cake with too much frosting. Beyond it the Swedish coastline stretched from Kullen to Landskrona, the sun's long beams gilding the windows of Helsingborg across the waters. This wooded coastline would have been Hamlet's view of Northern Zealand. And less than a mile away the tiny island of Hveen – near enough for Hamlet to have punted over for picnics with Ophelia.

In all of Elsinore the only salute to its legendary prince was a single statue, whose right hand floating on air offered a graceful perch for birds. The weather-beaten statue's face seemed to suggest a Victorian sailor more than the indecisive prince of dreamers.

The castle encircled a moonscape of cobblestones, a raised font in the centre, mullioned windows on all four sides punctuated by towers trailing blue silhouettes. Olivier and Guthrie envisaged a wooden stage to be erected on the west side where a gate led to the ramparts. A perfect place for the dressing-rooms! And that courtyard – it could hold at least two thousand. Yes, it could work!

Jorgensen had arranged modest aid from the Danes, provided the actors would work for a minimum. A benefit performance in the interest of British national prestige – who could refuse? Only two of the actors, who had prior commitments. Michael Redgrave would give over his role of Laertes to Anthony Quayle, and Cherry Cotrell was passing Ophelia to Vivien Leigh. Jorgensen wasn't surprised at the choice of the Leigh girl. As press rep on *The Mask*, he'd seen her in action. The only worry was, would her light voice fill that wind-swept echo chamber of a courtyard? Lilian Baylis was prepared to take the risk, and Laurence Olivier certainly would not have discouraged her.

Until they came to Elsinore, the mutual attraction of Laurence Olivier and Vivien Leigh might have been written off as one of those brushfire infatuations so frequent in the turbulent lives of film and stage actors. After Elsinore, or perhaps because of it, everything would change. Aage Sørensen, the Keeper of the Castle that year, remembers that production. He didn't find the English Ophelia so very beautiful as everyone said. 'Too small. Too dark. Too thin. Me, I like tall blonde women!'

And Olivier? 'A nice fellow, really,' Aage recalled. 'But I think sometimes this Ophelia she likes him not only on the stage, maybe. Because when I opened the gate, sometimes she did not walk through.'

Character analysis through gate openings? Sørensen forced his mind backwards: 'The gate. Always she would wait, the little dark Ophelia, for Mr Hamlet. She would look into the courtyard. If he was not there, so! She would wait then outside. Smoke a cigarette. Then when he comes they walk in together.' A smile of recollection curled the corner of old Sørensen's lips. 'I think these two have it nice together.'

The expedition had been Robert Jorgensen's brain-storm, but what he had not foreseen was a real storm. For two days and nights of outdoor rehearsal in the castle courtyard, rain had plagued the company. Wind screams had drowned some of man's noblest soliloquies. 'Is there not rain enough in the sweet heavens?' sighed John Abbott, a sodden Claudius, from beneath his umbrella.

Jorgensen recalls the dark-eyed Hamlet, a soggy towel draped around his neck like an oarsman, worrying with Guthrie that no audience, no matter how dedicated to tragedy, could be expected to tread water through a drowning performance in a language they didn't understand. Jorgensen, watching rehearsals wrapped in a tarpaulin, had reassured them that almost all Danes spoke English. Besides, with two thousand people already booked for opening night, what were they to do? Return their money?

The outdoor rehearsals continued in the downpour, from midnight until 6 a.m., since the castle was still open to visitors during the day. In the sharp glare of the work lights, forty Danish cadets who had volunteered to serve as 'supers' were driven on a great gust of wind across the vast stage area, their capes billowing like sails. Guthrie was trying to rehearse the scene of Ophelia's burial. They carried the slender Vivien wrapped in oilskins, the solemnity of their march destroyed not only by the storm but by their inability to keep in step. Guthrie considered the possibility of trying martial music, perhaps 'Rule, Britannia!'

Jorgensen recalls that Olivier seemed to draw power

from an invisible source. He had the ability to project this power, to make others pause and think. His strength was re-inforced by Lilian Baylis, who brought quantities of hot coffee and courage to her faltering company. She had reached the decision to abandon the castle. The largest indoor area in town, a fish-packing warehouse, had been suggested as an alternative. But unless they could exorcise the odour, there might be an unwelcome laugh on the line 'Something is rotten in the state of Denmark'.

The company retreated to their quarters at the Marienlyst Hotel for a conference. Of course it would mean a hasty restaging of entrances and exits, and they couldn't use the main double doors because the manager was a bird fancier and there was a pair of small birds who'd taken up residence in the architrave. They would have to improvise lighting, but they could make do in the hotel's vast ballroom, with its blue velvet curtains, flocked wallpaper, gilded sconces, and Art Deco crystal chandeliers. The audience might be uncomfortably crowded but the hotel could supply a forest of gilded chairs. Close enough to touch the actors. Perhaps Vivien was the only one who was relieved by the move. She, too, had been worried that her voice would not carry, and important London critics – Ivor Brown of *The Times* and George Bishop of the *Daily Telegraph* – were coming for opening night.

The ballroom opened into the main lobby. The grand staircase swept upwards to the rooms where the actors were quartered. Among them were Dorothy Dix, Leo Genn, Torin Thatcher, and an unknown young actor under-studying Olivier and playing the small role of Osric, Alec Guinness. All signed the register, still kept in the Marienlyst safe.

Now they had less than twelve hours to restage on a dance floor. Everyone pitched in. The stage manager, George Chamberlain, fitted 'bastard ambers' over the spots. He was assisted by Elsie Skoubol, Denmark's leading actress, who with her husband had volunteered to help. The rehearsal went on. Crosses and movements that had been stretched to fill a courtyard had now to be shrunk to the size of this waltz-worn floor. Guthrie's clipped, military good looks belied a sensitive nature and a probing mind. It was he who had enthusiastically encouraged Olivier's foray into the world of psychoanalysis when the actor first delved into the character of Hamlet.

Guthrie had discovered a work by Dr Ernest Jones, *Essays in Applied Psychoanalysis*,* and he introduced Olivier to the Welshman's Freudian interpretation: that Hamlet's reluctance to kill his uncle was because of hidden love-guilt for his mother.

The actor was by now discovering the growing sense of responsibility that stardom brings, the responsibility of living up to an image and the public's expectation. Not only believing one's own publicity, but justifying it. He drew the audience to him with his dynamic personality, his voice so soft during his first soliloquy that one had to listen with total attention.

In her room, while the first-night audience was assembling, Vivien donned Ophelia's heavy velvet gown, square cut at the neck, with full Elizabethan sleeves. A single glass jewel blazed from a thin silver chain at her neck. On stage it would sparkle like the real thing. She stared back at her reflection, pale as death's lilies. She was just nervous enough to be exhilarated. 'A fairy Tinkerbell with a kick in her tail,' George Brown recalled of Vivien at this period.

Ophelia would be Vivien's sixth stage role. Add to that six small parts in films, including *Fire* and *Dark Journey* with Conrad Veidt. These were roles that had forged a chain of self-confidence, strength on strength, with the certainty that Miss Leigh was headed somewhere. Now she had an added strength – Larry's love, a catalyst that would explode the past and change the future. Now, away from homes, mates, children, and prying eyes, they could at last explore this indefinable magic that had captured them.

Actors and actresses swept down the Marienlyst staircase

* Published 1923, Vienna.

towards the door marked, for tonight only: 'STAGE
ENTRANCE.' Olivier, in black velvet tunic, waited to play
before the real Prince of Denmark, who was seated in the
front row. And then the final rustle of chairs in that crowded
ballroom before darkness invented a curtain. For Vivien
and Larry, two people were about to live four lives.
Hamlet's note to Ophelia brought to life:

> Doubt thou the stars are fire;
> Doubt that the sun doth move;
> Doubt truth to be a liar;
> But never doubt I love.

There was no need for qualms. That performance held its
audience in rapt attention, bridging all handicaps of space
and brief rehearsal. When the drums of Fortinbras had
throbbed at last through the gilded ballroom, the standing
ovation lasted fifteen minutes.

Next day the weather permitted Hamlet to move back
to his castle, and not one of the two thousand seats was ever
available for the five remaining days of two performances a
day. Each night Hamlet fixed Ophelia in his heart's glance,
and the actor and actress lived the open secret that every
member of the cast and company could not fail to have
noticed. Often they might be seen together before the
performance seated in a quiet spot on the outer ramparts
near a line of old ordnance, rusting cannon pointing towards Sweden across the water. They would sit on the sea
wall and talk quietly or read the press notices, the North
Zealand breezes tugging at Vivien's unruly thick black
curls and riffling the printed praises in her hand. Like all
theatricals, they needed to be praised but they would
always remember the bad reviews more than the good ones.

So much was unresolved in their relationship. Words
and promises can be traps, when eyes are enough to convey
emotions. Could so much sharèd feeling be set aside like a
final curtain on their return to London? How well did
Vivien really know this mercurial actor, or he her?

Even in the enlightened thirties, adultery was still not

accepted openly by most people. So what would happen when they returned to home and England? Would they launch themselves into that subterranean half-world of married lovers, meeting in small dark cafés and anonymous museum corridors, plotting incognito weekends in out-of-the-way hotels? What would cause the lesser pain, resignation or assignation? For the actor-son of the Reverend Gerard Kerr Olivier, it would have taken more courage not to be completely honest.

So what must they do? Walk away from each other as though they had never met or discovered what life could mean together?

Olivier has always insisted that he had no hand in the invitation to Vivien to join that Denmark expedition. Nonetheless after their return they could never again settle back into the pattern of their former marriages.

In Denmark the love scene had grown into a way of life.

4 *High road to happiness*

It is said that anything can be hidden from a mate: illness, gambling debts, even extracurricular romances. But Larry and Vivien had agreed in Denmark that they must make their positions clear as soon as they got home – explain their feelings simply and naturally and plead for understanding.

But what is simple and natural when emotions are involved? No matter how gently it is broken, such news always hurts. Anyone who has experienced a marital break-up knows that all those brittle comedies popularised by the never married playwright Noël Coward have little place in reality, and 'understanding mates' are generally a myth. Too many elements are involved – pride not the least.

Both Jill and Leigh came to the same decision: do nothing for the present. They would wait, and possibly like a bad dream this romance would run its course. Their positions were reasonable, even logical. Life is not just moments lived at the summit of pleasure. Each of the lovers had a child, and Olivier's son, Tarquin, was only a few weeks old. But reason and logic have little to do with love.

For some time Leigh had watched Vivien's life drawing away from his. Each of her steps up the theatrical ladder separated them further. Leigh was not a man to indulge in recrimination, but he decided not to release her completely. He would let the matter rest for a year before making any legal break final. Vivien was determined to move immediately although she knew it meant giving up Suzanne. She accepted this with her usual fatalism: all would be right in the end.

Busy with her new son, Jill came to a similar decision: a tr.a separation before any formal action. And so with a sense of unresolved termination and minimal acrimony, Larry moved out of Dower House.

Having weathered the upheaval they had caused, actor and actress found a house in Chelsea. The arrangement raised few eyebrows in London's theatrical world. For the moment, their private lives could remain so, although international stardom was to change all that. Now they could go back to work at Denham and finish *The First and the Last* (later retitled *21 Days* and released in America as *21 Days Together*).

With Vivien relieved of wifely duties, her career drive shifted into high gear. Everything was going her way, for with Larry love blended with work. A curious incident was noted by film critic C. A. Lejeune, who had accompanied the cast on the last day of shooting down the Thames to Southend on a steamer. It had been raining and during the long wait between shots talk had turned to M-G-M's plan to make a movie of the current best-seller in America, *Gone With the Wind*. Someone suggested that Olivier would make the ideal Rhett Butler. 'Larry won't play Rhett Butler,' was Vivien's prophetic comment, 'but I shall play Scarlett O'Hara, wait and see.'

Larry and Vivien celebrated the end of the film and their new freedom with a holiday in Venice. That summer of 1937 the news about them had not yet reached the Rialto. They could safely linger in some little *ristorante*, perhaps over a chilled Soave, and pasta with white clam sauce, or a veal Marsala. Somewhere off San Marco Square listening to the two bronze Mori hammering out the hour from the clock tower as they had done for the last four centuries. Venice, a gilded spectre wearing too much rouge, was even in that summer of '37 beginning to drown – but it was much too soon for anyone to notice, especially the lovers from London.

Their charming little Durham Cottage, with its walled garden, in the heart of Chelsea, was already beginning to be

crowded with what Vivien called her serendipity, an accumulated treasure trove of fortunate finds, since there was
scarcely anything worthwhile that didn't catch her discriminating eye. She adored the house, but Larry found it
too finicky. He kept tripping over the furniture. Still, it
was their first home and it deserved a proper house-
warming. On their return from Venice they were going into
separate film assignments, and the party would help launch
them, too.

Friends arrived, bearing the usual gifts – candy, wine,
and bric-à-brac. At the height of the evening Ralph
Richardson made his entrance. Larry had first met Ralph
back in 1926 during a one-week tryout of a dismal comedy,
The Barber and the Cow, at Clacton. Earlier that year, Olivier
had been quite smitten with a charming actress, Muriel
Hewitt, only to discover that she had a husband – who
happened to be Richardson. The two actors took an instant
dislike to each other, which turned into a lifelong friendship.

Now Ralph entered bearing under his arm something
that looked dangerously like a rocket. When unwrapped,
it proved to *be* a rocket. An unusual house gift, perhaps, but
the ebullient Ralphie explained that it was to show the
bloody neighbourhood that Larry and Vivien had moved
in! Flourishing it like the mighty claymore of Scotland,
Richardson bore it into the garden where the launch was
toasted with a round or two of drinks. David Fairweather,
who later joined the Oliviers as a public-relations man,
recalls Richardson pointing his rocket starwards above the
Thames with pyromaniac glee.

In the split of a roaring second, the monster firework
spurted up, trailing a stream of sparks. Then it whirled into
a loop-the-loop and was returned to sender like a fiery
boomerang. As everyone in the garden ducked, it swept
across a flower bed, smashed through the drawing-room
window, and exploded in the delicately appointed room,
scattering guests out of its path.

Screaming with laughter, Larry clapped his deflated pal on his sagging shoulder. 'Do it again, Ralphie! Encore!'

Moon face clouding with guilt the accident-prone Richardson turned to his petite hostess wordlessly.

'Hollywood would say you knocked 'em in the aisles,' Fairweather commented.

Vivien rose to the crisis. 'Doesn't matter at all, Ralph. It was bigger than both of us.'

She was always one to put a friend at ease, though in this instance a good deal of shattered serendipity would have to be thrown in the dustbin next morning.

'To think,' ruminated Larry, 'that the insurance policy would have gone into effect at nine tomorrow.'

Vivien's old school chum of Roehampton convent days, Maureen O'Sullivan, already an international success, had been imported back from Hollywood to play the lead in *A Yank at Oxford*. Vivien had been loaned to M-G-M for their first English venture, to play the promiscuous wife of an Oxford bookseller in the film. The reunion of the two women seems to have been less than affectionate. But the abrasive atmosphere did not, it seems, rub off on Robert Taylor, who was enchanted by Vivien's beauty. And although her part was smaller than Maureen's, it gave her a chance for characterisation on the screen she'd never had before. She wore flashy clothes and a doxy hairdo and even impressed the venerable Lionel Barrymore, who played Taylor's father.

Meanwhile Olivier had been assigned the lead opposite Korda's most important discovery, the exotic Merle Oberon, in *The Divorce of Lady X*. He was also preparing to go into *Macbeth* for the Old Vic. This left little enough time for the lovers to be together.

Vivien had high hopes that Michel St Denis, who was being brought over from Paris to direct *Macbeth*, would cast her as the Laird's dominating mate. She had a concept of how the role should be played – a Lady Macbeth who stirs her husband to a froth of ambition by sex and feminine wiles. But Larry came home one night with the dampening news that Judith Anderson was being brought over from New York for the part. Vivien considered the news coolly. The powerful Australian actress could be expected to deliver the traditional husband-castrating interpretation.

For the moment, Vivien had to shelve all thoughts of such a theatrical stretch of her talents. But her disappointment was soon alleviated by Tyrone Guthrie's invitation to play Titania in his Christmas production of *A Midsummer Night's Dream*. She, too, was to work with an Aussie star, this one from the ballet – Robert Helpmann, who would for ever after be one of Vivien's inner circle. Helpmann was to play Oberon, his first speaking part.

As Christmas approached, Vivien chose a significant gift for the cast of *Yank*: copies of the bulky prize-winning novel *Gone With the Wind*. She apparently hadn't been able to get the part of Scarlett out of her mind.

As it turned out, Olivier might have been well out of *Macbeth*, successful though it was. For this production more than lived up to its theatrical bad-luck tradition. Almost any actor who has ever appeared in *Macbeth* can tell his own tale of some tragic occurrence. Indeed, this ill-fated masterpiece has supplied many anecdotes of disaster, and to this day is only referred to backstage as 'the Scottish play' by superstitious actors, who will not permit the mention of or even a quote from that play backstage. (The unfortunate miscreant who commits such a *faux pas* is required by tradition to exit the dressing-room, turn himself around three times, fart, and knock, begging re-entry.)

In this particular *Macbeth* production, first the director Michel St Denis, a somewhat *avant-garde* figure of the time, was hurt in a taxi-cab accident. Next Lilian Baylis's dog was killed by a car. Then Olivier himself came down with a wretched cold, which postponed the opening of the unready production for four urgently needed days. The tragic climax was the sudden serious illness of Baylis herself. A few days later, the cast in rehearsal was stunned by the news that the distinguished lady was dead of a heart attack. She had sent a last message: her illness must not delay the opening.

Vivien read the note stuck on Larry's dressing-room mirror: 'May you be as happy in *Macbeth* as in *Hamlet* last season.' It was Baylis's last message to him.

When it finally opened, the production was an unqualified success. Larry's make-up and costume made him almost unrecognisable. He wore an outrageous crown of horns, a malevolent beard and moustache, and huge chains about his neck. He had padded out his gums to make his lips protrude and designed an elaborate eye make-up and heightened cheekbones that made him look like some Genghis Khan who had blundered into the mists of Scotland. Vivien's gift to Larry for opening night had been the make-up box of the great nineteenth-century actor Charles Macready.

Vivien described his performance: 'Well, you hear Macbeth's first line, then Larry's make-up comes on, then Banquo comes on, then Larry comes on.'*

Despite Olivier's personal feelings that the production was a disaster, the month's run was a financial success for the Old Vic, and the play transferred to the New Theatre.

Olivier's mind was already racing to the next project. He was to begin rehearsals of *Othello* almost immediately, with Richardson playing the Moor to his Iago. Tyrone Guthrie was to direct, which prompted another dig into the subconscious to expose the curious psychological relationship between the two characters: Iago hated Othello because he loved him; the homosexual implications at last explained Iago's murky motivations. Love equals frustration, equals hate, equals destruction. But Olivier and Guthrie did not share this enlightenment with Richardson. Olivier wanted it to hit Ralph with sudden impact during rehearsals – when he kissed him on the lips! And this was exactly what

* Felix Barker, *The Oliviers*.

Olivier's Iago did at one rehearsal, much to the confusion of Richardson's Othello.

'Never mind your psychology. The beauty of the play to me is the magnificence of its rhetoric. Leave me my monumental alabaster' was Richardson's comment.*

Audiences watching *Othello* were understandably bewildered. No longer were they seeing the envious skulduggery of Iago's 'evil for evil's sake'. Instead they were being introduced to a mysteriously motivated instrument of perversion rather than mere perversity. Doctor-playwright James Bridie protested in the *New Statesman* that Olivier's Iago had 'a diseased and perverted sexual make-up'.

The season concluded with *Coriolanus*, with Sybil Thorndike. In spite of the occasional critical snort, Olivier was, at thirty-one, the acknowledged giant of the English stage. Now Vivien had to force her way through crowds at the stage door, aware that she shared Larry with most of theatre-going London. 'There is now no doubt in my mind that the only sign of a great actor in the making in England today is Mr Olivier,' declared one critic.

Larry and Vivien were finding it difficult to keep up with the increasing demands on their careers. It was as though the very act of breaking up their homes had rocketed them into some special orbit of desirability. Over dinner on the closing night of the season, they discussed the holiday both now badly needed. Her ninth film was in the can, and his season had ended at the Old Vic. The time would never be so in joint, Vivien pleaded, to go away before some irresistible offer 'fucked it all up'.

He always laughed at the way the most basic English fell from her elegant lips without ever seeming vulgar.

Where should it be, then, in that summer of '38 – summer of the last tranquillity? They decided on France.

Honor Earl, artist-niece of Somerset Maugham, recalls an incident that took place that summer when she too

* Felix Barker, *The Oliviers.*

happened to be heading for France. She had missed the main Channel boat and was forced to take a 'rather crummy little French boat'. Having recently completed a portrait of Vivien and other members of the Old Vic Company, she was surprised to see the actress, hiding behind enormous dark glasses, hanging on the arm of Laurence Olivier at the rail. Their relationship was still unknown to the general public, so Honor considerately pretended not to recognise Vivien.

But when the two bumped into each other in the 'loo', there was no avoiding the meeting. When they returned to the deck, they found Larry peering through his dark glasses at the little dog a film-director friend of Honor's was bringing back to his wife in Paris. Everyone was suitably embarrassed, since the lovers chose to assume that Honor and her travelling companion, Eugene Tuscherer, were also on an illicit adventure.

Once in France, for what was to be almost the last private moment in their lives, Vivien and Larry were able to let each day find its own rhythm and pace without plan or purpose. The Calanque d'Or, a tiny coastal hotel, became their fortress against the world. Vivien could look out of a window framed by white louvred shutters, across a half-tamed garden of cracked flagstones where Saracens had trod, and count the cats, eighteen blue-eyed Siamese, owned by the proprietor. The morning sun slanting across her black hair feathered it with a red halo. They would gather their things together and, armed with a picnic basket from the hotel, drive to the unpolluted blue sea. As always, she wore a large straw hat to filter the strong rays from her pale skin.

They avoided friends when possible, but there were brief visits with John Gielgud and Hugh Beaumont, a cassis and a chat with Peggy Ashcroft and Glen Byam Shaw and assorted film folk.

But hanging over their happiness was always the shadow of their binding marriages. The partners who would not 'consider at this time' any possibility of divorce. 'Renew your application in three months,' Jill had told him. 'Three years' trial. Live with him and see if it will last,' Leigh had told her. The lovers might well have wondered if they would ever really be free to marry.

Then, like a pebble rippling the surface of a still forest pool, the cable found them and spoiled the enchantment. An agent's enquiry concerning a Goldwyn film to start in Hollywood on the first of September. Would Larry play opposite Merle Oberon in *Wuthering Heights*, with the offer of a minor role for Vivien? Olivier was less than intrigued by the Hollywood offer.

His last experience there had been soured by the Swedish love goddess Greta Garbo, whose words he echoed: 'Life's a pain anyway!'

He had been tested for the part of Don Antonio in M-G-M's production of *Queen Christina* – the Spanish lover who encounters the abominable snow queen in an inn outside Stockholm. He had made no great impression. Garbo had greeted him in dark glasses, had blown smoke at him from her cigarette holder, and had failed even to remember his name. In the end she had insisted on her old screen flame, reedy-voiced John Gilbert, as her co-star. Walter Wanger, producing the film, had given Olivier the Hollywood handshake, and words to the effect: 'Splendid, dear Larry, we're all mad about you here at Metro. But Greta is a soupçon uneasy about your height.' Instead, Wanger offered him the chance to test for Romeo with Norma Shearer as Juliet. He turned it down, saying he didn't believe in Shakespeare on the screen. This was before he played with Bergner in *As You Like It*, which did nothing to change his mind.

But a reply had to be sent, albeit a less than enthusiastic one. And this, of course, had always been the ideal response to a Hollywood invitation: polite indecision, well-chilled at the edges. It positively insured that one would be in demand, since the unobtainable was always the irresistible. Olivier's coolness soon brought the arrival at their sun-baked retreat of a huge, packaged script bearing the names of Ben Hecht and Charles MacArthur.

The script itself was intriguing. But the part Goldwyn had offered Vivien was nearly an insult. She felt, and Larry agreed, that she could not go from leads in England to a supporting role in caste-conscious Hollywood. No, good as it was, the script must be returned. Besides, there was plenty of work for both of them in England.

But in his letter of refusal the actor baited one small hook for Goldwyn. He might be tempted into the role if Vivien was offered the part of Cathy.

It was mid-July when they headed home. The agent's letter caught up with them in a hotel in Roanne on the Loire. William Wyler, who was to direct *Wuthering Heights*, was in Europe and anxious to talk to Olivier personally. He would be waiting in London.

As a director, William Wyler had always been a perfectionist, a man who knew what he wanted, and got it if it took sixty takes of somebody walking through a door. He carried the finished film in his mind, had an eye for detail and an ear for nuance. Wyler had emerged from that curious garden of nepotism, 'Uncle' Carl Laemmle's Universal Pictures. He was proof of the truth that if being related is not always a guarantee of talent, it can occasionally produce an authentic genius. A quiet and deeply contained young man, he bore an air of modest purpose and tranquil confidence. He had a great shock of dark hair above a sensitive, slightly flat, almost Oriental face – the perfect face for a poker player. And he had come to Durham Cottage to play his best hand. Larry and Vivien were aware that they were confronting one of the great professionals, and regretted that they had not managed to see the director's current hit, *Jezebel*, starring Bette Davis.

Goldwyn had wanted Ronald Colman, but Colman wasn't available. Wyler had already tested Doug Fairbanks, Jr., and had agreed to test Robert Newton. But he knew that although they were all fine actors, none had that specific ingredient of wildness and smouldering earthy virility that he needed for Heathcliff and had seen in Olivier.

As for Olivier, nothing in his film experience to date had convinced him that there was any artistic satisfaction to be gained from that most popular of entertainment media. Its very popularity resulted from it being all things to all men. Art and cinema had yet to be mentioned in the same breath.

But Wyler suggested that as a serious actor, Olivier surely could not ignore the potential of film techniques compared with the limitations of the stage. Olivier pointed out that he did not totally ignore films. In fact he was starting another the following week: *Q Planes*, with Ralph Richardson. One of Wyler's countrymen, Irving Asher, was producing it for Korda.

Wyler looked properly unimpressed. He switched his tactics gracefully, bringing the conversation to the smaller part of Isabella, which he believed could be made as fascinating as the woman who played her.

Vivien bestowed one of her sweetest smiles on the director and suggested he try Geraldine Fitzgerald.

'What about Vivien Leigh?' countered Wyler.

Vivien arched an eyebrow, and stroked a purring, devoted cat. There was always an affinity between this female and felines. 'Afraid I can only see her as Cathy,' she replied.

Wyler advised that for a first Hollywood role, Miss Leigh could hardly expect to start at the top.

Vivien had never seen herself in any other position. His argument was wasted anyway. She had plenty on her plate at the moment. There was *Serena Blandish* at the Gate, with Stewart Granger. Then back to the Old Vic for the Christmas revival of *A Midsummer Night's Dream*. She recounted an amusing incident of the year before in which she and Bobbie Helpmann got their headdresses entangled while bowing to the Royal Family. Like two embattled stags.

Wyler laughed politely, sipped another whisky, and

turned back to his host, calling him Larry for the first time. He pointed out that in Hollywood people aren't so formal except with the people they don't want to work with. How many films had Larry made? Wyler had seen the actor in *The Green Bay Tree* in New York, with Jill Esmond, and in *The Ringmaster* at the Shaftesbury, so he knew what Larry could do on the stage. But if he were to play Heathcliff, Wyler promised him an experience like nothing he'd ever had before: learning the techniques of the medium, how to scale a performance down to the size of a close-up. And when they were finished, Wyler would ask once again if film work could not equal the challenge of the stage as an art form. 'Think again before making a final decision' were his final words to the actor.

But ultimately it was Vivien who was doing the serious thinking. Her question was simple. Did he want to play the part? Did he like it?

He was studying his lines for *Q Planes*, in which he was playing the part of a dashing young test pilot. He liked Irving Asher, he replied – a gentlemanly, considerate American producer on his first British assignment.

She returned the topic to *Wuthering Heights* and Heathcliff. But being with Vivien was more important to the actor than bounding through the Hollywood heather with Merle. Where would they get the heather, anyway? Ship it over, no doubt. Goldwyn had probably already bought Yorkshire! Hadn't Hearst bought a castle and shipped it over stone by stone? Well, Goldwyn wasn't going to buy Olivier that easily. He did not care to stir from Durham Cottage without Vivien.

The actress pointed out that one of the most important things about their relationship, about their love, was that they wanted the most for each other's careers, shared or not. Hadn't he always wanted that for her? Besides, it was only for three months, and she would be busy, too. Perhaps she could even come and visit him? They must be practical. Goldwyn couldn't write off his commitment with Merle. Vivien's playing Cathy was out of the question.

Besides, Vivien wasn't jealous of Merle, who, she knew, was deeply attached to Korda. They might even marry. Vivien wanted him to accept the role because it was right for him to do so.

On the set of *Q Planes*, Olivier brought the problem to Ralph Richardson. They had just finished filming a scene in the kitchen of Major Hammond, an eccentric British agent played by Richardson.

'What do you think of it?' Larry asked.

'Bit of comedy, you know,' replied Richardson.

But it was not the scene that concerned Olivier. It was the question of Wyler's offer – which Vivien thought he should accept.

'I should, old boy. Bit of fame. Good.'*

* Felix Barker *The Oliviers.*

5   *'Meet your Scarlett O'Hara'*

In her syndicated column datelined Hollywood, 15 September 1938, Louella Parsons wrote: 'I don't know what persuasion Samuel Goldwyn used, but Laurence Olivier, English actor, is coming here to co-star with Merle Oberon in *Wuthering Heights*.' The acknowledged but not totally unchallenged queen of the gossip columnists further noted that 'just about the time Olivier arrives in town, a very good friend of his and a fellow Britisher, Vivien Leigh, is expected to check in at Paramount for an important role in Cecil B. De Mille's *Union Pacific*'.

Right on one count. Olivier was indeed Hollywood-bound, having completed *Q Planes* by working nights, in time to sail on the *Normandie* on 5 November. As for Vivien, Louella must have been using her crystal ball. On that date, Vivien celebrated her twenty-fifth birthday in London. The possibility of her checking into the De Mille unit at Paramount to play Molly in *Union Pacific* can be categorically denied. As one of the screenwriters on that film, I happened to be present at a casting conference when Miss Leigh's name was suggested.

De Mille, attired in his customary highly-polished puttees and flared riding breeches, swivelled his gaze like a Gatling gun towards the casting director seated beside me. 'Egli, who in God's name is Vivien Leigh? I need a star for this part!'

'She made a very favourable impression on you, sir, in *Yank at Oxford*, which you will recall having liked when you screened it privately at home. On De Mille Drive, sir.'

'Don't tell me what I liked!' The great man glowered. 'And it might interest you to know that the Union Pacific

Railroad did not include Oxford on its scheduled stops, nor British postmistresses. But I suppose it's too much to expect you to produce an American actress for an American part?'

De Mille was later placated by the casting of Barbara Stanwyck, Robert Taylor's (the Yank at Oxford) wife, and Vivien Leigh missed what might have been her first Hollywood role – which might have led her to oblivion.

Although he had left his love in London, Olivier's journey to Hollywood aboard the *Normandie* was considerably brightened by the calibre of fellow passengers. The guests at the captain's table were like a Noël Coward play come to life. In fact Noël was one of the guests, along with Leslie Howard, Anna Neagle, Herbert Wilcox, Monty Banks, and Berton Churchill. They were enjoying the last glow of ocean-liner luxury in those pre-war, pre-package-tour times. This was a floating Grand Hotel, with the finest foods and wines, society balls, a gym with trainer, masseurs, Turkish baths, handball and squash courts, swimming pool, casino, and dinner dancing to two orchestras. The *Normandie* docked in New York on 10 November.

A week earlier, the film producer David O. Selznick had come home from the West Indies. From the beginning David had been marked by Hollywoodites as a man of destiny. He had the essential qualities: shrewdness, courage, and, most important, luck. He was of formidable stature and serious mien, with an iron will. And best of all, he was 'related': his father, Lewis J., had been an important film distributor, and his brother Myron had become the Napoleon of Hollywood agentry. Myron Selznick was not merely a good agent – he was the best of his day. Bulky, thickset, belligerent, and frequently rude, he, like his brother David, had a chip on his shoulder that was permanent and even organic, in the sense that it was a chip off the old block. Their father, Lewis J. Selznick, had been ruined by his colleagues and peers – the Schencks, the Zukors, and the Laemmles – caught in the crossfire of their wars with each other.

David Selznick's career was further enhanced by a provident marriage to a boss's daughter. Irene Mayer was the daughter of Louis B. – now the total power at M-G-M.

It just so happened that brother Myron had as a client Laurence Olivier. Beneath this loam of relationships would germinate the seed of the most fated piece of casting since Rudolph Valentino had been chosen to dance the tango in *The Four Horsemen of the Apocalypse*.

Olivier's agreeable ocean crossing was soon forgotten in rehearsals for *Wuthering Heights*, which began brightly enough on a sunny Monday morning, 28 November. The fact that there were rehearsals at all appeared, at first, enormously promising. Most films then were launched without even cast read-throughs, rehearsals being confined to brief walk-throughs for the benefit of the cameraman. Wyler had promised Olivier a memorable experience, but the director Larry confronted on the set was a far cry from the friendly, ingratiating theorist on film-making he had given drinks to at Durham Cottage in Chelsea. It was rather like meeting a general at a tea party and then actually serving under him on the field of battle.

Wyler could appear ill-mannered – or worse, barely articulate. He drove his cast on a quest for perfection but somehow omitted any explanation of what it was he actually wanted of them. He could exclaim that one of Olivier's scenes was 'lousy' without a clue as to why.

Nor was Merle Oberon the same charming, easygoing leading lady with whom he'd enjoyed working at Denham Studios. 'Must you spit in my face?' she demanded coldly after a close-up love scene. Olivier apologised, and Wyler took the scene again.

'There! You spat again!' she snapped in the middle of the scene. Now, as anyone who has performed on the stage knows, it is one of the tribulations of actors to be caught in the spray of a fellow actor's plosives. Film acting does not require this intensity of enunciation, and no doubt

Olivier was overprojecting. But now it was his turn to be angry. He walked off the set, limping badly, for he had developed an agonising case of athlete's foot for which there seemed to be no cure.

Not to be outdone, Oberon also walked off, announcing she could be found in her dressing-room when Mr Olivier had left the studio. Wyler allowed sufficient interval for temperaments to cool, then sweet-talked his stars back to the set. And though at that moment they may have been hating each other's guts, they were troupers enough to convey love's tenderest emotions into the all-seeing camera eye.

Nor was Goldwyn happy with his choice of stars. After viewing the rushes, he complained bitterly to Wyler in a voice intended to be loud enough to carry to the actor's dressing-room. 'Willy, Willy, for the money I pay he could at least wash his face!'

'He's playing a stableboy, Sam.'

'Just because he's overpaid he shouldn't overact. Hold him down, Willy. Hold him down!'

'Sam,' Wyler told him, 'you're a great producer but you're not directing this picture. Now kindly leave the set, or I will!'

Temperaments continued in this state throughout the filming. Worst of all, Larry had not expected to miss Vivien so much. His letters to her grew more and more misery-filled, culminating in the painful revelation of his un-glamorous affliction. Now he was stumbling about the set on crutches between takes, and the growing feeling of manic persecution was dissolving in the realisation that Wyler and Goldwyn were not wrong about his acting. In this gothic epic of emotional storms, any over-emphasis of voice or gesture came out pure ham. Olivier's fundamental problem in this exacting role was to diminish melodram-atics to the microscopic register of the camera. For the first time in filming, he was being made aware that his performance was simply too large for the screen. With this self-laceration and gradually developing technique, a new understanding was growing, a respect for the medium which always before he had dismissed as a quick means to earn far more money for far less effort than the stage had ever offered.

His letters brought Vivien to a reckless decision. With less than a three-week break between engagements, she boarded the *Queen Mary*, having booked a flight from New York to Hollywood – an enormous expenditure, since travel time would leave only five days with Larry. She was covering twelve thousand miles, and a prompt return was essential since rehearsals were due to start on *A Midsummer Night's Dream* her first day back. But along with the need to see Larry went the secret dream that somehow, some way, a door might open to her growing obsession with the role of Scarlett O'Hara. She had brought her much-thumbed copy of the book on board ship, and read and re-read her way across the Atlantic. Rumours, false reports, and talent-searching had gone on for so long that only Selznick and God could say for sure if the coveted part was still available. The part fascinated her, as it did every other actress under the age of thirty-five with two arms, two legs, and a real or bogus Southern drawl.

On 5 December 1938, Louella's formidable rival, Hedda Hopper, announced: 'The cute English vamp, Vivien Leigh, is in our midst, but not doing a picture. Her romantic interest seems to be Laurence Olivier, in spite of the fact that some here are trying to link his name with Merle Oberon. Are we laughing, because Alex Korda is on his way over.'

Vivien sat on the patio drinking in English tea and California sunshine. It was Sunday and Larry didn't have to be at the studio. They were reading the 'trades' and revelling in a whole day together. The Hollywood *Reporter* noted that the role of Scarlett O'Hara had still not been cast, yet the film was due to start the following week. Was it possible? Vivien's face was a book in which sometimes Larry could 'read strange matters'. He considered with some amusement that perhaps she had not come to California only to see him. For, after all, how was she to occupy herself all day while he was spitting at Merle? No harm in mentioning her to Myron in the same breath with Scarlett. His agent not only knew where all the bodies were buried, he'd buried a few himself.

Myron Selznick was a combination wailing wall, mine detector, espionage agent, drinking companion, occasional pimp, and available father confessor to his famous clientele. And it was true that in all Hollywood history no man had better filled the functions of international purveyor of talent and wheeler of deals. As Olivier's agent, he could only have regarded Vivien's arrival as a minor godsend; his client definitely needed a morale boosting. But in a sense that no one yet realised, her timing could not have been better. However, at the moment Myron was only concerned with Larry's happiness.

When the actor mentioned her to Myron as a possible candidate for Scarlett, the agent reacted with his customary poker face, polite but non-committal. It was true that on both sides of the Atlantic there wasn't a likely actress who hadn't already been considered. They'd been at it for three years! So, he conceded, they might as well have a look at Vivien Leigh.

Now, after years of preparations, delays, and manipulations, David O. Selznick was succumbing to the pressures of his backers and associates. Ready or not, he must launch principal photography on his epic. When they were not feuding, the brothers Selznick could be extremely useful to each other. But although Myron had an inside track at David's studio, Olivier knew the odds were against Vivien when he went to see Myron in his sumptuous Beverly Hills office. The strongest contender, the flamboyant Paulette Goddard, was also Myron's client.

Olivier assured him that Vivien was not just a great

beauty but was considered a fine actress. Myron took that in his stride. Weren't they all, always? Besides, Louis B. Mayer was putting up the money and the biggest male star in the world for *G.W.T.W.* Not that L.B. was overly devoted to his son-in-law. David was well educated and not without polish, which made him socially acceptable in stratas where L.B., with his humbler roots, moved uneasily. The younger man was something of a challenge, even a rival, in the power plays of Hollywood. Perhaps L.B. could recognise behind David's smooth façade the same ruthless brand of ambitious opportunism that had ignited his own rise. And Mayer knew the enormous appetites that accompanied the power drive, the insatiable need for women even on the periphery of a comparatively happy marriage. It made David a rather too dashing mate for L.B.'s beloved daughter. So the deal he made with his son-in-law was as hard as he would have exacted from any other studio head. For Clark Gable, David had to forfeit to M-G-M the lion's share of distribution profits.

And Mayer would be certain to take exception to Vivien Leigh because of what had happened on *A Yank at Oxford.* It was M-G-M's first British-made film and Mayer had descended on London to supervise it personally. He had been enraged to discover that his British producer, Michael Balcon, had hired a comparative unknown in Miss Leigh for the second female lead. Mayer's screaming attack on Balcon reverberated throughout the studio, and Balcon's honour demanded the hara-kiri of resignation. Oddly enough, when the dust had settled, Vivien was allowed to remain in the film. To further disqualify Vivien, Myron knew that David had already screened *Yank* with George Cukor, who was set to direct *G.W.T.W.* They had thought Vivien pretty enough but far too sleazy for the tempestuous Scarlett.

Olivier reminded Myron that in that film Vivien was playing the role of a tart.

'And a very British one,' Myron said pointedly. He assured Larry that he was pursuing a lost cause. They had already discarded Vivien as a possibility. After such a high-level turndown, it would take a séance to bring anyone back. But Olivier persisted, and Olivier was too important a star to give the brush, so Myron considered the angles. And maybe there was an angle. If Vivien was as hopeless a candidate as he expected, perhaps it would make Paulette seem more right for the part.

Myron agreed to meet her. Olivier revealed that she was ready, waiting, and at this moment in his outer office.

'With you as her agent, she doesn't need me!' Myron observed, buzzing in his secretary. 'Sunny, tell Miss Leigh to come in, will you?'

'Yes, Mr Selznick.' Sunny beamed, all eyes for the actor. The willowy blonde from Texas was a recent arrival in Hollywood and still starry-eyed at most of Myron's clients.

'I warn you, Larry, I'm still pushing Scarlett O'Goddard, as Louella is now calling Paulette.' Myron rose, pacing the Colonial-styled office with its antiqued leather armchairs. Behind him in bookshelves, the authors he controlled marched row by row to the ceiling.

Sunny could hear his summary: So far, one thousand four hundred candidates had been interviewed and turned down. Out of those, more than ninety had actually been tested – and turned down. Paulette would have the fucking part right now if she hadn't been mixed up with Chaplin. Then there was Joan Bennett, who went to the right fucking parties, with Jean Arthur, who was a fucking great actress but could only be photographed from one side. And Miriam Hopkins and Tallulah, who the whole fucking South were screaming for because they were actually Southern. Then there was Norma Shearer, who owned half the fucking stock of M-G-M, only she was fifteen years too old. David had had his ass in a sling ever since he announced this damn movie! Suppose Louella got wind of their love life? It could blow *Wind* right out of the window!

Olivier assured Myron that they were both trying to get their divorces and would marry the same day they succeeded. At which moment Vivien walked into the office.

Myron stared, and stared some more. 'Well . . .' he breathed. 'Well . . .' he repeated. 'You're not the girl in *Yank*?'

'I am an actress, Mr Selznick.'

'Sunny, get Nat Deverich in here, will you?'

'Yes, Mr Selznick.' The eager secretary was gone in a flash.

Myron explained that his assistant, Deverich, used to be a jockey. His connections at the Santa Anita race track were very useful with Myron's horsy clientele. The dapper Deverich bounced in, wearing a bright plaid jacket. Known to be a smart dresser and a hot golfer, he was one of the leading lights of the 'Divot Diggers' – a high-powered group who closed some of Hollywood's biggest deals on the nineteenth holes of the Rancho, the Hillcrest, Lakeside, and the Riviera. Between the race track and the golf course, more business deals were wrapped up than in all the inner sanctums of the studios.

Myron suggested that Deverich try to set up a screen test, explaining that although he knew David 'like a brother', he believed in taking a curve on the inside before hitting the straightaway. Besides, he admitted, he'd had a slight brawl with David several nights earlier at the Ambassador's Coconut Grove. Potted as the prop palms, both had been discreetly ejected.

'Does D.O.S. know her work?' Deverich asked.

'Yeah, but for God's sake don't remind him. Just let him look at her. Like I am.' And in truth, Myron had scarcely taken his gaze from her. The owner of one of the most jaundiced pair of eyes in the industry was plainly impressed.

That afternoon Deverich paid his normal visit to Santa Anita and ran right into one of David Selznick's aides, Danny O'Shea. In exchange for a tip from the ex-jockey, the screen test was arranged in the following manner: Danny slipped Vivien Leigh's name on to a memo to D.O.S. recommending a test. Selznick, who lived in a plethora of memos, automatically approved it with no recollection of having already turned her down. This second-generation mogul was obsessed with perpetuating his own thoughts and ideas in highly explicit memorandums that trickled from his office in a perpetual stream like Chinese water torture on the heads of his underlings.

With three days left before she must return to England, Vivien's hopes were fading, for she had heard nothing. Dining at Romanoff's Beverly Hills restaurant, Vivien and Larry tried to talk of other things under the scrutiny of the beaming bogus White Russian prince from Brooklyn, Mike Romanoff, who lavished imperial hospitality with an elegance only a facsimile could exude.

Suddenly Myron appeared at their table and sat down beside Vivien. He'd been looking for the two of them all over town. David was shooting the burning of Atlanta that very night and Myron had fixed it to bring them over to the set.

'Pay the cheque and let's get going before David burns down the whole damned Culver City,' Myron urged.

Production designer William Cameron Menzies was creating the biggest holocaust that California had seen since the San Francisco earthquake. Up to the sky in streamers of dancing flame soared the painted false fronts of obsolete movie sets acquired for the purpose. *Little Lord Fauntleroy*'s drawing-room became a sirocco of consuming sparks. Temples from *The Garden of Allah*, forests from *The Last of the Mohicans*, miniature skyscrapers from the first *King Kong* – going, going, gone, in a cremation of dreams. Tonight these façades, doubling as antebellum Atlanta, were playing victim to Sherman's accurate pronouncement: 'War is hell.' David's inferno was the first footage to be shot on the greatest cinema epic in film history, and one might well wonder whether the original burning of Atlanta could have matched this re-enactment.

Like some beefy Nero, David O. Selznick viewed the scene of capital consumed, so auspiciously reddening the skies above Culver City. His brother Myron was at that moment driving into the studio past a nervous fire chief who had marshalled a huge force of fire fighters in case the conflagration got out of control.

The fireman glanced at the pass and waved him through. 'You're late, Mr Selznick.'

By the time he rolled his car to a stop near the back-lot location, the flames were guttering low. He led Larry and Vivien to the top of the platform, where his brother and a few of the upper echelon surveyed the scene.

Since no principal actors were involved in the filming, this was technically considered 'second unit'. The vast forest of burning building fronts was fed by an ingenious system of oil sprinklers, through which water could also be spurted intermittently when necessary to control the fire between takes. Three sets of doubles for Scarlett and Rhett skirted the fire in horse-drawn buckboards, also carrying doubles for Melanie and her baby, and Prissy, the slave girl. Since nobody yet knew the final size and shape of Scarlett, they had protected themselves with assorted Scarletts who would, in any case, only be filmed in long shot. Even Selznick couldn't afford such a bonfire twice.

Vivien watched, thrilled, her skin burnished by the re-flected glow, hair stirred by the breeze, eyes like fire opals beneath the circle of her wide-brimmed black hat. Watching her, Myron thought that perhaps in no instant of his experience as an agent did his instinct scream louder: right girl, right place, right time. He caught his brother by the sleeve, dragging him around.

'Hey, genius. I'd like you to meet your Scarlett O'Hara.'

Bulking large, hair tousled, red-eyed from the smoke, the producer turned his glance around behind his thick tortoise-shell glasses. He looked, then returned his attention to the acres of embers – then looked back again, then stared. Myron knew, if he knew anything, that the impact had not been slight. And with this flash of knowing, all things became suddenly possible.

The director, George Cukor, was looking, too, with the

discerning eye of the connoisseur who can judge the merit of a work of art – or the validity of a fleeting expression on an actress's face.

'Scarlett O'Hara, eh?' pondered David.

'Vivien Leigh, Mr Selznick,' said Vivien, annoyed by the cavalier ways of Hollywood.

The producer could not seem to drag his gaze from that poignant face so amazingly composed in the reflected aftermath of holocaust. Why hadn't he heard of her? Or had he? Could it be possible that his brother might actually have come up with the answer to his great dilemma? He invited them all back to his office. The VIPs descended the platform, leaving the crew to extinguish the last embers under the worried eyes of the fire chief.

In the office, David was all shrewd affability. What was this British girl doing in Hollywood? How had she fallen into Myron's clutches? He glanced at his brother, now restored to grace. Why hadn't Myron mentioned her before? Only three days in Hollywood? Just for a visit? And yet she had read the book – read it and re-read it, she confessed. And what films had she been in that he might have seen?

Vivien stressed her theatrical background: Ophelia to Olivier's Hamlet. West End leads. Nobody was foolish enough to mention *A Yank at Oxford*.

And then the question they had all been waiting for: would she like to test for Scarlett?

Behind the producer's back, Myron threw Vivien a warning glance, and she said nothing about the fact that her name had been on the list for days. Olivier, waiting with as much anticipation as Vivien, mentally applauded her perfect reading in accepting the offer with neither overeagerness nor lack of confidence. Myron swallowed the fear that his brother might have recognised her as someone he'd already turned down.

The producer suggested that Cukor take her into his office for a chat. Give her a reading. Then he poured the actor a drink and offered a bone. 'Too bad we haven't got you as Rhett, Larry.' Gracious, of course, but everyone knew what a coup it was for him to have Gable.

George Cukor's office was a vast clutter of costume sketches, a dozen versions of the eternally unfinished screenplay, shooting schedules, model sets, photos of authentic Southern settings which they would match on the back lot. The director indicated a chair across from his desk. Vivien sat, crossing her thin, shapely legs beneath the flare of her black silk dress. He asked her to remove her hat, and studied her features, his mind seeing her face from every angle with the eye of a camera. Then he sorted through some scenes on his desk and handed one to her.

'Read this,' he said curtly.

She scanned it. 'Will you read with me?'

He nodded. He would read Ashley, which he did in a dull monotone, giving nothing, not indicating what he thought of her. When they had finished, he frowned. She felt a cold twinge.

He must have hated her!

But he hadn't. Aside from her obvious beauty, Cukor rather liked her straightforward approach. 'Cold reading' that it was, there was something honest and uncloying. And her beauty was anything but vacuous. It was alive, vivacious, sparkling. And somehow you wanted to know more about this girl. One could sense the layers of complexity. To a man like Cukor, who had worked with all the great female stars and had been satiated by the two-dimensional plastic beauties of this town, it was clear that he was sitting in the presence of a strong personality and a unique talent. But his face gave no clue to his thoughts.

'Once more, Miss Leigh. And this time, no honeysuckle and moonlight, please.'

They read it again, and she studied him for reactions. The director was small-boned, round-faced, wearing thin metal-framed glasses, his dark hair short and brushed back in the American style. An ample nose gave a comfortable, lived-in look to the sensitive face. His expression was enormously contained, urbane. There was something about him immediately likeable, but for the moment he was holding it in reserve. When they finished the scene, he only nodded.

'Well?' she asked.

'I have three other tests to make. You'll be the fourth. Now let's just read it through one more time.'

After the day of the test, Vivien related the studio gossip to Larry. The first test was to be Jean Arthur, who had locked herself in her dressing-room in near collapse from nerves and tears. Cukor had finally coaxed her out and in front of the camera, where an instant metamorphosis took place – from wilted lettuce into crisp confidence and charm. But she seemed a bit too wholesome for the part.

Next came Joan Bennett, highly polished, very social – more New York deb than Southern belle, and a shade too glib withal. Then the favourite! Paulette – tanned all over and overconfident, just back from Bermuda and partying with the Whitneys, Selznick's backers. She had been 'backer-dropping' all over the set. And word was that the test was great. Finally came Vivien. They did the scene in which Scarlett tells Ashley she loves him. She had plunged right in, her English more clipped than sugared water-melon, because suddenly Cukor had said: 'She's not a fucking Peter Pan, darling.' And from that moment Vivien felt he was on her team, even though she knew his own choice would have been Katherine Hepburn. And she knew something else: she absolutely adored him.

After the test, Vivien thanked the charming Leslie Howard for all his help. He had liked her performance. Effective, he thought. He liked the arrogance – no drippy magnolia nonsense. Of course he'd never read the book.

Vivien was stunned. Well, he admitted, he'd avoided it until now. Couldn't stand the part of Ashley, actually – great limp tower of patriotic jelly. But he'd accepted be-cause David could be damned persuasive, particularly with a cheque book. Howard had much preferred his role in *Berkeley Square* at Fox, but Lasky worked from a smaller pocket.

'Do me a favour, Leslie. Read the book,' Vivien advised. And she told Cukor that whatever the outcome of the test, she wanted them to be friends. He had invited her and Larry to his Christmas party. The place would be throbbing with all manner of people, some even friends. She would probably have heard David's decision long before that. It was six whole days away.

Cukor was careful not to show any sign of preference among the finalists. George understood actresses. He enjoyed a well-justified reputation of being the finest 'woman's director' in town. He could sense the gem-like play of light and shadow, the swift flickering dart from mood to mood, and, like a conductor before an orchestra of emotions, his ears and eyes were tuned to recognise any false note. In Vivien he saw that behind her eyes lay authentic mystery, the enigma of the eternal Eve. Deeper still, something else flashed through the quips and wit and professional polish – an inner silence like the tenuous dusk when the last bird sound is stilled in the forest.

'Thank you, Vivien, that was fine' was all he had said, his tone punctiliously neutral. But Vivien had read the message. Here was the man who could guide her performance perfectly – *if* she got the part.

She reported this thought to Larry. The scuttlebutt was that David was scared shitless of the kind of publicity he might arouse if he had a Limey playing the flower of old Georgia – especially with half of America pretending Europe wasn't even there, so they wouldn't get mixed up in the brewing war.

And there was that other not so little problem – the two of them. Adultery didn't go down well in Bible Belt-Women's Club America.

The five-day visit Vivien had come for was running into weeks! For the third time, she cabled for another delay. Again Tyrone Guthrie graciously agreed. And still she waited for Selznick's decision. She wrote a confusing letter to Leigh and sent off a Christmas box of books for Suzanne. And then they called her in for another test. This time to probe the possibilities of her Southern accent. Susan Myrick, a Georgia journalist and friend of Margaret Mitchell's, had been hired to teach Scarlett and Melanie (played by Olivia de Havilland). Vivien later confided to Olivia: 'Don't worry, sugah. All you've got to do is learn to say, "I've got a foah-doah Foahd," and that will carry you.'

The silence deepened from the Selznick Studio, and Vivien knew that she would not get the part. Only Larry still believed in her chances, but then Larry loved her.

In Myron's office, a great deal of whispering was going on behind closed doors. One day, his secretary paused outside the door and thought she heard her own name mentioned. As she returned to her desk, the door opened and Harry Ham came out. Ham, tweed-clad, pipe-smoking English assistant to Myron, leaned across Sunny's desk. He always managed to appear polished, cool, and less rumpled than his boss. He studied the pretty blonde for a moment and then enquired: 'Sunny, how do you like your job in the Selznick Agency?'

'Marvellous, Mr Ham. I love it.'

'How would you like to do something even more interesting?'

Could Harry Ham of the London office be propositioning her? She had been warned in Texas that all Hollywoodians would. 'Depends on what it is, doesn't it, Mr Ham?'

'Well, there's a little English actress testing for Scarlett . . .'

The idea was straightforward enough. The agency had rented a house for Vivien and would move Sunny in as companion-secretary, and (more important) chaperon. This might help keep the gossip queens away from their typewriters. D.O.S. couldn't risk a hint of scandal about anyone he was considering for Scarlett, whose salacious activities must be limited to the screen.

Sunny agreed to move into 520 North Crescent Drive,

Beverly Hills. The house had two large suites of bedrooms, one at each end. She and Vivien hit it off perfectly from the start. When Larry paid his discreet visits, Sunny made herself scarce.

The days went by and still there was no decision. The silence was driving Vivien mad. 'I don't even want the bloody part any more!' she insisted to the actor.

Sunny recalls a vivid picture of the lovers: 'He was always kissing her. Holding her hand. Or his arm around her shoulder. She was most responsive. They were more like teenage lovers than two adults who had been married before and each had a child. She was kittenish, green-eyed, a complexion like Dresden, with a will-o'-the wisp waist. He would say, "How's my pussycat?" "I'm fine, puss. How are you?" "What kind of a day did you have? Well, sit down and tell me about it." She was always so dramatic and so excited about everything, like a little girl hearing a story for the first time.'

Myron had said David was screening all the tests at least thirty times. 'He sits in the projection room like a petrified mummy, mentally constipated.'

And still they waited. Now they had a whole day alone together. Vivien gave Sunny the day off, and the lovers retreated behind drawn shutters. Sunny arranged for food to be sent in – veal and avocado soup. And Player's cigarettes from Schwab's Pharmacy. Vivien smoked far too many.

Often Sunny would hear them quoting Shakespeare.

'By the Lord, this love is as mad as Ajax; it kills sheep; it kills me.' He, holding her face in his hands.

'*Love's Labour's Lost*, puss. Act Four, Scene Two.'

'Three. Now let's get dressed and go carolling to dear George Cukor under the eucalyptus trees.'

'Happy Christmas, puss, my puss.'

They could not be expected to know that from this moment their lives would never again be completely their own. They were on the threshold of that most rarefied peak, the heights of international fame, where private life no longer exists – and the worst of it was that they would learn to need it!

Christmas Day, 1938: on Cordell Street in Beverly Hills, beautiful cars were discharging beautiful people. At George Cukor's home imposing gates and high walls excluded the inadmissibles from one of Hollywood's innermost circles. In the Elysian setting provided by the connoisseur-director, the privileged flow of guests was welcomed into a graceful hall hung with paintings and lined with Georgian silver-leafed shell-shaped chairs. (There's a similar set at the Royal Pavilion, Brighton, George IV's fantasy folly.)

Vivien and Larry moved through a circular panelled lounge, dominated by a serene gigantic Buddha head. Her discerning eye recognised a Braque and beside it a sizeable Rouault hanging in the circle of Impressionist paintings. There were drawings by Augustus John, Picasso and the like – personal acquisitions of a man of taste, a confirmation of what she had immediately sensed about this director. A beige circular sofa followed the curve of the window, and beyond it they could glimpse across the pink flagstones a pool of unruffled turquoise, mirroring the sensuous curves of Greek statuary.

George collected people as he collected art. The Christmas spirit flowed through the house and out to the sun-bright garden where eggnogs vied with mint juleps – a not so subtle concession to the epic at hand. Never had Hollywood seemed more isolated from world troubles.

On this day, a sweating Santa rode on a motorised sleigh down Hollywood Boulevard and strangers embraced like orphans out of a storm in the garden of George Cukor while Hedda and Louella, wherever they were, made notes.

Larry and Vivien were shepherded around the garden and introduced to members of the cast of the film. Those guests on the 'inside' carried themselves with mysterious importance, for they already knew that 'Olivia, darling' and 'Leslie, darling' were set in their parts. Now it was only a question of 'who, darling' would pluck the plum from the pudding. The smart money was still betting on Paulette, and Bette Davis was probably still fuming somewhere else that day for having been passed over as a logical contender. Local gossip was going the rounds about the new cabochon ruby-and-diamond bracelet La Goddard was sporting.

'Definitely *not* given her by Charlie!'

'More the glitter of a Whitney.'

'Jock? You're mad!'

'No, not Jock . . .'

Voices drifted away as Cukor came over to draw Vivien aside to a quiet corner. 'Well, it's finally settled, Vivien. David has made his choice.'

She was trying very hard and almost succeeding in pretending that whatever the choice it didn't really matter. 'It must be a great relief to you, George.' His face had given no hint.

'Oh, vastly relieved,' he said. The garden glittered with cut glass and laughter, high strident actresses' laughter. Later she told him her thoughts at that moment: it didn't matter. It didn't matter because it was never more than the most fragile of hopes anyway. Larry was the only thing that really mattered. But now she would have to leave him. Return to London. Console herself with rehearsals and exuberant Bobbie Helpmann taking her mind off the disappointment, and to hell with Hollywood; except for Larry being here and the prospect of working with George – who would want it anyway?

'I guess we're stuck with you,' Cukor said. The director smiled at her through a slanting sunbeam that almost blinded the eye, and she was certain she had heard wrong, and she had to take it calmly and not cry or do anything silly like shouting! . . .

'Me?'

'You, Vivien! Congratulations.'

She looked across George's shoulder to where Larry was chatting with Leslie Howard and Olivia de Havilland. Her skin was chilled in the hot December garden, and she felt all pins and needles. 'Larry?'

The actor moved to her in an instant.

'George says . . .' She could scarcely form the words.

Cukor told him the news. The actor remained wonderfully cool, but he was quite as excited as she.

And Cukor said that if either of them breathed the news to a living soul before David broke it to the press, he would smother them in prop magnolia leaves and loan them out to Monogram.

But another party later, dropping by Merle Oberon's bash for Myron (her agent, too), they ran smack into Korda who drew Vivien aside. He began by asking her whether anything he had ever told her had *not* been true.

'Not that I ever found out, Alex.'

Then he was telling her right now, she shouldn't do it. In Mississippi and places like that, she'd be burned in effigy. In Georgia, she'd be lynched. In Boston, they'd drown her in tea. Bad enough she was English, but in his opinion she was wrong for the part. He reminded her that she was still under contract to him. Anyway, he was certain that Selznick would never start principal photography, and if he did he wouldn't finish it. What a budget! His father-in-law had him over a barrel, and the barrel was Gable. Difficult man. It could be worse than what Laughton did to him, Korda, in *Cyrano*, he assured her.

Looking across a tray of hors d'oeuvres, Merle noted with less than enthusiasm her fiancé and the porcelain Miss Leigh, head-to-head, exchanging whispers.

Vivien pleaded with Korda not to stop Selznick from using her. He shrugged. There was always the possibility he was wrong. And if he was, he would ask for a clause in his agreement to loan her out. The third picture after *Gone With the Wind* would have to be for him.

Vivien heaved a sigh of relief and hoped it would be with Larry. The thing they wanted most in the world – next to being together – was to work together.

6 *The perils of Scarlett*

> *If I don't with my name*
> *Scale the heights of fame*
> *Like Mrs Siddons, Réjane, or Cornell,*
> *Please believe me I choose*
> *And hope not abuse*
> *A seat on the heights of Cordell . . .*
> To my darling George with my dearest love, Vivien

That inscription on Vivien's photograph, which still hangs on Cukor's study wall, celebrated an affection that time and changes of fate would not diminish. Cukor loved Vivien, and treasures a collection of photographs of her. Olivia de Havilland remarked of them: 'They are so elegant and so curiously very sophisticated and strangely poetic and wistful, all at the same time. I don't know how she managed that, but she did, and she was unique – absolutely unique! Whenever George Cukor mentions her name even now, he says, "and *darling* Vivien". He can't just say, "Vivien".'

The first time Olivia met Vivien was in David Selznick's office: 'It was all a great secret that I was going to play the part, that she was going to play the part, and Leslie Howard was going to play the part. I got this secret phone call that I was to arrive and go in by a special entrance, and all of that – so the press wouldn't trail me. I can remember so clearly entering David's office and there she was. She came across the office to shake my hand to greet me. She was very composed. That's what struck me. There was this coolness and composure, and, of course, charm. It was a cool charm, quite individual. Very polite. I can see her now, so clearly – coming forward like that, which was a nice thing for her to do, very gracious.'

With the casting finally set, David Selznick was firing off his customary volleys of memos, augmented by his final giant step of decision. The wise producer avoids decisions as long as possible, since only by doing nothing can mistakes be safely avoided, and the *status quo* maintained. But now that what was done could not be undone, the begetter of the action must protect his flanks. The massive commitment of making a movie could no longer be avoided. Selznick had finally put down the flag on the meter, and the cost of forward movement into full-scale production must now tick into the millions.

4 January 1939: Selznick sent a memo to John Hay Whitney about Korda, the lucky Hungarian having a third-picture commitment with an actress who would, via Scarlett, become the most valuable star of the age . . . A memo to assistant Henry Ginsberg: On his (Selznick's) terrible worry over 'the accent problem' . . . A memo for the urgent attention of Lee Garmes, cameraman: On the need for further photographic tests to experiment with hair, eyebrows (one seemed to be higher than the other), figure, 'including particularly her bosom!'

And the national press was pap-fed by the wet nurses of the studio publicity department to counteract any build-up of resentment against a foreign Scarlett or a scarlet woman who had left home, husband, and child to co-habit with an actor who had left home, wife, and child. They published harmless tidbits about Vivien celebrating with Olivier and co-star Leslie Howard at the Bublichki Russian Café. The same trio was seen taking in a USC football game where the fans mobbed Howard, completely ignoring the unrecognised lovers.

At the studio, Lee Garmes, a cameraman and an old friend from the days of the *Cyrano* tests with Korda, was singing that old swan-neck song again. He had complained that he'd have to keep the camera angled high or get her to wear something around her neck. One of David's memos ordered Wardrobe to dress her only in high-necked gowns, and Garmes had thought to soothe her by promising to throw a shadow on the right strategic spot. All this wretched concern with the anatomy connecting her head to her trunk!

Meanwhile a fat script had arrived with a note to Olivier from Myron. Larry had not yet found the right moment to mention it to Vivien.

'But David doesn't really give a shit about my neck. He's worried about my bosom.'

'And all the time I thought they were perfectly lovely,' he sighed.

As Dorothy Parker once noted, what God had forgotten could be stuffed with cotton. They'd had Vivien in and out of brassières all day, pushing her up and down and sideways – but nothing ever looked right to Selznick. He had sat there smoking a giant cigar and ordering, 'More pointed! Now lower the left nipple!' and similar grains of wisdom. He seemed obsessed with mammaries. At last Vivien managed to tell him that she had her own idea. Everyone waited with bated cigars while she disappeared, took off all the padding, put her gown back on over her own natural assets, and then emerged before the battery of scrutiny.

'What did you do?' shouted David, absolutely ecstatic. 'Now it's perfect! Exactly right!'

'It's just plain me, David,' she told him.

The perils of Scarlett . . .

Larry was wearing the polka-dot silk dressing gown she had given him to celebrate the finish of his filming. (But films have a way of never quite finishing and Wyler's retakes were dragging on and on.) And now Vivien took note of the script in his lap. He tossed it aside, launching quickly into another subject. He was beginning to fathom the mysterious Willy Wyler. These movie monsters were perfectionists within their own orbit. He actually had learned a great deal on this film. Wisdom through suffering, perhaps, but Larry was the eternal student of acting. So would she learn, he assured her, by this unique challenge that awaited her.

A challenge, all right, Vivien agreed. Hard to believe but there was still no shooting script for *Gone With the Wind*, though God knew they'd shot down enough writers. Sidney Howard's original draft still seemed the best, she thought, but it would have lasted for ever on the screen. Howard had been followed by Ben Hecht, Jo Swerling, Oliver H. P. Garrett, F. Scott Fitzgerald, and Donald Ogden Stewart. All that expensive talent rewriting each other for two and half years and Selznick himself rewriting all of them! David had even asked Margaret Mitchell to try her hand at dramatising her own book, but the lady wisely refused to set foot in Hollywood. Selznick had rarely looked at the book since the day he had paid a fortune for it.

Vivien's eyes came to rest on the bulky manuscript Larry had carefully avoided mentioning. Now he told her it was the new S. N. Behrman play, *No Time for Comedy*. Sam, as always, wrote bright dialogue – the American Noël Coward. This was a light triangle sort of thing. Katharine Cornell was to do it in the spring. And they wanted Larry. But nothing was definite yet. He wasn't even sure if he wanted to do a Broadway play just now.

'Opposite Kit Cornell? Don't be daft!'

He watched her busy herself with deft fingers arranging a mass of freshly-cut blooms Sunny had brought in from the Japanese gardener: California flowers, always paler, less aromatic than at home where the sun didn't drain them. When Vivien arranged flowers, it was like a great pianist improvising. Her fingers danced through patterns of shape and colour until the flowers seemed to fall into perfect array by themselves.

Larry reassured her he was not about to rush off to New York and leave her trapped in a bloody Civil War with Gable and Leslie Howard, two of the most renowned womanisers in the world! She came over to him from the floral still-life created out of chaos.

'Larry . . .' She was looking at him with that combination

76

of wonder and knowing, and at this instant she was unbearably beautiful.

The conversation about the play went on for weeks. He could find all sorts of reasons for not doing it. He assured her Myron could find him another film. There was one coming up at Metro that would fit him like a codpiece.

She reminded him of the pact they had made in the beginning. Whenever the right parts came, they wouldn't let their need to be together stand in the way. They had promised they would try to work together, but if it wasn't possible they'd go their own ways for better or for worse. And there couldn't be anything better than a Behrman play with Cornell. He agreed, but there was one thing about the offer that bothered him slightly. He kept wondering if maybe there wasn't a Selznick in the woodpile, pulling a few strings to get him out of town so that the women's clubs wouldn't ban his picture, even though the Daughters of the Confederacy had given Vivien their blessing! But perhaps they were just relieved that the part hadn't gone to a Yankee.

'Well, fiddle-de-dee – as Scarlett would say.' One day she had slipped and said, 'Fiddle-de-fuck'. Actually, it wasn't a slip at all; she hadn't wanted Cukor to print that particular take, so botched it deliberately.

Vivien promised that if Larry accepted the Behrman play they wouldn't be apart for very long, because she would move heaven, earth and Selznick, drive the company like a Simon Legree, shoot day and night to get the picture done. And when it was finished, David would know what the word 'slavery' really meant.

The actor did want the play, and he could console himself that Vivien wouldn't have time to be lonely. As usual, she'd make good friends. Thank God she had Cukor and not Wyler for a director.

Vivien avoided mentioning the terrible rumour that had slipped out on the set the day before. It had sent her and Olivia de Havilland into a frenzy of alarm. Cukor might be replaced. They were sure it was only studio gossip – but whispers persisted that David was considering another director because Gable was unhappy. However, she knew if she breathed any of this to Larry he'd never accept the Behrman play, and she also knew it was right for him to do it now. They were both professionals, possessed and obsessed by the demon of work – driven by the need to excel.

The rules they made for themselves could brook no compromise. Never fail the company or the audience. Never short-change the role, great or small, with half an effort; never cheat for an effect; never be late on the set; never leave a line unlearned. That's the way it was for both of them. Always the search for illusive perfection, the final reality, if you had to rebuild every feature of your face, re-shape the muscles of your body, change voice, change heart, extend and stretch to the limit and beyond – that was what made it all worthwhile. Worth building a life on.

With Larry the actor, Vivien was like an anchorite in the desert dedicated to one God – an anchorite who wanted to share the altar. Referring to this, Olivia de Havilland said, 'She had to be successful because she had so much regard for Larry. It was not competing; she wanted to measure up, to be worthy, to keep his esteem. He idolised her and she didn't want to lose that. She was sure that she had to succeed on every level in order to keep his admiration and his love.'

Every morning Larry watched her prepare herself to be at the studio on the set by 6 a.m. And in make-up and costume by 8 a.m., to face the clinical eye of the camera that could read through any phony note or false gesture. The camera dissects a performer like a pathologist searching a cadaver. It finds the weakness and disembowels. This was what they didn't know – the kids dreaming of platinum stardom. This was the difference between being a 'personality' and being an actor. Olivier knew the cost and the toughness that would be needed not merely to survive the little failures that are the daily bread of this art, but to survive the more destructive prize: success.

And now there was a new and deeper hunger between them, caused by the almost unbearable knowledge that they would be parted again. In a way it was made easier by the presence of filmdom hypocrisy that erupted one day in David O. Selznick's office. The magnate had never looked so ominous. He'd had – horror of horrors – a call from Louella! A call and a question.

Was it true that Larry had been observed leaving Vivien's house on Crescent Drive *early* in the morning?

Of course it was true. He still had to report to his studio.

Solemnly David reminded her of what he considered to be their clear understanding of the situation *vis-à-vis* the American public. And it was no good telling him that their private life didn't concern him – because it did, to the tune of his four-million-dollar investment,* and they both knew the score when she signed her contract.

Vivien reminded him that her relationship with Larry could hardly have come as a revelation to him or even to Louella. All of London knew they were living together.

David remained frozen to such logic. Perhaps Myron had neglected to read her the small print in her contract. There was a clause called 'moral turpitude', and if she violated it David could pull her off the picture and see to it that she'd never work again in Hollywood. He had a film to protect and Larry was going to move out of Vivien's house. And from now on he was barring the actor from visits to the set! End of conversation.

What she had no way of knowing at that moment was that it was mainly Selznick's money financing the Behrman play that would remove Olivier from the scene.

For the few remaining weeks, Olivier moved in with

---

* A minute sum by today's blockbuster standards, but even twenty years later the cost of making such a film was estimated at ten times as much.

Leslie Howard, though ironically Howard also happened to be in residence with a lady to whom he wasn't wed.

M-G-M's publicity factory had fashioned the perfect totem image for the current virility cult. Hailed as 'the King', this Hemingway-like deity had a cynical squint that could appraise a woman or a charging rhino with the same detachment, both to be gagged, stuffed, and exhibited in his game room. Clark Gable had become the leading all-male star.

No matter that his career had been launched and bird-dogged by his ageing drama-coach wife or that Carole Lombard, his current wife-to-be, let it be known that he was not exactly Mount Vesuvius under the sheets. The image had been created and it persisted. Gable helped it along by turning up everywhere with machismo companions, actors and directors who might be imagined outsnarling a grizzly bear, who were quick with fist and gun and liked their whisky neat.

Most Hollywood personalities come to live up to their publicised images – or down to them, as the case may be – in the show-biz syndrome called 'believing your own publicity'. Working as an M-G-M film writer at that time, I used to accept Gable's invitation to shoot skeet with him during the lunch hour, at a range not far from the studio. I never beat him at shooting, which was perhaps why I continued to be invited. I found his personality larger than life, a kind of vigorous accumulation of all the parts he'd ever played. He was somewhat anti-social, avoiding the Hollywood party scene and more at ease with cronies like the rugged character actor Ward Bond, Ernest Hemingway, and the director Victor Fleming.

Vivien Leigh knew nothing beyond the fan-magazine gossip about her co-star when his huge mobile dressing-room was towed on to the Selznick lot. She soon discovered that Gable was by no means comfortable in the part of Rhett Butler. Not only did it place strong demands on his acting ability, but he was especially unhappy with the choice of Cukor as director. Cukor's reputation for favouring his women stars, and his aesthetic sensibility, left Gable cold.

Selznick himself was becoming dissatisfied with the direction, despite the fact that Cukor was an old friend. The producer was worried by what he considered the director's fussy touch on the tiller. Instead of the scope and sweep of history, its drive and tempo, the director seemed more concerned with the authenticity of detail, like petticoats of genuine Val lace beneath Walter Plunkett's costumes. Even Ann Rutherford, playing Scarlett's sister Careen, remarked on the extravagance.

'Nobody will ever know what we're wearing underneath, Mr Cukor.'

'But *you* will know, my dear,' the director pointed out.

Cukor goaded dialogue coach Will Price, as well as Susan Myrick, to keep the Southern accents authentic. Margaret Mitchell had warned that the South would rise again if subjected to any more of Hollywood's treacle. But Gable ignored the accent entirely. He had no intention of losing his fans by altering his image.

Often it took a long time for relighting or changing a set-up. Vivien would sit in a corner of the set with Gable and Olivia de Havilland, playing a then popular game called Battleship. What surprised Olivia at the time was Vivien's capacity to rise from the game (if the make-up man had checked her out while she was playing) and go at once on the set to shoot the scene. Olivia, like most performers, would have to stop a good ten minutes before they needed her. She would stay quiet in her dressing-room, making the transformation into her character for the scene. But Vivien had the capacity to make that adjustment instantly, and it amused and pleased her that the others couldn't.

Gable's unease with Cukor prompted Selznick's increased presence on the set. Few directors will put up with a producer breathing down his neck, and Cukor wasn't accustomed to heavy-handed supervision. Doubts of the director's suitability were being leaked by Gable to his paternalistic boss, Louis B., and Mayer's harassment of his son-in-law accelerated with Gable's dissatisfaction. Mayer could find a new son-in-law more easily than another Gable.

The King didn't merely communicate his discontent through grumbles and sulks. That was not his way. He simply refused to report for work. In fact, he didn't even refuse; he simply didn't show up. At first Cukor just shot around him, hoping he would cool off. But his absence was not making hearts grow fonder. Rumour was that Metro might appease its disgruntled gold mine by withdrawing him from the Selznick picture – a move that could mean cancellation of the whole project or at least a takeover by Mayer. Such a possibility could not be ignored, and the producer could procrastinate no longer.

On Friday the thirteenth of January, Cukor had posed cheerfully with Vivien, Olivia, and Leslie Howard for a press photo. One month later, on the thirteenth of February, Cukor was fired by Henry Ginsberg, Selznick's general manager, known as 'the hatchet man' for his efficient, clean-cut executions. Selznick was not one to let friendship stand in the way of business.

When the news reached Vivien and Olivia de Havilland, they were on the bazaar-sequence set. Both were in black dresses because by now in the story, Melanie had lost her brother, Scarlett's husband, Charles Hamilton. The two invaded Selznick's inner sanctum – and took over three hours of his time. 'Poor man!' de Havilland recalls. 'We wept! We had these little handkerchiefs with black borders around them – our mourning handkerchiefs.' She laughed. 'And we took them out and we wept, wiped our tears with them. I don't know how he resisted us, but he did manage to.' As far as the actresses were concerned, the whole film was being created in Cukor's mind, because God and Selznick knew there was still no script.

Selznick protested that he'd had eleven screenwriters on the picture. No property had ever received more attention and work, and if they didn't have a final script it was because they never *would* have! He concluded sanctimoniously that while he, too, loved George, he had put aside his personal feelings in the interest of the picture.

The picture or Clark Gable? the actresses demanded. Their argument was simple. Although the King might insist that Cukor was essentially a woman's director, he had directed many male stars with great success. The producer peered out at them from his fleshy face, exhausted eyes couched above pillows of abused health. He was surviving on a mixture of benzedrine, thyroid tablets, and sleeping pills. The uppers and downers did not improve his disposition. Now he wearily reminded his two female stars that Gable was the biggest box-office draw in the world. He also knew that Vivien was playing a part that any actress on earth would have screwed Quasimodo to get. And Olivia had cost him his shirt to borrow from that son of a bitch Jack Warner!

Far too shrewd to risk losing his female stars, Selznick opened a bottle of scotch, and as he poured he let them have a few facts of film-making that might save them from doing something their lawyers would regret. No script? True. But a moving picture was more than a script, or a directorial attitude, or the artistic bias of any one person. And it wasn't just a matter of ego or a great performance. You could take the damned movie and flush it down the can when the director or any of his stars started taking over the screen! But there was one man who had finally to decide what values were being wasted, what possibilities were being neglected, what chances were lost. The producer. And he was the heavy if anything went wrong. But when it was right and the result was entertainment, half the audience didn't even know his name. No, it would be Gable, Vivien Leigh, Olivia de Havilland – and, of course, Leslie – whom the audience would walk out remembering. And whose salaries would go up accordingly.

Oh, yes – and one thing more. That God-damned book. One thousand thirty-seven pages. Sixty-five thousand dollars he'd paid for it. Had either of them considered how many hours that book would run on the screen? Of course not. They only viewed the whole through the peephole of their own parts. As Louis B. kept drumming into him, 'They'd stone Christ if he came back and spoke for four hours.' A book is not a film. It's a seed, a beginning. Selznick carried this picture on his conscience like original sin. And if it failed it wouldn't be just a loss of Whitney's money or a pain in the bank's ass, or a waste of their fine talents. It would be one man's fault. And this picture was going to be a success if he had to direct it himself!

The thought, however chilling, would eventually father the deed. But at this moment he quietly informed them that after considerable soul-searching, he had decided that George's replacement would be Victor Fleming, Gable's closest chum and L.B.'s own choice.

If the blow was bitter, it was scarcely a surprise to the actresses. They left the office knowing they were just the hired help. And for Vivien any chance of enjoying the filming was gone with George Cukor. She was determined now to drive herself and the others to get the picture finished. She had only one goal: to rejoin Larry, who had left to start rehearsals for the pre-Broadway tour with Cornell. She was alone now, with only Sunny to look after the everyday details of living.

But, in fact, Cukor hadn't entirely gone with the wind of change. Olivia de Havilland began going quietly to Cukor for coaching in her part, feeling a bit guilty about it, and not mentioning it to Vivien. When she did happen to confide her secret to someone, she was told, 'Oh, don't be silly! Don't feel like that! Vivien has been doing the same thing all the time.'

And so she had. Sunday after Sunday, limp and exhausted, Vivien reported to Cukor's house for secret guidance in interpreting the mercurial Scarlett. All Fleming would say when she asked for help on a line reading was 'Ham it up!' Such advice might work for Gable, who only played himself anyway, but Vivien wanted more than a two-dimensional performance. She felt that she

The love scene unfolding – *Hamlet* at Elsinore, 1937. *David Fairweather.*

The actor's first film role: *Too Many Crooks,* 1930. *Rank*

The actress's first film role: *Things Are Looking Up,* 1934. *Gaumont British*

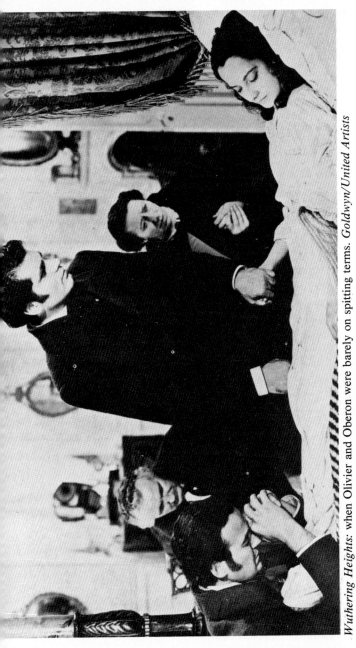

Wuthering Heights: when Olivier and Oberon were barely on spitting terms. *Goldwyn/United Artists*

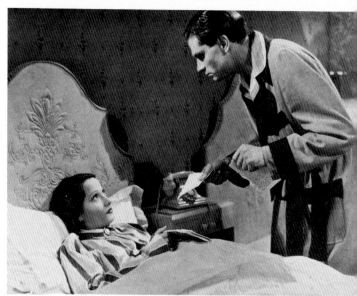

With Merle Oberon in *The Divorce of Lady X,* 1937, when they were on speaking terms. *London Films/United Artists*

A less than affectionate reunion with Maureen O'Sullivan, in *A Yank at Oxford. MGM (London)*

Gone With the Wind, 1938. Vivien with Olivia de Havilland and (left to right) George Cukor, David O. Selznick, and Leslie Howard. (*MGM*)

The tour that failed: *Romeo and Juliet*, U.S.A., 1940 . *Sunny Alexander (Lash)*

Olivier with old friend Douglas Fairbanks, Jr., *circa* 1939. *Douglas Fairbanks private collection*

Lieutenant Olivier, R.N.V.R., 1942. *Copyright Keystone Press Agency Ltd*

needed to find a way to make the audience like this self-centred girl, so intent on destroying to survive. Cukor helped her see and understand Scarlett on many levels: what the war did to her, her struggle to come through the devastation, and the gradual stripping away of the false façades of custom and environment when the moonlight and roses went out of her world.

How ironic. Any woman would sell her soul to play this part, and all she wanted now was to be with Larry! She came again and again to Cukor for help and sympathy. But she could find little for herself. One day she told George, 'There is no greater bitch than a woman who steals a man when his wife is expecting a baby. I know. I did it.' She would fall asleep on a chaise in his garden, and he would take a blanket to cover the body growing thinner in the rust-coloured slacks. She wouldn't be much good to Larry or the picture if she ruined her health, he advised her. She was now working sixteen hours a day, six days a week, and forcing everyone else to keep up her pace. Selznick was only too delighted with the speed-up of his shooting schedule and the hundreds of thousands it was saving him. On the set she would rail against the interminable delays. 'What are they fucking around for?' she could be heard saying, over and over.

'I just can't get anything from Victor Fleming,' she told Cukor. 'He may be Gable's hunting, shooting, and drinking mate, but he's a poor thing and he seems very confused. I'll be surprised if he doesn't end up with a nervous breakdown before the fade-out.'

What she did not mention to George was a rather naughty trick she had played on her new director. It happened on his first night of shooting, during the church scene in which Belle Watling gives Melanie and Scarlett the handkerchief tied with money bearing Rhett Butler's initials. Vivien, intent upon showing her displeasure in her own subtle fashion, had invited de Havilland and Selznick to dine with her in her dressing-room. She so regaled and entertained the producer with her loquacious charm that the actresses, de Havilland recalls, were both late reaching the set, and kept the director waiting – a discourteous, unprofessional thing to do. But no one could fault Vivien, since she had been with the producer and the other leading actress in the scene. Selznick was totally unaware of how he had been manipulated.

Vivien's letters to Larry were more and more filled with bitterness and disillusionment. It seemed that nothing could go right. Except, of course, the results, which even Selznick couldn't have foreseen in those dark days.

'How I hate film acting!' she told Olivier on one of her nightly long-distance calls. 'Hate, hate, and never want to do a film again! Puss, my puss, how I do miss you . . .'

He understood, because he had been there, too. He had been up to his eyeballs with Wyler, until he discovered that the director was, in his own strange way, so often right. But it hadn't made Olivier love him at the time.

Vivien didn't hate Fleming, Gable, or anyone. Just the job. Much as she had loved the book and had wanted to play Scarlett, she detested the reality of making the picture. Nothing was ever filmed in continuity, and she sometimes had to play four different ages in one day to accommodate the sets. What a jigsaw the movies are! How could they ever fit all the pieces together? But they would.

During the shooting, when Larry was gone, Vivien would sometimes invite a few of her new friends to Sunday lunch – the only available time, since they were filming six days a week and at night. Olivia de Havilland recalls that Russell Birdwell, the publicist, Sue Myrick, and Will Price were among those present. They would sit out by the pool, dining on lobster and champagne, organised by Sunny.

One talk she had with Vivien stays in Olivia's mind: 'We got into a conversation about childbirth. I was fascinated because Melanie had to give birth in the film and I'd done quite a lot of serious research about that. I found that talking to a doctor and talking to a woman who'd had children conveyed absolutely nothing at all. Doctors simply don't remember the type of sound a woman makes, or what she does with her hands. They can't remember anything, isn't it odd? So George Cukor said, "I think you've really got to go to a hospital and see some births . . ." So I did, and I was deeply impressed. I found it so moving. Enormously moving, beyond my wildest imagination. I spoke to Vivien about this, and she said, "Oh, I didn't care for it at all. I found it humiliating." "Humiliating" was the word she used for having a child. I have never heard another woman say that – ever. It fascinated me. I found it absolutely incomprehensible, an attitude of superiority to this basic and fulfilling experience, for no matter how much trouble it causes a woman, most would hardly think of it as humiliating.

'And yet I'm sure she was very sensual. She must have been passionate and was surely erotic. On the set I saw one thing that surprised me. Someone had an engraved antique cameo ring of an erotic subject. We were shooting the scene when Melanie comes down the staircase with the sword, after Scarlett has shot that awful Yankee. It was the set of Tara after the war – after the burning of Atlanta – and there she was in that pathetic cotton lavender dress. She was always so cool, so polite, so exquisite, so *raffinée* – and then suddenly she was told about the ring, and said, "Let me look at it! Let me look at it!" It was quite surprising that she looked at this rather explicit carving and took a strange, lascivious, and very obvious pleasure in looking at it. It was out of character with all this tremendous coolness, and the "I found it humiliating" surprised me. A frank spontaneous "low down" reaction in front of the crew, when normally, her attitude was one of ladylike, exquisite discipline.'

On one of the nightly phone calls, Larry asked how she would like a visitor for the weekend. It was a sixteen-hour flight. He could leave after the Saturday night performance, land at Burbank at 4 p.m. her time the next afternoon, and be back for the Monday curtain. As long as Selznick didn't find out, a little touch of Larry in the night would be heavenly . . .

Sunny went alone to the airport to collect Larry in her nondescript Plymouth. He emerged from the plane behind dark sunglasses, his clothing rumpled, his hat brim turned down. She bundled him into the car and whisked him off to Beverly Hills. As manager of Vivien's household, she had stocked the larder with food from Victor Hugo's restaurant, plenty of Beluga caviar, and bottles of Mumm's Extra Dry, and she had given the house servants the weekend off.

As they headed over the Cahuenga Pass, Larry asked what was for lunch.

She reminded him that it was almost five o'clock. 'Miss Leigh has ordered a veal dish for dinner. I had suggested Southern smoked ham, but you know what she said? "Sunny, just because I'm playing Scarlett doesn't mean I have to like ham".'

'How is she, Sunny? Really?'

'Impossible as ever. Driving herself to exhaustion. Insists on working far into the night. Only four hours' sleep sometimes. I don't know where her energy comes from!'

'And how are she and Fleming getting on?'

'She's too much in a hurry to finish to make problems. And Mr Fleming very soon learned to respect her. The poor man's ready to be carried off himself. He hasn't even had time to read the book. Once he lost his temper and told her what she could do with it. Shove it up her Royal British ass, he said. Then Fleming went home and got drunk with Johnny Lee Mahin, his favourite writer. But everything was patched up when Miss Leigh, Gable, and Selznick arrived at Fleming's beach house with a peace offering. A cage of lovebirds. Miss Leigh's idea, of course. But frail and exhausted as she is, I think she'll outlast the tough Mr Fleming,' said Sunny.

The car stopped in front of the house. Sunny made no move to go in with him. Only assured him she'd be back to whisk him to the airport in time to catch his plane.

Larry's play was going beautifully. As usual, the critics

worshipped Cornell and Sam Behrman's dialogue. The newspapers were calling him the new matinée idol – again. In fact, he was getting a bit fed up with some of his fans. One hid in his car and actually tried to tear his trousers off. The price of fame.

As for the subject of their divorces, Vivien was still writing friendly letters to Leigh. His answers were prompt, sending Larry his best wishes, worried about her overwork, but not seeing his way clear just yet to give her freedom. It was the same with Larry and Jill. They would still need to be patient.

She told him how she'd had to 'tick off' Leslie, who was blowing his lines, still hating Ashley because he felt he was too old for the part. He hadn't read the book yet. Not surprising, really. Olivia had worked with him once before, in a film with Bette Davis, and had found him of a distracted frame of mind, and felt little sense of connection with him. He was always rather late on the set, and would say, 'Well, what scene is it today? What is it? What is it?' But he had been just as disturbed as the two actresses over the change of directors – and also the endless 'blue pages' of rewrites they kept getting on the set. Much of it was by Oliver H. P. Garrett, which seemed to Leslie nowhere as good as the original scenes. In that department, at least, he was an ally.

Everyone hated every part of it except Clark. And she hated his false-teeth whisky breath when she had to kiss him. Filming was so fucking slow sometimes she thought she would go mad! Everyone fiddled about and adjusted fringes. She told him about the weird game she'd thought up for a party. It was a new charade called 'ways to kill babies'. She'd pantomimed driving a car and 'chatting up' a child. Then she rolled down the window and tossed the child out. David thought she was really losing her mind, and maybe she was.

Larry's heart felt sore at the tiredness he saw in her behind the rattle of words. He put a small velvet box into her hand. To puss with love. It contained a large heart-shaped aquamarine ring from Van Cleef & Arpels. It fitted on her fourth finger, left hand.

Suddenly their idyll was over and Vivien was watching Sunny's old Plymouth taking Larry away from her. All the tension and loneliness engulfed her again.

'Don't let her smoke too much, Sunny,' the actor said. 'And try to get her to eat a bit more.'

'I'll try, Mr Olivier. But she's a dainty eater, you know. Though she does love avocadoes. I do think it's the one thing about California she likes.'

Sunny sighed, thinking you couldn't be around these two people without wishing you were in love, too! Because they made love into the greatest reality. 'If I didn't have a sweetheart, Mr Olivier, I'd sure feel pretty sorry for myself about now.'

Larry's return flight was delayed and brought the actor back to New York too late to make the Monday curtain. Miss Cornell was not amused.

Vivien continued to write to Leigh Holman, and her letters revealed her state of mind. 'It is really very miserable and going terribly slowly. I am such a fool to have done it,' she complained. Then in another letter: 'Every scene is so hard to play because of the appalling dialogue . . .' And so the filming dragged on. Tara exteriors were being shot at Lasky Mesa in the San Fernando Valley (so named because some of my father's early films were shot there in the dawn of Hollywood).

It seemed as though they would never get out of Georgia. Only this Georgia happened to be fabricated flimflam as artificially coloured as an Easter egg. At 3.30 a.m., while a sickly first sunray crawled up a California hillside sprayed red to represent the burned-out fields of Tara, hungry Miss Scarlett could be found grubbing for a radish. But no dawn light ever seemed quite Georgian enough in the projection room to receive Selznick's blessing.

One evening after rushes, Vivien buttonholed Selznick and demanded a weekend off. She made no bones about where she was going – to meet Larry, a safe distance from

Hollywood, in a hotel in Kansas City, Missouri. Selznick was less than thrilled with her plan. What would happen to his film if her plane crashed? The production insurance wouldn't cover that.

Then, she suggested, he had better pray that someone up there loved him, because she was going to the Meulbach Hotel, where the press was unlikely to find them. And he shouldn't worry about her not getting enough rest. She intended to spend the entire weekend in bed. Reluctantly, Selznick agreed.

Larry arrived in Kansas City from New York, deeply concerned at how weary she looked. There was much to tell about the filming, like the day she was supposed to retch in close-up. She hadn't wanted to do it, but it should have been easy. All she had to do was think of the two directors now on the film. Plus Selznick. With so many people telling her what to do, she'd have taken direction from the script girl. She had to cope with Fleming one day, Sam Wood the next. Even the indomitable Fleming was on the verge of a nervous breakdown. David wasn't satisfied with her retching, so Olivia de Havilland had dubbed in a more obnoxious sound track.

In New York, Larry had become the object of wild-eyed adulation. He had found himself torn apart by loneliness, by the press, by his new movie fans, who mobbed and hounded him.

His outbursts fed the press: 'Life is very dull for Laurence Olivier,' snidely remarked Elliott Arnold in a June interview in the New York *Telegraph*. 'Being a matinée idol is very dull. Having a couple of dozen adoring women waiting in the alleys of the Ethel Barrymore Theatre is very dull. Giving interviews is ditto, and playing opposite Katharine Cornell in the hit *No Time for Comedy* is also very dull. In fact he's going stale in the role, so he is leaving the cast in the beginning of July.' But Arnold went on to admit: 'Mr Olivier is quite without question the matinée idol these summer days. First he sent so many women into a mild nervous breakdown in the motion picture *Wuthering Heights* and now he is sending them into some other dream world with his performance in the stage comedy at the Barrymore . . .'

Larry's interview with the *New York Times* film critic, Bosley Crowther, hadn't increased his popularity in movieland: 'He doesn't mind telling the world that he has no use at all for motion pictures . . . he finds the screen demands much more literalness than the stage. This is due partly to the fact that living actors are able to establish a personal communion with their audiences which the screen cannot achieve; partly due to the embarrassment of movie audiences before anything which is tenuous or intimate.'

But, whatever his ambivalent feelings about movies, every play revue was a rave, while Hedda Hopper drooled embarrassingly about *Wuthering Heights*: 'When Laurence Olivier says, "Come here, you're mine!" – how gladly you'd go! And even suffer a third-degree burn and love it when he puts his head on your arm.'

Back from the Kansas City hotel, Vivien met Selznick. 'Well, how did it go?' he asked.

How could such a question be answered?

'Oh, David, I'm so grateful to you. Larry met me in the hotel lobby and we went upstairs and we fucked and we fucked and we fucked the whole weekend.'*

The wrap-up party for *Gone With the Wind* was given on Stage 5. It brought no real sense of completion. The stars put in a perfunctory appearance – and some of the crew got perfunctorily drunk. Everyone knew there were still too many scenes to be shot to say farewell.

Through all the filming, Vivien had felt no satisfaction in her performance. It had been physically destructive, mentally depressing. It had taken such a toll on her health, left her so drained, that Olivia de Havilland, who hadn't seen her for about four weeks, actually didn't recognise her when she returned for a last day of shooting. She passed

---

* Roland Flamini, *Scarlett, Rhett and a Cast of Thousands*.

Vivien on the set, failing to recognise her or 'sense her aura, because she had lost so much weight, and looked so diminished by overwork. Almost depleted. Her whole atmosphere had changed. She gave something to that film which I don't think she ever got back.'

She wasn't the only one. At one point, Fleming had threatened to drive his car off a cliff. Selznick wasn't happy with his replacement, Sam Wood, and ended up directing the final scene himself. He did two versions of Gable's last words: 'Frankly, my dear, I don't give a damn.' The censors made him revise that to 'Frankly, my dear, I don't care,' though the original version was released later. Selznick had wanted to reshoot the opening of the picture, where Scarlett is first seen as a sparkling teenager in antebellum Georgia, but one look at Vivien's face decided him to postpone it until she had at least a month's rest. And she was going to New York to join Larry. Now he could afford to be generous. He told her to enjoy herself, to take in a few plays. His office would get her all the tickets she wanted.

Vivien told him that Larry's father had died. Since Larry was leaving the play, they planned to spend a month in England. Selznick was delighted. It would keep them out of the clutches of the American press.

When he noticed that she was crying, she explained, 'David, you won't believe this, but all I've wanted was to get the bloody filming over with. And now that it is – I feel like weeping for Scarlett. She's dead, you see, and we've been together so deeply.'

'The hell she is! You two will go on for ever.'

Selznick had bought the screen rights to Daphne du Maurier's brilliant gothic novel *Rebecca*. His selection of Olivier to play the moody Max de Winter could not have been more ideal casting – as the author enthusiastically agreed. The producer gave Vivien the latest revised scenes for the *Rebecca* screenplay to take to Olivier, carefully avoiding the question still under consideration: whether Vivien would play opposite Larry. Selznick knew how much they both wanted that, but he had strong reservations about Vivien as Daphne du Maurier's mousy heroine. The American public still liked their stars to be typecast.

Vivien and Sunny got aboard the next plane – a night flight to New York. Vivien was too excited to sleep. The two women cuddled together in the double berth and chatted through the dark hours above the steady vibrating rumble of the propellers.

Larry met them at the airport in a chauffeur-driven limousine. Sunny climbed in beside the driver. Black curtains entirely masked the back seat for the lovers' reunion. There was a healing atmosphere in New York that summer. On Fifth Avenue, Vivien met the important Hollywood columnist Radie Harris, whom she had phoned on arriving. Loyal friend Radie could be counted on to remain silent.

That afternoon, Vivien went to Larry's last matinée before Francis Lederer took over. She sat with Radie Harris in the darkness of the theatre and heard the house rock with laughter to the perfectly-timed lines. Vivien could hardly wait until the final curtain to go back. She hurried Radie to Larry's dressing-room, where he dropped out of character for a clinging embrace.

Sunny saw them off to England on the *Ile de France*, queen of the floating palaces: small figures behind the confetti and streamers floating down from an upper deck. And as the graceful ship backed into the current of the old Hudson River like a wealthy dowager dogged by poodle-tugs at her skirts, the band played 'Should auld acquaintance be forgot . . .'

Travel has changed. And so have morals. The lovers had separate cabins, and their names were discreetly absent from the passenger list. They met 'quite by chance'. With Vivien blanket-wrapped in steamer chairs and pampered by stewards, the tiredness soon drained away from her face, the sea spray painted colour back in her cheeks. She was regaining that appreciation of every instant of living that was her special gift.

Once in London, they could move back to Durham Cottage, but of course the visits to the children would be made separately. And they had something marvellous to look forward to: fulfilment of their desire to work together when they would return to Hollywood to co-star in David Selznick's *Rebecca!* Life had assumed a dreamlike quality in which nothing could go wrong.

7 *War and hoopla*

The royal 'we'. Vivien sighed, looking up from Selznick's
cable, which had reached them aboard the ship. It went on
to say that playwright Robert Sherwood, the screenwriter in
this case, and even George Cukor, who was to direct, both
had the identical reaction. The words threw the last shovel-
ful of earth on a buried hope.

Oliver had also received a cable:

DEAR LARRY: PLEASE SEE MY WIRE TO VIVIEN. (As though
he wouldn't!) I KNOW YOU MUST BE DISAPPOINTED BUT
VIVIEN'S ANXIETY TO PLAY THE ROLE HAS IN MY OPINION
BEEN LARGELY IF NOT ENTIRELY DUE TO HER DESIRE TO DO
A PICTURE WITH YOU WHICH WAS BEST DEMONSTRATED IN
PART WHEN I FIRST MENTIONED IT TO HER AS POSSIBILITY
AND UNTIL SHE KNEW YOU WERE PLAYING MAX . . .

It was a letdown, a disappointment, but after all *Rebecca*
was only one film out of a lifetime ahead. They could still
raise champagne glasses and drink to England, to each
other, to all the decks they would ever stand on together,
all the theatre stages, all the studio sets – and, as Vivien
was often heard to say, David be fucked!

On 28 July 1939, tugs pulled the great ship into
Plymouth, where the actor faced a swarm of journalists
while Vivien remained aloof. What about Miss Leigh, they

wanted to know? Was it pure coincidence their travelling on the same ship?

Everything is coincidence, isn't it? No, Mr Olivier understood that Daphne du Maurier was actually pleased that he would be playing Max de Winter. But he imagined that Mr Selznick would have preferred Ronald Colman, who hadn't been available. Miss Leigh to co-star? A little too vivacious for such a dowdy role, wouldn't they agree? He avoided mentioning the two cables in his pocket.

Mark Twain once said: 'Rural England is too absolutely beautiful to be left out-of-doors, it ought to be under a glass case.'

In the churchyard of Addington, a charming village in Buckinghamshire, Larry said his final good-bye to that sometimes distant shadow on the backdrop of his life, the Reverend Gerard Kerr Olivier, a year short of his seventieth birthday. It was a sun-blessed day in the English country-side, and yet one could sense the gathering turbulence that people called with understated optimism, 'a state of emergency.'

The sandbags being filled, trenches being dug, air-raid shelters in Hyde Park, gas masks doled out at town halls – all somehow seemed a foolish gesture, like amateur theatricals. Vivien did not feel the same measure of serious-ness as she had the summer before, when, after Munich, she had rushed off to volunteer for Civil Defence. More likely, this would be another false alarm, with the politicians patching things up again, extending the good life another year, another five or ten. Hadn't one of the Mitford sisters been to tea with Hitler? Hadn't Chamberlain promised 'peace in our time'? Yet greedy eyes were devouring Danzig on the map, and there was a hollow ring to the Prime Minister's reassurances.

Thus, with a certain feeling of unease, Vivien and Larry visited their children and friends until it was time for them to sail back to the States. Vivien took her mother back with them for a holiday. Although she adored Larry, Vivien's mother was understandably troubled by the impending divorces, but still she went with them in good spirit.

Three weeks later, in Hollywood, they were all invited on a yachting party by Doug Fairbanks, Jr., who had chartered a comfortable boat for the long Labor Day weekend of September, 1939. As Doug related the weekend to me, the boat was nothing ostentatious – just large enough to provide several staterooms – and it was to be a particularly British weekend. Young Doug, who had contracted anglophilia at an early age, had invited (along with Vivien, Larry, and Mrs Hartley) the superb blustery actor Nigel 'Willie' Bruce (everyone's favourite Dr Watson), David Niven, and Robert Coote; also aboard were Doug's wife, Mary Lee, and her doctor, as she was expecting her first baby. They sailed for Catalina, the isle that rears itself above the blue-green Pacific, twenty-five miles off the California mainland. You could always see Catalina on a clear day – and every day was clear in those days. The Labor Day weekend had attracted a number of fine yachts to Emerald Bay, among them the *Dragoon*, owned by Ronald and Benita Colman. Nearby was the popular resort town of Avalon, where, according to the song of the day, one's love was left 'beside the sea'.

And so Doug had brought together a yachtful of Englishmen, escaping for a few days from the studios and the speculations of whether or not their country might possibly find itself at war. Most people were trying to believe that Hitler, the ranting little man with the bristling moustache, could still be appeased. Only two days before, German armies had invaded Poland, and, though nobody aboard the Fairbanks yacht could yet know it, at this very moment the British passenger ship *Athenia* was about to be torpedoed, with thirty Americans among its victims.

It was early Sunday morning on Doug's chartered yacht. The sun, sparkling on the crystal water, brought the guests out early to the deck.

'Think you might pick up something on the radio, Doug?'

'Can but try, old boy.'

Doug manipulated the dials of the powerful radio; everybody strained to hear. The tranquil morning was broken by a crackling voice – the British Prime Minister Neville Chamberlain, weary, solemn, with nothing left of the old bowler-brolly confidence. Now he was announcing that the flirtation with Hitler was over. Germany had been given until 11 a.m. to promise withdrawal from Poland. 'I have to tell you now that no such undertaking has been received, and that consequently this country is at war with Germany . . .'

Vivien felt tears coursing down her cheeks. Even now, the bombers might be over London.

'Oh, God . . .'

Larry put his arm around Vivien's pale, thin shoulders. A comforting gesture but, under the circumstances, useless. His thoughts were the same as hers. The same as those of all the British on that boat. Everyone wanted to say something, but what was there to say? It was like walking suddenly on stage without being given the lines or the actions.

Silently the group separated, going to their cabins. Doug and his wife slipped away first; the others followed. It had been in Doug's mind that when or if the time should come, he owed a debt to the place and people he knew almost better than his own homeland.

'Mary Lee,' Doug said quietly, 'I suppose I'll join up right away, if they'll have an American. Which sounds as melodramatic as a subtitle in one of father's old pictures. But it's what I'm going to do.'

In their cabin, Vivien and Larry considered what must be done. Olivier identified himself deeply with his country's history, having portrayed so much of it on stage. He may have disliked the blatant jingoism of Prince Hal, yet he'd made of it a thunder that shook even the most dedicated isolationist in the audience.

They would go back as soon as possible. Naturally they couldn't just drop everything. They each had a film to finish, and contractually a war couldn't be considered an act of God. They had been told the plan would be to call up by age groups; it would be months before the military started taking the thirty-two-year-olds. Meanwhile, they'd arrange to bring Tarquin and Suzanne to America. It seemed selfish to be thinking only of their own, but it was all they could think of until they knew where they could best be useful.

The tiny cabin did not seem large enough to hold Larry now. He would report to the British Consul in Los Angeles first thing Tuesday morning. If they weren't prepared to send him back immediately to join up, he'd start flying lessons in California.

Vivien nodded, holding back the fear she felt. Whatever was going to be, she was glad they had found each other first. What a rotten trick it would have been to have shared the same lifetime without sharing their lives!

In his cabin, Nigel Bruce tapped his damaged leg, a permanent memento of France, 1917. He glanced up at Robert Coote. 'Jolly unfair, Bobby. One war going to keep me out of another. It'll be the same for "Bart" Marshall and Leslie Banks. Had his whole face rebuilt, you know.' He rose, looking at himself in the mirror. 'Willie Bruce, pipe-smoking, blithering fool of stage and screen. What – I ask myself – would Watson do now?'

'He'd leave it to Holmes,' replied Coote.

'Can't just do nothing, even with a gammy gam. But the bloody question is what?'

But Robert Coote was busy making up his own mind. He would leave for Canada to join the RAF or RCAF – whichever would have him first.

In David Niven's cabin there were no decisions to be made. He had been in the Regular Army and was now in the Reserve of the Highland Light Infantry. He would report at once and probably be sent directly to his old regiment. Simple enough, now that the political dithering was finally over. He was to be the first from Hollywood's English bastion into uniform. Rather like a man going home . . . To celebrate, he got out his smart Savile Row dinner jacket. Might as well get a last bit of wear out of it this bright sunny morning before God knows how many months of mothballs.

Since there was really nothing else to do, they all drifted quietly back to the deck. Doug had brought up a case of champagne. Corks popped, and glasses were passed.

'Well, here's to whatever it is!' Doug toasted.

'To victory,' Larry said solemnly.

The sun crept up a little higher and empty champagne bottles accumulated. Either get sloshed or go to church. And who could find a church on Catalina? asked Willie Bruce.

'It happens, though you may not have noticed, to be one of the most highly churched hamlets in the hemisphere, dear boy,' Doug said. 'In fact, the whole island is a kind of altar. To chewing gum. St Spearmint, St Juicy Fruit, and St Tutti-Frutti.' He was referring to the fact that Catalina Island was owned entirely by William Wrigley, the chewing-gum king.

'That's an ice-cream, old horse.' Dapper in dinner jacket, Niven slid his feet into water skis.

'No patent-leather skis? Damned poor show, David.'

'No fear, I shan't lift a foot above water.' Niven swung over the side of the yacht, signalling the waiting motor-boat, and he was off in a cloud of spray.

'Lucky bugger's got a regiment to go back to,' complained Willie, lighting what appeared to be the world's largest straight-grain gold-banded Dunhill. Fairbanks recalls what happened next.

'Somebody should bloody well tell them!' Olivier frowned, finishing off his glass of champagne. He was referring to the tinkle of unseemly laughter that had drifted to them from one of the other yachts.

'Tell whom and what?' asked Doug, thinking his friend might have had enough to drink.

But Olivier was adamant: they had to be told. Nobody quite knew what he was referring to until he hopped down into the bobbing dinghy. Off he shoved among the fleet of swaying luxurious yachts on whose decks unnautical captains lolled with their sun-oiled guests.

Like an admonishing Isaiah of the Pacific, the actor raised his clarion voice to announce the approach of doomsday, sounding an end to the world they had known. They had best drink their last, eat their fill, copulate, and be merry, for tomorrow would bring bitter wine! Olivier plied his oars on down the line of boats, castigating the flotilla as he rowed. Astounded yachtsmen leaned across their well-burnished rails to stare down at the passing prophet. Was the man raving mad? Who the devil was he? Some actor, probably. No wonder they kept them out of the Los Angeles Country Club!

Olivier, rowing on, seemed to gain in vehemence from his own performance. 'O God of battles, steel my soldiers' hearts, possess them not with fear! Take from them now the sense of reck'ning, if th' opposed numbers pluck their hearts from them!' He rounded the stern of a sleek pleasure cradle rocked gently by the tide and switched to *Julius Caesar*. 'Cry "Havoc!" and let slip the dogs of war, that this foul deed shall smell above the earth with carrion men, groaning for burial!'

Leaning over the rail, Vivien had lost sight of Larry, but she could still hear him. 'I think somebody better leash Larry,' she suggested.

A yachtsman's wife focused binoculars on the offending oarsman. 'Heavens! It's Ronald Colman!'

'Should be reported to the Committee!'

Which, of course, was done. Sometime after Olivier had rowed himself back to the Fairbanks yacht, an immaculate brass-gleaming motorboat carried the Commodore of the Yacht Club over to the sixty-seven-foot ketch that had been transformed into one of southern California's loveliest yachts. Ronald Colman and his Benita moved to welcome the official aboard.

'Splendid morning, Commodore. Have a drink?'

'Thank you, no, Mr Colman.' The Commodore's face was starched with purpose. 'Sorry to bring complaints from a number of our members. They have informed me of your insulting behaviour this morning.'

'Mine?'

The Commodore pursed his lips. 'I think we need hardly go into it further, Mr Colman. I'm sure it must be as embarrassing to you as to me. However, I feel I must ask you to make a formal apology in writing to the membership.'

'For what?' asked Colman.

The Commodore was growing angry. 'If it isn't on my desk by tomorrow, we'll have to request your resignation.'

For once, the perpetual Colman poise showed signs of ruffle. 'But, my dear fellow, I can scarcely apologise until I know the nature of the crime.'

The Commodore drew a long breath. This unpleasant chore could hardly be compensated by the pleasure he might derive from presenting silver trophies for victories over tuna and marlin. 'No good playing the innocent with me, Mr Colman. You were reported by at least ten yacht owners and heard by most of the island, I'd guess. Damn it, I don't know what you said, but it was in the worst possible taste. After all, this is Sunday, you know!'

'But Ronnie hasn't been off our boat all morning!' protested Benita, justly indignant. Colman's glance lighted on the Fairbanks chartered yacht, at that moment slinking cravenly out of the harbour. The truth visited him in a great flash of knowing. The Commodore's glance followed Colman's.

'Isn't that – ?'

'It is.'

'I think I owe *you* the apology, Mr Colman.'

'Not you, Commodore. But I have a fair suspicion who does! And he'll damned well appease me with a case of that champagne he's been drinking all morning!'

Benita sighed. Young Doug, doing his Richard III again.

On Tuesday morning, the British Consul in downtown Los Angeles was besieged by a distinguished all-star cast. Old and young, leading men, character actors, they all crowded into the small office, many with luggage already packed – volunteers for immediate war service. In the forefront was Laurence Olivier. To one and all, the Consul's instructions were to do nothing at that time. His Majesty's government had a most difficult situation to be dealt with, and the untimely arrival of British subjects who were not actually trained members of the Army, Navy, or Air Force Reserves could only add to the confusion. In fact, he informed them, the British government requested that actors who were under contract to American companies should fulfil their obligations. They should continue to portray Englishmen in films with dignity and charm, and help eradicate the unfortunate impression shared by so many Americans – that England was a nation of blithering, monocle-sporting, tea-sipping types who only knew how to brandish a croquet mallet. To gain the sympathy and friendship of the United States for their embattled cousins would be a far greater service than rushing to arms.

In short, the story was: 'Don't call us. We'll call you.' The drama of reality does not always match the pace of melodrama, and the weeks began to pass with little real news or excitement. The French sat on their Maginot Line. The British trained and prepared – and not a single Frenchman was killed except in motor accidents.

'This war will end up on the cutting-room floor,' said a yawning British film director. And since there was no real war to get on with or into, film-colony Englishmen got on with their own careers – except for Niven and a handful of 'old sweats', as the British called them. As the autumn of 1939 came on, it seemed that nobody would be going anywhere. But the four horsemen were waiting in the wings.

'Larry and I got fucked out of working together in *Rebecca*, Myron, darling. I'd awfully like your assurance that it isn't going to happen this time.'

'Will you stop worrying, sweetheart? It's in the bag!'

She hung up the telephone. Vivien had learned, among

other things, never completely trust a Hollywood agent.

Later, over lunch at the Beverly Hills Brown Derby, the agent radiated confidence – and reweighed the prospects. Vivien and Larry had two chances of working together on the next film. M-G-M was preparing an adaptation of Jane Austen's *Pride and Prejudice* with George Cukor set to direct. George wanted them both.

So what was the problem? she asked.

The problem? Nothing that couldn't be solved. If they didn't cold-deck Vivien.

What, the actress asked, was that supposed to mean?

Deal a queen off the bottom. A queen named Greer Garson. M-G-M had just signed a contract with her in London and she was arriving on the next boat. Myron had been getting signals from Casting that Benny Thaw and Eddie Mannix, two of Metro's top production executives, thought she was perfect for the part. It would take a fast shuffle to keep Vivien in the winning hand.

It seemed elementary to Vivien. Simply get her signed for the part before Greer arrived.

That, Myron intoned, was the other problem. Louis B. had pegged Vivien to play the dame in *Waterloo Bridge*.

Then, suggested Vivien, why not get Larry the lead in that?

Impossible. Not only was Larry practically set for *Pride*, but Robert Taylor was in rail position for *Waterloo*. After playing *A Yank at Oxford*, he was a natural for the British officer.

But Larry's accent might be a shade *more* natural, Vivien suggested.

The agent gave her a hard look. She was not thinking Hollywood. Not tuned in on the big box office. Americans still didn't buy foreigners that quickly. Even foreigners playing foreigners!

'But you said it was in the bag, Myron.'

Myron admitted that the bag had a couple of holes in it. Not that he was giving up without a struggle. He'd be needling L.B. all the way to the post. As Vivien looked depressed, Myron patted her slender hand like the all-protective daddy agents always pretend to be. 'Who pays who to do the worrying?'

'Whom.' She withdrew her hand from his solicitations and lighted a Player's. Her decision was clear. She simply would not do another film – any film – unless it was with Larry. And Myron could tell that to L.B., C.B., D.O.S., or even to God.

But God didn't come into it. L.B. was alone on this one. Myron promised he'd get with Thaw and Mannix right after lunch and kick it around. But he also promised something else. He was not letting her screw up her career by turning down *Waterloo*. Taylor was right up there with Gable, and until *G.W.T.W.* hit the screens and the public bought her, she was not dealing from strength. 'This is a crazy town, sweetheart. Let Uncle Myron call the plays.'

Vivien was beginning to understand what lay behind Hollywood's glitter. She was enough of a realist to see that the blossom-scented air was faintly drugged. One had to struggle to keep one's balance. How many of the beautiful bitch-goddesses destroyed themselves on their own altars in fear of growing old? The sense of it was chilling.

In her heart, Vivien knew that her battle was lost. Selznick was trying and succeeding in keeping her and Larry apart, on screen and off. She suggested this possibility to Myron.

How could he disagree? David had poured four million dollars into *G.W.T.W.* Did she expect him to risk that because of her sex life? She knew the damage a bad press could do, and most columnists would skin their mothers for a scoop. *G.W.T.W.* wasn't just *any* movie. It involved the moral sensitivity of the United States of America, he told her solemnly. And to a Hollywood studio, four million dollars was a lot of moral sensitivity. But surely she knew how sympathetic he was to their problem.

And she was sympathetic with his and David's. But if Larry wasn't invited with her to the world première of *G.W.T.W.* in Atlanta – in the immortal words of Sam

Goldwyn, they could include her out!

And even the wily Myron fathomed that this time there would be no swaying her.

'Jesus, you kill me, Viv!'

'War is hell, darling.'

He tossed a five-dollar tip on the table and arose, knowing he had won one and lost one.

Georgia, Georgia – peachy, memory-soaked citadel – the state you couldn't get off your mind. Lazy as golden summertime, land of swamps, grey dust, and red mud still bearing the scars of the wagon wheels that hauled cotton. Now Georgia would light up on the map of the world for the greatest movie ever made, from the book of her own honoured daughter! Who in those ink-splashed publicists' days to come would ever get Georgia off his mind? Hollywood's invaders would change the land almost as much as Sherman's fire and swords, with the crackle of typewriters, blasting ballyhoo around the world.

Larry handed Vivien his printed invitation to the première and was surprised that she wasn't surprised. Selznick, in his slightly nagging Eastern accent, had given in: 'Larry, we have decided to include you at the opening as a kind of live trailer for another great Selznick film. I have ordered publicity photos of you as Max de Winter and news releases on *Rebecca*, which I trust may draw some attention in the rather considerable hoopla attendant on our opening.'

Vivien wanted to know whether he had really said 'hoopla'.

Olivier nodded. No doubt a Red Indian word to denote organised insanity.

Vivien whisked out a ball gown designed by Walter Plunkett that she and Sunny had been packing for Atlanta. A hoopskirt for the hoopla! 'Fiddle-de-dee,' she said as she held the gown in front of her, singing, 'Oh, I wish I was in the land of cotton . . .'

'*Were* in the land of cotton.'

'No, *was*. It's the song they wrote for the picture, puss.'

'An old Southern song, Miss Leigh. Authentic,' Sunny assured her.

'Lawdy, Lawdy, massah! An' I jes' gave an interview sayin' they wrote it 'specially for *Gone*. They'll think I'm an idiot.'

'Only British.'

'Same thing.' She sprawled over the pile of gowns in joyous exuberance. Sunny handed her a folder of papers.

'It's the schedule for Atlanta, Miss Leigh. They haven't left you time to powder your nose.'

'I'll think about it tomorrow,' she sighed, in her Scarlett mood.

The Hollywood *Reporter* noted: 'Before junketing to Atlanta, Ga., for the première of *G.W.T.W.* the cast of the picture was advised to prepare speeches for the event. Fortunately, someone thought of asking Vivien Leigh what she planned saying. "Oh, I've prepared a splendid speech," La Leigh replied. "It's very short, but I'm sure they'll like it. I'm going to say, 'I'm just as happy to be here in Georgia as General Sherman was!' "'

For the first time at a motion picture première, television would cover the event. N.B.C. would broadcast and telecast with four Iconoscope cameras via coaxial cables to two mobile transmitter trucks located opposite the theatre. On that glorious Friday, two cameras at the main entrance would capture highlights. In command of the operation was Howard Dietz, publicist-in-chief, whose authority on this occasion would be second only to D.O.S. himself. Not to be outdone by the Mayor, the Governor of Georgia declared a state holiday; it was an act no politico could afford to avoid.

The parade moved down Peachtree Street, with brass bands in Confederate uniforms blaring the anthem of the Old South to the enthusiastic cheers of some million and a half spectators, many in costume. Fifty flower-decked automobiles bore the cast from the airport through a storm of glittering confetti to the Georgia Terrace Hotel for a mammoth civic reception attended by ten Southern governors.

Olivia de Havilland rode with Olivier in a car in that parade. He made a strong impression on her because of something he said. It was a cold, rainy afternoon, and the sight of the people eight deep, come all the way from five different states, was depressing to the actress. It seemed extraordinary to her that people would come so far just to see other people who'd been in a movie. She told that to Olivier, who replied, 'Oh, it doesn't depress me. I think it's marvellous that people can feel so strongly about something and come so far to express their feelings, and that it is ourselves they want to see. That what we give them means that much to them.'

In the hotel elevator, Larry and Vivien did not hide their affection. William Paley's wife found this display adolescent and in bad form. But de Havilland found it rather appealing, and thought it wonderful.

De Havilland has a vivid image of Vivien at this time: 'There was something quixotic about her. Her quality was less robust than Scarlett's, more delicate. And her very precise English accent added something to her personal atmosphere. She suggested not so much fragility as delicacy. If you thought of an animal – it would be a Siamese cat, elegant and imperious. Or the delicacy of a fine porcelain cup. She also made me think of Japanese wind-bells, of tinkling suspended glass. Those three images of Vivien come to mind.'

That night Vivien and Larry attended the Junior League *G.W.T.W.* ball in the large red-brick auditorium, where eight thousand of Atlanta's élite cavorted with the cast to the music of Kay Kyser's band (which performed gratis because the publicity for them was so stupendous).

Kyser told us how, during the Grand Waltz, one local belle's Scarlett O'Hara costume caught fire, and the blazing hoopskirt had to be extinguished with mint julep ladled from the nearest cut-glass punch bowl. To Rebel yells of 'Yee-aay-ee,' 'Waa-hoo-ee,' and 'Yaaa-yee,' the squealing girl was divested of her hot pantaloons.

Gable met Margaret Mitchell for the first time, and, slightly embarrassed at seeing her hero in the flesh, the petite authoress hustled him away from prying eyes to the privacy of the ladies' powder room, where she promptly locked them in. What passed behind those doors will never be known.

Amid the wild commotion, Larry seized Vivien's hand. He had been amused to see Vivien and Clark, leading the Grand March, practically hissing at each other under their breath. Gable had arrived by separate plane, in a foul mood, bearing a grudge against Selznick and a hangover from a booze session with Fleming, who had refused to attend the première. The King was furious because some newspaper had quoted Selznick as saying that he, Selznick, had had to 'direct' the directors.

'Clark and I have signed a neutrality pact,' Vivien confided. But the lovers found few moments for private whispered words, with socialites bearing down on them from every direction. Larry's face froze into the required mask of polite detachment as he watched Vivien being whisked away by Jock Whitney to meet some Vanderbilt, Swope, Rockefeller, Morgan, or Astor. They were all there, and all the names were beginning to form a blur of sound no longer attached to faces. Her glance found Larry's and she kept up the barrage of banal answers to senseless questions.

'An' they do say the scalpers have been askin' and *gettin'* two hundred dollahs for a ten-dollah ticket. An' even so they were all sold out in two minutes, Mizz Scarlett . . .' Already she was losing her identity.

'What did you do in the picture, Mr Olivier, suh?'

'Admired it, madam.'

Finally, they were watching the film, and in the darkened theatre Larry switched seats so they could be together. Hands could touch unnoticed by the mighty Selznick, riding his crest of glory as reel after reel re-created Civil War Atlanta for the deeply-moved progeny of the Old

South. And even Margaret Mitchell and her husband, John Marsh, were satisfied. She sat a little forward in her seat, bare-shouldered in a light silk dress, her short hair bobbed and held neatly in place by a small bow. Until the lights dimmed, Vivien – in long white ermine cloak, an orchid pinned to her handbag, a flimsy veil over her hair fastened by her blazing aquamarine – had been the target of every eye. For the next two hundred and twenty emotion-packed minutes, nineteen thousand, eight hundred feet of film ground through the projectors.

Perhaps no audience had ever been more moved by any moving picture. They wept, they cheered, they relived the memories and stories of family forebears. For the people of Atlanta, *G.W.T.W.* was far more than a film opening – it was a drama that involved their heritage and wrung their hearts. When it was over, the cheers and calls for 'Author!' brought the slight, nervous Margaret Mitchell to the stage. It seems unlikely that at any time has a film opening brought the book's author to the stage by demand of the audience. But almost everything to do with *G.W.T.W.* made film history.

And yet the new star hardly saw the screen. Her thoughts went back to the agony and exhaustion of those lonely days of filming; she relived the driving frenzy and tension of trying to capture the image that had grown in her mind since she first read Mitchell's saga. The birth of this screen Scarlett had in some measure been a series of crises for Vivien – mental, physical, emotional. A film of this magnitude was a war from which no actress could emerge unscathed. Never again would it be possible for her to be the old Vivien. All that rubbish about success going to her head – of course she had changed! She had been rubbed by the philosopher's stone of Hollywood, which could transmogrify any salesgirl into pure gold. Only one thing would not change, ever: the way she felt about Larry. No starry heights would diminish her dependence on and need for his guidance, her respect for his infinite talent.

With her remembrance of the deep weariness of the

filming was a surreal sense of the incongruity of these events. This circus of Southern nostalgia hardly seemed suitable against the very real war preparations her mother had just written her about from London. On 9 December the first British soldier had fallen, shot dead on patrol on French soil. But here all minds were on the past and the profits it would bring.

By the next day, when they had reached the final 'Grande Bouffe' – a luncheon given by Margaret Mitchell at the Piedmont Driving Club – Vivien had begun to feel like an automaton, smiling at strangers, countering flattery with a modest answer. She and the authoress had hit it off from the first, and they were both a little overwhelmed. Now she listened to Mitchell's kind words while the press noted for posterity the actress's jaunty wide-brimmed hat, short silver fox cape, and that same blazing jewel on a chain at her neck.

'An' why have we seen nothin' of Ashley, Mizz Scarlett?' enquired a Daughter of the Confederacy.

'Mr Howard returned to England in August. The war.'

'An' when will you be goin' to join the colahs, Mistah Olivier?'

His eyes searched and found her glance. Oh, to be an actor, not a star! Oh, rather the reality of any work on any stage! . . .

'I've been honeyed and sugared so much I've got diabetes,' groaned studio photographer Norman Kaplan to Howard Dietz.

'Be grateful you're not one of the stars.'

At the Washington opening, Vivien was seated in a box facing Olivia de Havilland's. They were the only members of the cast who were there. Gable had had a bellyful, and even the great Selznick couldn't stop him from heading home with his bride of nine months, Carole Lombard.

When Scarlett was introduced at the opening, Vivien rose and acknowledged the applause with only a graceful nod of her head. 'It was the attitude you'd expect from royalty – an imperial highness, quite fascinating and un-expected. Something instinctive in her that expressed two things: her own personal sense of style, and a genuine attitude, too,' de Havilland recalls. Selznick had given out his star's age as twenty-four, but Vivien had just turned twenty-six, two years older than Olivia.

New York proved to be a ritual replay, with hordes of screaming fans and three hundred extra police to get the celebrities into the movie house. D.O.S. and his backers basked in the certainty of a winner; and indeed, *G.W.T.W.* would be one of the greatest moneymaking films of all time. In 1977, it was still receiving awards: the Photoplay Award as All-Time Favourite Movie, accepted by the only surviving star of the film, Olivia de Havilland.

But in December, 1939, Vivien's reaction was less than enthusiastic: 'I couldn't have looked at it again. I was beginning to hate my face,' Vivien complained as she and Larry slipped away to the privacy of a quiet supper at the Chambord Restaurant. At the opening they'd made their entrance; then, as the lights dimmed, they ducked out a side exit. He chuckled in the candlelight, remembering the Mayor of Atlanta's ambiguous introduction of him at the ball. Larry had remained carefully in the background, but finally his presence had to be acknowledged.

Mayor Hartsfield attempted discretion – with dubious success: 'An' now ah want to introduce an actah who came here on his *own* business!'

8 *Romeo weds Juliet*

'In January I devoted a whole column in a seething, scornful denunciation of David O. Selznick because he couldn't find in this country, a Scarlett – therefore chose an English girl. And now, by golly, I've got to congratulate him and everyone concerned for choosing Vivien Leigh. In fact she didn't play Scarlett, she WAS Scarlett,' commented 'Hedda Hopper's Hollywood,' 18 December 1939. 'Now Vivien's problem will be, in subsequent pictures everything she does will be coloured with Scarlett!'

Vivien hoped to God that Hedda was wrong. To prove it, she felt she simply had to find a play again. Larry was in full agreement. In fact, he'd given the matter a lot of thought and come up with an answer for them both. Since the fates and David O. had contrived that they were not to film together, what would Miss Leigh say to a spot of Shakespeare?

'I'd say: Wherefore art thou, Romeo?'

Her response was instinctively right. For Larry was indeed considering a production of *Romeo and Juliet*, as soon as he had completed *Pride and Prejudice* and she had crossed *Waterloo Bridge*.

The winter of 1940 was showing promise for the new year. The Oliviers-to-be had moved to 1107 San Ysidro Drive, next door to Danny Kaye and his then wife, Sylvia Fine. (Danny was to remain a friend for life.) Each day they made the trip to M-G-M in Culver City, but their dreams were all in Verona. Between takes on *Pride* – in a part ideal for Olivier – the actor, in tight-fitting fawn trousers, sat in his folding chair and plotted his production. This was to be the most impressive, lavish, dynamic, mobile *Romeo and Juliet* ever to tour the States or anywhere else. The production would ensure their theatrical stature in America and it would be their last great effort before returning to England and war.

Mervyn Le Roy, who directed *Waterloo Bridge*, told me he considered Vivien Leigh 'one of the best actresses that ever lived'. But he added that 'she was also one of the dirtiest-talking women that ever lived. She was so cute about it, though. Used all the swear words you could think of, but the way she would do it, you would pay no attention. It just came out . . . innocent.'

The admiration was mutual. Vivien liked Mervyn and working on *Waterloo* far better than *G.W.T.W.* Author and friend Alan Dent later described her Myra as 'a daffodil just beginning to peer . . . as though Anna Karenina had fallen under the wheels of a streetcar named Desire.' In this part, Vivien was desperately trying to create a character that would make Hedda eat her words.

Since they were working at the same studio, separated by only a few sound stages, Vivien and Larry were able to spend their spare minutes together. But now all conversation was directed towards their pending stage production. They would finance it themselves, and Larry would produce and direct it. Their plans didn't worry Mervyn, who was about as relaxed as any director could be. Youthful and full of bounce, Le Roy has remained boyish into his sixties.

'Hairdresser for Miss Leigh, please!' Le Roy would call before a take.

'If they're going to be looking at my hair, they won't notice the fucking scene, Mervyn, darling.'

'Wind machine for Miss Leigh's hair!' he called, with a merry smile.

Vivien was using every spare moment on voice lessons to strengthen her projection and on coaching in the part of Juliet. She had found the perfect teacher, that great English actress Dame May Whitty. The ageing actress had known all the great Juliets of her day. Larry and Vivien were trying to persuade her to take the part of the Nurse, but she had declined, saying: 'No, no, my dears. I'm much too old for a tour; though I must say I'm sore tempted.' Dame May would visit Vivien's dressing-room while Sunny stood guard.

Sunny recalls an incident when they were working together on the scenes: 'A forty-year-old bottle of bourbon!' The throaty slightly rasping voice belonged to Gable. Finger on lips, bottle in hand, he'd slipped past Sunny, who was quite in awe of him. Vivien set down the text.

'Might as well come in, Clark. Now that you're in.'

'Brought you a little anti-snakebite.' He kissed her on the cheek, uncorked the bottle with his teeth, and poured. She declined, saying she had to be back on the set in ten minutes; Mervyn was driving her like a Georgia mule.

'Like you drove poor old Vic?' he asked. Clark tossed himself into a chair, stretching his legs. Vivien passed him a copy of the *Hollywood Reporter*.

'Did you see what Leslie Howard is quoted as saying about the war?' "A dreadful exhibition. Costumes tasteless, lighting shocking. It can't possibly run long." '

'Maybe M-G-M will loan me out to the war,' he sighed. 'Incidentally, I just gave out an interview about us.'

'Oh? Did you say how I used to sink you at Battleship?' The angled eyebrow again.

'Nope. I said to begin with that I'd like to state that despite what a lot of papers said, there never was any feud between us. We neither fought nor fell in love. And as for that possibility, I knew that was out at first glance!' He took a swig of his rare old 'mule kick'.

'Did you really say we neither fought nor fucked?'

'I sure as hell did, but not in those words.'

Dame May tittered. Vivien sat on the arm of the elder actress's chair in her sleazy *Waterloo* costume. 'How did you know at first glance there would be nothing between us? Did I look like a bad lay?'

'If I'd seen you in that get-up, maybe I'd have felt differently. But never have I seen any girl more completely hooked on a guy than you. You couldn't think or talk about or dream of anything or anyone else on earth! I really began to think I was slipping! As for my falling for you – I'm sure that could have been plenty pleasant, except that, added to your lack of interest in me, my heart was already staked out. And I mean Carole would have put a stake through it if I'd looked sideways at you!'

He hoisted himself to his feet, pouring one last bourbon as an afterthought. 'Like I used to say to Harlow when I poured one or two into her to cheer her up when she was having a rough patch – "This'll take the bumps out of the road, sweetheart." '

Vivien smiled. 'Make it the road to Verona, and I'll join you, Clark.'

Laurence Olivier's hand travelled down the long ivory keyboard. He was composing his own entrance music for *Romeo*. Vivien handed him the letter which had just arrived from Ralph Richardson. His London oracle had finally answered. He read it and frowned, surprised. It seemed Ralphie thought *Romeo and Juliet* 'a bit too luxurious for wartime.'

Since Richardson was already on active service in the Fleet Air Arm, things might look a bit more grim to him, across a vista of shortages, rationing, and the like. Olivier tossed the letter on top of the piano, played a series of measured chords adapted from Palestrina airs, and considered whether Ralph could be wrong this time. He had bettter be, because they were too far into production plans to count pennies now. The Motley sisters had been brought over from England to design sets and costumes. Everything was costing a bloody fortune, but it was Olivier's idea to re-create Renaissance Italy. It was hard enough for Americans to absorb the words of Shakespeare; he didn't want them to have to strain their imaginations. There must be a real staircase to Juliet's bedroom, a real garden wall for Romeo to vault. He wanted them to smell the dust and feel the Verona heat.

And now the house had become a vast production office

– bedrooms crammed with all manner of fabrics, photos, bits of scenery, props, and miniature sets. Olivier had definitely decided to use a stage revolve to present the twenty-one scenes in sequence. The cast was shaping up nicely: Edmund O'Brien as Mercutio, Alexander Knox for Friar Lawrence. Dame May had finally agreed to play the Nurse; she would be the oldest member of the cast.

The youngest was Jack Merivale, son of the actor Philip. Jack recalls: 'Larry knew a bit about me and first of all said I should play Paris. But he wanted Paris played in a certain way. He explained it very lucidly. It wasn't me at all. I couldn't do it the way he wanted it done, so I said if he really wanted it played like that he should get my step-brother John Buckmaster. And he said, 'Well. oddly enough, that is, what Vivien said. But I didn't know anything about his acting, and I know a bit about yours''

An unattached young British actor of more than average good looks, Jack Merivale was chosen to play Balthasar, and understudy Olivier. The part he would finally play in Vivien's life was then not even imagined.

Rehearsals were held at night at Warner Brothers Radio Studio on Sunset Boulevard. The Motleys were working at the old Vitagraph and also the Curran Studios in Los Angeles. It seemed as though preparations for the production were spread out all over southern California! Up to now, Vivien's and Larry's bank accounts had been emptied of some fifty thousand dollars and Larry was luring extra financing from Warner Brothers.

Vivien was still worried. The critics always said that no actress could play Juliet until she was too old for the part. Cornell was – and did! Bernhardt played it in her seventies, on one leg! Larry, however, truly believed she would be the greatest Juliet ever – and at least no critic could dare say they didn't know how it felt to be in love.

Thoda Cocroft was hired to do publicity for the tour, and recalls that Olivier thought it unnecessary to spend money on exploitation. 'No three sheets [lobby posters] for the front of the theatre or mail-order blanks?' wailed the press agent.

'We don't need them A small ad in the newspapers will be sufficient,' Olivier replied. Eventually he was persuaded to post three sheets and invest in a minimal number of mail-order forms. But he ruled out other customary American methods of exploitation. In England, such tactics were unthinkable.

Cocroft's impression of Vivien is revealing: 'Her naïveté and her wisdom, her warm beauty that could instantly freeze if Olivier were criticised, her juvenility and her matronly dignity . . . paradoxically combined to give this slip of a girl a refreshing wine-and-water personality . . . The screen fails to register her utter delicacy and daintiness, the changing colours of her eyes, the transparent quality of her skin . . . the most beautiful skin I have ever seen.'*

Variety of 12 February 1940, suggested (erroneously) that the stars didn't figure on making a dime on this tour, because the tour was too brief (twenty weeks, including rehearsals) to pay back the high initial cost of production. 'Personal satisfaction would be their reward,' the trade paper noted.

But if satisfaction was ever an end in itself, Vivien's Oscar Award on 28 February was totally gratifying. At the *G.W.T.W.* table with David and Myron Selznick, the Doug Fairbankses, the Bob Benchleys, she had been the centre of all attention in floating green chiffon, white ermine draped over her chair, a heavy antique bracelet, and sequins adding sparkle where none was needed. In her brief acceptance speech, she was the only person who remembered to pay tribute to Margaret Mitchell, 'that kind lady from Atlanta.' She ended by thanking Spencer Tracy, who had come from a hospital bed to the Ambassador Hotel to make the award.

Seated next to Olivia de Havilland, Larry appeared pre-

---

* Thoda Cocroft, *Great Names and How They Are Made.*

occupied, even through the glorious clowning of Judy Garland and Mickey Rooney. He was always a little bored with social events, and his mind was filled with the new project. He looked up to see Hedda, who was making a brief return to acting with a role in C. B. De Mille's *Reap the Wild Wind* – Paramount's answer to *Gone With the Wind*'s triumph, starring the girl who didn't get the part, Paulette Goddard. It replaced the burning of Atlanta with a giant squid (a scene I had the misfortune to write).

'I asked an extra on the set today what she thought of you and Vivien. She said, and I quote, Larry, dear, "Any love that's as great and sincere as that will always have the sympathy of the public and not its condemnation." Now isn't that swell?' Hedda kissed his cheek and wished him and Vivien luck on their San Francisco opening. This was against theatre tradition, but then this was Hollywood.

In that jewel among cities, San Francisco, the most complicated and expensive Shakespearian adventure in American theatre history was about to open. There were friends and well-wishers aplenty. Olivia de Havilland came up with Jimmy Stewart. Margaret Sullavan, Leland Hayward, John Swope, and Kay Aldrich made the trek. Alexander Woollcott was already there; the critic had donned greasepaint himself at the nearby Curran Theatre in *The Man Who Came to Dinner*. Woollcott devoted his nightly curtain speech to the forthcoming Olivier production, proclaiming it the greatest of all *Romeo and Juliets* – although he had not yet seen it.

So far, the production had cost sixty thousand dollars, but the entire San Francisco run was an advance sell-out, so the exhausted actor-manager and his Juliet were not too worried. Larry had revised his earlier London Romeo, giving the role a more poetic, lyrical interpretation. Perhaps the love scene he was living was making his Romeo more romantic.

Romeo's vault into the Capulet garden had worked perfectly at every rehearsal. But at the première exhaustion finally caught up with him. A few bounding steps, and he leaped for the wall, only to find himself dangling by his fingertips, unable to hoist himself over. For a fraction of a moment too long, the audience saw a struggling helpless Romeo. The magic was destroyed in a snicker of laughter before the stage manager had the presence of mind to black out.

'I felt such an awful fool hanging there with my legs kicking weakly,' he recalled later. But the critics were generous and lenient, though they generally seemed to prefer Vivien's performance to Larry's.

The cast put on a special matinée performance attended by their great admirer Alec Woollcott. The proceeds were donated to British and Finnish war relief.

As the train sped them through the prairie night towards Chicago, Vivien and Larry could hardly know that San Francisco would turn out to be the highlight of their tour. They could feel a new sense of joy. In six months or less their respective divorces would be final. After abandoning all possibility of reconciliation, both mates had become co-operative.

For weeks the Chicago movie palaces had been announcing the coming of 'the great lovers – *in person*!' The response was a welcome at Union Station resembling a political rally. More than a thousand upturned faces beneath a huge banner: 'WELCOME LAURENCE OLIVIER AND VIVIEN LEIGH.' The press agent had been doing his job – perhaps too well. The advertising in Chicago actually promised: 'See real lovers make love in person.'

'I trust they'll not expect us to copulate on the platform.'

'Afraid it's in the New York papers, too, Miss Leigh. I wasn't going to tell you,' revealed Sunny, who had come along as private secretary to both.

Police fought to clear a lane. Grubby hands thrust pencils for autographs. Someone caught and tore a bit of Vivien's dress. Hysterical fans always terrified her. There was a built-in savagery in this American brand of adulation, something beneath it that hungered to tear at you, drag you down, rip your clothes, pull at your hair, make you one of them. This was no reverent awe, only the rape of worship. But then Chicago always did everything in a big way, from steaks to gang-war funerals. Carl Sandburg called it 'the city of the big shoulders'.

Ensconced in a comfortable suite at the Ambassador beside the long lakeshore, Larry could give himself to the more pressing production decisions. Chicago would be their last chance to make important corrections. The stage revolve had been giving them problems, and they would need a stronger P.A. system, since they were to perform in a vast auditorium that seated thirty-five hundred people. Olivier was still not satisfied with the blocking of the last sword fight, and Jack Merivale would have to work on his fencing. They would need to have another lighting rehearsal, and the new equipment had not yet arrived from New York. But the bills had arrived along with the funereal-faced business manager, who handed the actor-manager pages of astronomical figures.

'Are we going broke, lover?' Vivien asked, concerned, as she combed out a newly-arrived wig. Not while Larry could still sign cheques with the golden fountain pen Vivien had given him.

At rehearsals he guided her performance with love and a gentle rein.

'It's this way, lovey,' he would tell her with a fond pat or caress, recalls Thoda Cocroft.

'No darling, turn here, so we can have your face. Downstage like this, sweetheart. There, now you have it!' He was gallant, tender, ardent . . . She was unselfish, thoughtful, pliant. They were in love both with each other and their work . . .'

The Chicago critics were not as enthusiastic as the adoring fans of the two stars. One called it *Jumpeo and Juliet*. But the audience had come to see what the press agent had advertised: 'The world's greatest love story enacted by the most picturesque couple in the world.' If Vivien's voice didn't always carry, the audience had come to see movie stars – not to hear Shakespeare.

In *Life* magazine of 20 May 1940, Noel F. Busch reviewed their stage and real-life love affairs. 'At the present time, instead of being sealed up in a tomb, like Romeo and Juliet, or muttering at their mates, like many other persons, Laurence Olivier and Vivien Leigh are in the best of condition. Their dispositions, though not perfect, are compatible ... (Perhaps he was referring to a story circulating at the time. At a private party to celebrate Vivien's Oscar, she became so arrogant and high-handed that Olivier brought her down to earth by throwing her Oscar out into the garden.) Olivier has apparently put on weight, which makes him look less neurotic, and Vivien Leigh has taken off weight, which makes her look more neurotic.

'A question arises as to the whereabouts of Mrs. Olivier and Mr Leigh Holman. Both are in England and both are divorced. The divorces symmetrical and simultaneous. Mr Holman named Laurence Olivier as correspondent and Mrs Olivier named Vivien Leigh as correspondent. In neither case did any scandal arise ... Olivier says: I don't suppose there ever was a couple so much in love. Vivien Leigh says: Our love affair has been simply the most divine fairy tale, hasn't it? ... They intend to get married as soon as their divorce decrees become final ... They will then join the select company of great American lovers – the Duke and Duchess of Windsor, John Barrymore and Elaine Barrie, and John Smith and Pocahontas.'

After a brief but satisfactory Chicago engagement, the company came to New York's 51st Street Theatre in May with the certainty of success. They came, trumpeted by their own publicist, celebrated by Hollywood, and even forgiven by movieland's most eminent arbiter of the private morals she so publicly exposed: 'No matter how one feels about divorce, the honesty of Olivier and Miss Leigh must be respected.' Such bull from the papal Louella Parsons was equivalent to absolution.

Their New York hotel suite (now unabashedly shared)

and dressing-rooms fluttered with cabled and telegraphed wishes for success. Even from war-locked Britain, friends found time to offer advance congratulations. No spring-time had ever seemed more kindly disposed towards visiting lovers.

Vivien worried that they had ordered enough champagne for the opening-night party. One might have thought they were launching a fleet, not a play. She wandered about the suite, looking delicate as the child-woman Juliet, while Romeo's golden pen autographed another batch of cheques. Broadway success! Friends pouring into town! If Vivien hated public adulation, she felt quite different about it on a personal level. Friendships and parties were a vital part of her existence – and even at this early stage in their relationship she realised that Larry's dedication to work would always push pleasure into second position. Yet he fed her whims, and had ordered their California chauffeur, John, to drive their limousine out from Hollywood. They'd need it, since they planned to spend much of their spare time at Kit Cornell's house at Sneden's Landing on the Hudson, wedged in among all those millionaires.

Larry smiled over at her, recognising the slight hint of nerves. Not that nerves were ever a bad thing before a first night. Controlling them produced the right tension, a sharpening of all the senses. He had known nerves bad enough at openings so that he had to force himself to leave the dressing-room. But this time it was *their* cast, *their* theatre, *their* New York – because they were in it together and because nobody had ever been so in love. More than anything, Vivien wanted the world to know that Laurence Olivier was the greatest actor in it.

David Fairweather, who was their great friend and long-time press agent, has said: 'To suggest that Vivien was jealous of his achievements is so ludicrous it hardly bears investigation. She thought him the greatest actor in the world, as indeed he is, and was very unsure of her own ability. As a film star, yes, but as a classical stage actress, no . . . If anyone dared to criticise Larry in her presence, she would flash with rage, and God help the offender . . .'

As the play moved towards its final curtain on opening night, Vivien, alone on stage, raised the poison vial to her lips. A door banged somewhere backstage. She drew breath and continued her last soliloquy. Through it came a rising noise of scuffling, curses, laughter. A group of celebrity-crazed fans had actually penetrated the exit doors and were doing battle with the ushers.

'Cheap Hollywood publicity stunt!' hissed a critic.

The play ended to less than wild applause, and the dressing-room (where the mood of a night is always reflected) was hardly a riot of adulation. Friends managed non-committal comments on costumes and the excellence of the sets. Sam Goldwyn appeared with his elegant wife, Frances.

'Well, you're still Olivier – and you're still beautiful, Vivien.'

Vivien offered the producer a glass of champagne and the sweetest of smiles. Neither deterred him.

'I think you should quit all this Shakespeare baloney and make another picture for me.'

Very kind of him, but they'd be going back to England as soon as they finished the run.

'That soon?' the producer asked bluntly. Polite good-nights. A number of bottles of champagne managed to retain their corks.

The critics' reactions to the event could be summarised this way. A couple of Hollywood stars had drifted into New York to toss a few Shakespearian pearls before the local swine and buy themselves theatrical immortality. Their efforts could not be mentioned in the same breath with the art of the serious theatre. One critic pointed out that the 51st Street Theatre just happened to be owned by a movie company, and had even once been called the Hollywood Theatre.

Although Walter Winchell noted on 22 May that they

did not exit from the same stage door 'so's not to interfere with each other's autograph fans,' the critics were not cheering: 'The worst Romeo ever!' 'Olivier talked as though he were brushing his teeth.' 'The audience remained quiet. They were fast asleep.' Brooks Atkinson, dean of New York drama critics, complained, 'Much scenery – no play.' And more of the same: 'Plodding and uninspired.' 'Incomprehensible.' 'Hollow.' The A.P. dispatch capped it: 'Ouch! Vivien and Olivier panned by critics!'

The decision was simple: instant economy. Give the hotel back its suite, the caterers their cases of unused champagne. They'd accept Cornell's offer to stay at Sneden's Landing. Sunny handed Olivier the phone. The box office was calling. There was quite a long line of people, stretching all the way around the block.

But the spark of hope was immediately doused when the manager went on to explain that the people weren't queued up for tickets. They wanted their money back! Larry was silent for a moment; then grim-faced, he ordered: 'Give it to them. Every penny.' He put down the receiver, flashing a crooked smile at Vivien.

'You know what I feel like doing? Going down to that box office and handing back the money myself.'

'Wonderful idea, my darling. I'll go with you. We could even autograph the bills.'

They were broke, but it didn't matter. They were together.

In fact, the total loss to the actor, actress, and Warner Brothers (their filmland investor) would come to over a hundred thousand dollars.

Embarrassed silence greeted their entrance to Noël Coward's party at Radio City Music Hall for the British war relief, but Noël's greeting was warmer. 'My darlings, how brave of you to come.'

And when they returned to the hotel, Sunny announced that the forgotten John had arrived after his three-thousand-mile drive, with their Packard limousine. Well, at least they wouldn't have to drive to the poorhouse in a taxi.

Notwithstanding, on 1 June, the Broadway Association chose Vivien Leigh as Broadway's First Lady – since her name was appearing simultaneously on four marquees. Aside from her unhappy stage début at the 51st Street Theatre, she could be seen at the Capitol in *Waterloo Bridge*, at the Rivoli in the newly-released four-year-old *21 Days Together*, and at the Astor in *Gone With the Wind*.

'At least I thought Ralphie could have got me into the Fleet Air Arm,' Larry complained, waving Richardson's letter at Vivien. Now his friend and eternal Cassandra had written that the R.A.F. wasn't taking anyone over twenty-eight unless he already had a pilot's licence. What did they think this was – another Children's Crusade? How old did one have to be to get killed?

Vivien continued knitting calmly on one of the many balaclavas she was making for the troops. 'You don't even like flying.'

'Yes, I do. It's you who don't!' But the point was rhetorical. Duff Cooper, the Minister of Information, had cabled that Olivier might be more use where he was – and Cooper must be better informed than they. Of use doing what? The actor sprawled into an enormous red damask chair in the study at Sneden's Landing. At his feet the newspaper vividly described the Nazi tide now engulfing the Low Countries. France would be next. And then . . . It was easy to imagine miles of barges and landing craft cascading their conquering hordes into England. And where was Romeo? In his final, feeble fourth week, forced to finish out his contract, flourishing a prop sword at empty houses.

Across the Hudson from Sneden's Landing was a sea-plane base. He was giving serious thought to taking flying lessons. Unless there was a bloody age limit for that, too! It was easy to feel unneeded – downright unwanted. And every shipload of ammunition that went over to

England now came back full of children. They had already discussed moving their own children to Canada and had written to their mates for permission. The British government was relocating thousands of children from Central London into foster homes in the countryside. But only money could take them to the safety of another continent, one unlikely to be bombed.

The actor had been gazing out towards the seaplane base. His glance did a perfect take-off following a plane as it lifted above the river. With sudden purpose he stepped out of the room. She watched him go, heard him dial the hall telephone, and then ask to speak to the instructor in charge. Her heart sank. He knew her innate fear of flying, that she could never quite adjust to humans being hoisted aloft into that boundless blue wilderness. And she knew that this was what he wanted and she would never say a word to stop him.

And so the flying lessons began, precariously. Whatever his abilities, no one could ever have called Olivier a born aviator. It was a mark of Vivien's titanic courage that she ventured aboard Larry's fragile training craft, braving the winds above the Hudson on a wing and a prayer.

Bumping high above the Rockies *en route* from New York to Hollywood, Alex Korda, a man who had undoubtedly influenced the course of their lives, clutched the arms of his chair. He tightened his seat belt and tried to read. On his lap tray were two bulky blue volumes by the naval historian Admiral Mahan. They chronicled another war against another conqueror who had also threatened the existence of Great Britain. Napoleon's failure to invade England had largely been due to an undersized, one-armed, one-eyed, frequently sea-sick sailor, Horatio Nelson. What a subject for a movie! It got better and better as Korda read on. What drama! What a film! And what a coincidence that the books just happened to have been sent to him by Duff Cooper, Minister of Information. For here was the ideal propaganda vehicle to put England back in her ex-colony's good graces. Here was an England that might totter on the edge of annihilation, but would find a hero in time of need. There was no harm in making a profit from patriotism, decided Korda. Why, Churchill might even reward him with a knighthood!

He would call the film *Lady Hamilton* so that nobody could get the idea they were making British propaganda. He would direct it himself. Brother Vincent would be art director. And the script? A masterpiece, by R. C. Sherriff, who wrote *Journey's End*. It would be the greatest part for Vivien since Scarlett – only better. And who else could play Nelson but Olivier?

When Vivien and Larry considered it, they saw that beyond the fact that the assignment sounded worthy, it would replenish their purses and enable them to bring over the children and keep them in Canada through the war. But Larry had one provision. He still wanted to get into the RAF. When he told Korda he intended to continue his flying lessons, the producer had a mild seizure.

RAF? Flying lessons? Was the actor crazy?

'I'm not asking you to fly with me, Alex.'

What would Korda tell the insurance company? How could he expect anyone to insure the film with a flying Nelson?

'Why not try "England expects every man to do his duty"?'

Reluctantly Korda agreed, provided Larry didn't tell him anything about it. If Vivien couldn't stop such madness, the producer wouldn't try. 'Now, have I got myself a Lady Hamilton and a Nelson?' he asked.

'Vivien has leased a small unpretentious cottage, while Larry maintains bachelor quarters at a nearby hotel.' Radie Harris was covering the fact that her friends were actually sharing a house at 9560 Cedar Brook Drive, off Coldwater Canyon. It was owned by screenwriter Sig Herzig, who had bought it from Dorothy Parker and her husband-collaborator, Alan Campbell.

For Vivien the place had an intangible atmosphere of melancholy, as though it had absorbed vibrations from the moody lady humorist who had originally owned it. Long shadows off the hills of the canyon crept down at four o'clock with a lugubrious chill. Vivien mentioned this oppressive feeling to Cukor, who later recalled it. Vivien had a perfectionist's sense of décor and a preference for delicate eighteenth-century furniture. Perhaps it was the heavy Victorian furnishings, deep plum shutters, and trumpet vines swarming over the roof that she found so overpowering. Dorothy Parker had also been affected by the gloomy atmosphere.

At the bottom of the garden was a small pool house, with tall eucalyptus trees hovering over it and writer-director Garson Kanin for an occupant. The sitting-room had white stone walls and a charming fireplace.

By a curious coincidence, in the fall of 1942 this property was occupied by Olivia de Havilland. Her reaction to it was completely different: 'I had the tenderest feelings in that house – and associated it with the happiness of the other couples who had been in it. Two great love affairs. I loved that house!'

Although Vivien and Larry had been longing for the opportunity to do a film together, now that they had it it seemed that the financial benefit was uppermost in their minds. On 9 August, the day her divorce from Leigh became final, Vivien wrote him one of her curiously affectionate letters, beginning, 'My darling Leigh . . .' In it she protested that 'we are certainly doing this for financial purposes which are useful in these days . . .' No doubt some feeling of guilt prompted this letter. Later, in October, she wrote again: 'The Nelson film is nearly over. We have rushed thro' it because apparently after Thursday there is no more money! – Alex's usual predicament . . .'

Naturally Vivien was worried about Larry's flight training – and well she might be! He was taking lessons at Clover Field from Cecil Smallwood, who taught most of the film-colony air buffs, including Jimmy Stewart, Katharine Hepburn, Frances Langford, Jon Hall, Margaret Sullavan, and Olivia de Havilland.

De Havilland says: 'When I would fly with Jimmy Stewart to various places, it seemed that no matter where we went or to what airport, Larry would have come in just before that and sideswiped some plane with his wing. One day we went to Monterey and we learned we'd have trouble landing. And we no sooner got on the ground (Jim was a grand pilot and we never had any adventures) when someone said, 'Well, Olivier's been here – and part of the field is out of commission!' There were at least ten incidents and it was really hilarious. Larry was undaunted, fearless, oblivious.'

John Cottrell credits Olivier with smashing up three training planes while completing his two-hundred-hour flying course. All of this generally occurred at five-thirty in the morning before he reported to the studio. He did manage to complete his training and qualified at Metropolitan Airfield, out in the Valley.

Of all this, Korda officially knew nothing, except that Larry was no Lindy but surely had guts. The flying was making Vivien terribly nervous and she wasn't sleeping well. Would his bones still be in the right places when they could finally wed?

One evening she was surprised to hear him say, 'I realise it is a wicked, inexcusable thing to do and I am ashamed of my weakness in surrendering to this adulterous passion when I am already married to a fine woman.'

It was only part of the new scene required by the Hays Office. They had insisted on Nelson's recanting to his cleric father for the sinful liaison with the notorious, Lady Hamilton. Hollywood always dared to change history in the interests of American morals. Joe Breen, filmland's official censor, had warned Korda that if he wanted a release for his film, there would also have to be a new opening scene for Emma, showing her sad end as a boozy, blowsy, derelict adrift in the port of Calais. In 1940 evil was still being punished and virtue rewarded on the big screen.

On the set next morning Korda was rehearsing Vivien's first meeting with the British Admiral at the British Embassy in Naples.

'What you first hear is the salute from the guns.' Of course the sound would be dubbed in later. 'For this I want a big reaction. And then I want you got something in your heart – like a portention!'

'A *portention*, Alex?'

'You know. That is coming something important.'

And something important was coming. The good news, brought by Sunny, that Jill and Tarquin, Suzanne and Mrs Hartley had all safely completed the dangerous Atlantic crossing to Canada.

Another shipload of children had been less fortunate. The *City of Benares* had been sunk in mid-Atlantic by a submarine almost the same day, and only thirteen of the hundred children on its passenger list had been rescued.

And there was more news. The Olivier divorce decree had become final on 28 August. Now they were both free to marry. They had waited so long it seemed unreal. Tears filled her eyes. 'Oh, puss, we're so lucky!'

That night they dined with Ronnie and Benita Colman and discussed wedding plans. They wanted privacy, and the press kept at bay. This meant applying for their licence outside Los Angeles, since the local registries were haunted by newspaper spies. Colman suggested Santa Barbara, an ultra-respectable backwater often used for sneak previews. Nothing ever leaked out of Santa Barbara, not even money. They would need to register there three days ahead, but the Colmans would arrange everything, starting with the ring. Benita would order it from her own jeweller, and since her finger was smaller, she'd use the excuse that her hands always swelled in the August heat. The simple gold circlet she chose was later to be deplored by the Hollywood *Reporter* as being 'a mere half inch wide'.

Colman had a business partner named Al Weingand, who owned the San Ysidro Ranch, a rustic cluster of bungalows in the Montecito Hills, in the environs of Santa Barbara. Here marriage could be committed as privately as sin. And the newlyweds could honeymoon aboard Colman's *Dragoon*, observed only by the flying fish.

At the last moment they invited a few friends in for a drink without revealing what they were celebrating. Watching them, Alan Mowbray observed to Sunny, 'Those two are an aphrodisiac! Positively electric, dear girl. Don't know how you can be around them all the time. Makes me randy enough to want to sleep with my own wife!'

Sunny recalls nostalgically the contagion of their romance: 'It was so powerful it rubbed off on everyone around them. They were the most popular couple in Hollywood – received more invitations than they could ever accept. Vivien never wanted to offend anyone and she made full use of her great skill in being diplomatic and tactful in declining invitations. She could be so charming and warm on the telephone that the caller had to hang up happy, even though disappointed, and Larry would say, "Clever girl, puss. You jolly well got us out of that one." Married couples were always after them, especially those whose sex lives I imagined might be growing tired. After an evening with Viv and Larry, it had to be like a hormone injection or better.'

'The great passion and adoration these two had for each other was truly electric. The way he looked at her, and vice versa – their responses were pure delight – almost as though "Wait till I get you alone", and "Yes, love, how soon?"'

'A well-known British actor, who shall remain nameless, would quite frequently be invited to dinner. He made a classic remark that I'll never forget, one that had everyone roaring with laughter. It was "I start getting an erection when I ring the doorbell here". It typically describes the vibes emanating from our adorable Vivien and Larry.'

Garson Kanin and Katharine Hepburn were among those admitted to the conspiracy about the wedding.

Hepburn was having a romance with Kanin, after Howard Hughes and before Spencer Tracy. The great Kate was somewhat annoyed at being disturbed from an early night, as she was filming the next day. But since Garson was to be the best man, she slipped into her flying gear, tucked her hair into a scarf, and – though it was after 10 p.m. – donned a pair of dark glasses.

Garson, at the wheel, insisted on a short cut, which got them lost. In one of the bungalows at the San Ysidro Ranch, Al Weingand was doing his best to tranquillise Fred Harsh, Justice of the Peace. The official had not been told just whom he was expected to join in marriage, but he knew they were very, very late. Weingand recalls keeping him in tow with alcohol and eloquence – and the help of his wife and a friend.

How could Al be sure these folks would actually show up? Harsh asked. Plenty got stage fright before facing the altar.

'I don't think this couple will get stage fright, Fred,' Al assured him.

At this opportune moment, the sound of a car brought them to the terrace. In the moonlight, Larry and Vivien came up the steps, followed by Kanin and Hepburn.

'My God, it's Scarlett O'Hara! Why didn't you tell me, Al?'

'Didn't want *you* to get stage fright.'

Vivien wanted the ceremony held on the terrace. Larry looked across the lemon orchard away from the sea towards the rim of hills. 'Mind if we face that way, Judge?'

'No, sir, Mr Oliver. But why?'

'Olivier. And *that's* the direction of England.'

After more than three years of waiting, it was all over in a moment. Harsh had used his capsule version a minute after midnight, 31 August 1940, which legalised their three-day wait.

'Please do it again, Judge Harsh,' Vivien asked.

'You're legally hitched, Miss Leigh. I mean, Mrs Olivier.'

But Vivien insisted that they had come a long way and they wanted to hear all the words. Harsh took a breath and repeated the ceremony, this time the full version. For a final effect, he joined their hands and shouted over them: 'I now pronounce you man and wife. Bingo!'

The judge savoured a close-up kiss. Green eyes shone in the valentine face, and then the newlyweds were gone like a final fade-out, back in the car, with a long drive ahead down the coast to San Pedro yacht harbour.

'Good-night, Judge Bingo! Your encore was better than the first show!' Vivien called back as the car made its caoutchouc descent through the platinum pepper trees towards a moonstruck sea. 31 August 1940.

The floating bower of flowers in the Oliviers' stateroom on the *Dragoon*, so lovingly prepared by the Colmans, appeared a bit wilted in the bright Catalina morning. Gardenias were turning brown, and the champagne was stale. There was an essence of anti-climax about the whole thing.

The Colmans had organised their security perhaps too perfectly. Theatrical people, who live their lives in a series of peaks, come to accept – even expect – the obstacle course of celebrity. Where is the joy of escape if there is no hue and cry of pursuit? As the day wore on and they swam in the crystal waters toasting each other and their skins, they would casually flip on the radio. Nothing.

Surely someone would have leaked the news to Winchell by now? Where were Hedda's spies? Imagine the embarrassment if they had to go back and announce it!

At ten o'clock that night, they were relieved when the story broke and they heard that they were reported to be honeymooning 'on land or sea' – which left few other possibilities.

Only Louella quibbled, in her column, 'Your Hollywood and Mine': 'I am not saying that Olivier and Vivien Leigh and that other romantic duet of today, Norma Shearer and George Raft, will meet a similar disastrous fate (to Francis X. Bushman and Beverly Bayne) in their lives, but looking

9 *Wings of war and Agincourt*

Few films have ever been shot with more speed and less nonsense than *That Hamilton Woman*, as it was finally titled for American release. For Korda, it was a labour of patriotism and love. And if a certain amount of on-the-spot invention was required by the pace of production, it would not damage the final results. Seventeen miniature sets for the Battle of Trafalgar had been built at General Service Studios, ranging in cost from three thousand to fifteen thousand dollars each, paltry sums by current standards. Korda even hired antiques from East Coast museums to dress his sets. Olivier, whose role was in the end rather too brief, produced an amazingly authentic Nelson, down to the red-dyed hair. His characterisation was right on target. As usual, he'd done his homework well. Vivien, perhaps a too piquant Emma, was nevertheless exquisite, and her performance was touched with welcome moments of comedy. If the real Lady Hamilton had been a rather more heroically proportioned goddess, full-blown in the years that followed Romney's celebration of her Grecian 'attitudes', nobody who saw the film would care, and few would know.

On 6 November 1940, the day after her birthday, Vivien celebrated with a coruscant froth of a party on the sound stage. Since her birthday coincided with Guy Fawkes' Day, the English sky always seemed to be sprayed with fireworks in her honour – and in Darjeeling, too, a local festival had lit up the sky on the very day she was born.

For this party, the actress appeared on stage in costume – a huge leghorn hat and a short-waisted flowing-skirted gown of palest gold chiffon, which *Photoplay* recorded as being 'so overwhelmingly feminine that every man on the set reacted to it, while Larry . . . gave off such a visible glow of possession that you could have lighted bonfires with it.'

During their secret Atlantic meeting, Churchill was to screen this film for Franklin D. Roosevelt. The Prime Minister would by then have seen it at least five times, for it became his favourite film.

The press was having a field day with the legalised lovers. Hedda, aware that more readers were caught on the fly with acid than with honeymoons, noted: 'Vivien Leigh evidently never read the book *How to Win Friends*, etc. The editor of America's best national magazine (Luce) having put her coloured picture on the cover (*Life*) now wanted to contact her for a story about Bundles for Britain. He could only get her maid on the phone.'

Louella countered with a flabby jab at Vivien's eating habits: 'She munches chocolates while working, to keep her weight up to 106. Some people have all the luck. Chocolates, and that gorgeous new groom sweeping her clean off her feet.'

The ladies of the press were less generous than Vivien and Larry, who, when the filming was completed, gave gifts to every member of cast and crew. But there were other news items with more far-reaching consequences. The filming over, Vivien flew to Vancouver where her mother, Mrs Hartley, had enrolled seven-year-old Suzanne in a convent school. As Felix Barker relates the incident, it was perhaps the last time Vivien would see her daughter for the duration of the war. Her visit under the name of Mrs Holman, coupled with the fact that Suzanne's real identity at school had been kept secret, brewed a tempest in a teapot. The sniff of a story brought reporters to the door. Her host's son improvised a well-meant fabrication: Miss Leigh had been avoiding publicity because of kidnap threats. *Kidnap threats*?

Headlines!

With the Lindbergh tragedy still lingering in the quaking hearts of mothers whose daughters were attending the same school, the Mother Superior insisted that Vivien remove Suzanne. Mrs Hartley was forced to remain in Canada and place Suzanne in a day school.

Shortly before Christmas, 1940, on a rain-drenched Sunday afternoon, Vivien and Larry hovered ghostlike over a last drink with friends.

'Hollywood's weeping raindrops for you, darlings.' Dame May Whitty embraced her beloved Juliet.

As a final gesture, the Oliviers had participated in a two-hour broadcast to be aired on Christmas morning, organised by Alan Mowbray. It was the biggest transcontinental 'airer' (as the *Reporter* called it) ever attempted coast-to-coast on NBC and throughout Canada. The British colony of some eighty stars, including Philip Merivale, Doug Fairbanks, Jr., Brian Aherne, Gladys Cooper, and Greer Garson, appeared *en masse*. Cukor and Garson Kanin brought Vivien a friendship ring to wear in England, showing two hands clasped over a ruby heart. And Larry had spent an hour at the jeweller's designing the engagement ring to match the wedding ring he had already placed on her finger.

When would they see these friends again? They were already becoming estranged by the future, their voices somehow artificial against the more immediate reality ahead. The war was imposing its question mark, and life was moving into another dimension.

'What will you do with him?' Cukor indicated the sloppy-tongued sheep dog, who seemed to be panting premonitions.

'He stays with the house. Old Tom, too.' Vivien stroked the arched back of the cat, so familiar with the Beverly Hills garbage cans where rubbish came gift-wrapped. Over a battlefield of luggage obstructing the hallway, the actor wished them all good-bye.

'Glad?' he whispered as they walked down the familiar path for the last time.

'You know I am, puss.'

'Whatever?'

'Whatever.'

Around them, California was indulging in the usual imitation Yuletide encountered in subtropical climes. At least they wouldn't have to endure another sleigh bell over the radio. They'd be trading them in for the wail of air-raid warnings.

Whistles signalling relief at a safe crossing, the American ship *Excambion* disgorged four hundred unrefreshed passengers into New York and collected twenty-five hardy souls to sail back to Lisbon. Only a madman would have chosen a European holiday in that winter of 1940. Madmen, spies, patriots, and the Oliviers – the *Excambion* held them all.

Lisbon's cafés were crowded with refugees, fugitives, black-marketeers, and informers; an honest Portuguese hardly dared show his face. How to get on a flight to England? The local cinema helped solve the problem. Max de Winter's burning glance just happened to be scalding packed houses, which added clout to the Oliviers' appeal at the harassed British Embassy.

Three days later, they were packed into an aircraft with blacked-out windows, heading home. And a very changed home it would be. From now on, with strangers dropping bombs on strangers, there would be no safe place or time.

She held his hand tightly. Below now, unseen, would be that familiar coastline, chalk cliffs on the blackboard of night.

'It was the war which stopped us being sucked into Hollywood. We were probably naïvely patriotic . . .' That was how the actor would recall it to Jim Walters of the *New York Times* many years later. The war had indeed saved them from languishing in Lotus Land.

In the aircraft, the pilot's door suddenly opened, revealing a flash of flame above the cockpit. Vivien froze.

'Someone's fired the bloody recognition signals and forgotten to open the window,' Larry reassured her authoritatively.

Amid the sad wail of sirens, the plane descended near

Bristol – a city racked by the cough of anti-aircraft fire and powdered by the dust of bombings. The heart had come to where the home was.

What price patriotism? Perhaps a rather stiff one, as Vivien's agent had warned. But for her the course had always been clear. It did not take into account obligations to David Selznick. She knew he could, if he wished, sue her for violation of contract – if she survived the Luftwaffe.

'When Larry went back to England for the war, Vivien went with him unquestioningly, leaving her career in Hollywood,' recalls George Cukor. She packed it away like a suitcase of old clothes for the duration, and many local realists considered her demented. Larry, too. If one had to joust at windmills, why not build one on the back lot at M-G-M?

London, pounded for fifty-seven nights after Dunkirk with 20,000 tons of high explosives and 37,000 canisters of incendiaries; 177,000 people sleeping underground in the tubes, praying, snoring, dreaming, and occasionally copulating. But in the extremes of those nights, the courage of the human spirit glowed to a higher candescence

The Oliviers returned to find Durham Cottage badly damaged by bombings. But Leigh's house in Little Stanhope Street had been levelled – a slate of memory wiped clean. Vivien could only be grateful that Suzanne had been in Canada, and Leigh away in the Navy. The bad news for Larry was that the RAF could get along very well without him. A medical exam disclosed a damaged nerve in the inner ear, which disqualified him. He had to pull strings to get accepted at all. The strings led to Ralph Richardson, the Fleet Air Arm, and non-operational flying. They were first posted to Lee-on-Solent and then on to Worthy Down.

It was incredible how elegant Vivien always managed to appear even in an open car crammed with luggage and furnishings. She rode to war like a fragile Boadicea at the wheel of an open four-seater with a broken clutch. But she wasn't in command of this unworthy chariot. It was being towed by a decrepit Invicta, driven by Larry in his new uniform. Vivien's passenger and companion was Tissy, their black-and-white cat. Larry was confident that his wife would be the hit of the post. She had been a bit edgy at times, but wasn't that to be expected?

His three-week course at Lee-on-Solent had scarcely fitted Larry to convert from American training planes to the worst of British aircraft – which was the best that could be allotted to this backwash division of the Fleet Air Arm. Yet he felt that once aboard, he could wangle the chance to make operational flights against the enemy. Wars become less discriminating as they drag on. The top-of-the-barrel pilots were fast being used up. He avoided confiding such hopes to Vivien.

Word had been spread around that Squadron 757 of the Fleet Air Arm was welcoming and commissioning all volunteers with licence in hand. It was a great attraction. World War I memories made the infantry unpopular, and from a naval standpoint, an Air Arm commission kept you from sleeping in hammocks and wearing bell-bottomed trousers. Squadron 757 hadn't exactly collected the cream of the crop. The RAF had skimmed that off. The Navy's few fully-trained pilots were wanted immediately on the carriers. Like beggars combing the dustbins after the feast, Squadron 757 collected the leftovers: air-minded ex-cons pardoned for the purpose; a couple of Grand National jockeys who somehow equated flying hoofs with wings; a jaunty young solicitor, Commander John Dykes; a volant nobleman – Lionel, Lord Tennyson; a jester named Jack Bissell; and a group of thespians, including Robert Douglas and Ralph Richardson. It would seem the squadron hardly needed more actors.

His new role as pilot hadn't altered Richardson's singular proneness to accidents. Dykes recalls with a shudder receiving a phone call from him. 'A slight mishap to my aircraft on the outskirts of Winchester, sir. Me? Oh, perfectly fit! Returning to duty immediately. That is, as soon as I can borrow a bicycle.' Richardson neglected to mention that the aircraft had been completely wrecked.

The story, when he heard it, brought Larry an upstage smile, but Vivien did not find the incident amusing. The prestige of theatrical people was therefore somewhat in question when Olivier arrived on the scene. Domestically his introduction was auspicious. The Oliviers rented a house at King's Worthy, some three miles from the airfield. The actress set about making it homey with a few personal treasures from Chelsea, including Indian rugs, an Aubusson carpet, and oil paintings by Sickert and Boudin, which replaced the owner's watery seascapes. Olivier somehow acquired a magnificent motorbike, a German BMW twin-cylinder of a type none of the men had ever seen before. To add to their glorification, Vivien obtained and grilled enormous steaks for Larry's fellow-officers. She cooked them herself, and the diners were not too overwhelmed by her beauty to tuck away a hearty meal.

The field itself was hardly promising, as the actor soon noted. Worthy Down may have appeared worthy enough to the RAF back in 1916, but it had been condemned as unsuitable by 1920. It was only reasonably functional for older-type aircraft in which wireless operators could be trained on huge antiquated sets jammed into the back of the old planes. Here the initiates learned to send and receive Morse Code and try to keep in touch with the station. If contact was lost, the pilot was supposed to haul his crate back into communication range and start out again. It was rather like stretching an elastic to discover the breaking point, and it would be the duty of Acting Sub-Lieutenant Olivier, RNVR to fly one of these planes. Other inspiring assignments would range from training Air Scouts of an average age of twelve, and taxiing aerial gunners on prac-tice runs.

But for the moment he was girding himself for his first day of actual flying. Vivien tried not to think of his training misadventures in California. 'They're not going to let you fly in combat?' she asked hopefully, making it sound as though he could lose the war single-handedly.

On the bumpy field at Worthy Down, Blackburn Sharks, those heavy, antiquated bi-planes, useful only for training purposes, were lined up in a neat row, almost wing tip to wing tip, chocks bracing wheels. Clearly there hadn't yet been any German daylight bombing here or the planes wouldn't have been displayed in such a compact target. Larry roared up on his BMW to find the entire squadron waiting to see this famous star launch himself into the firmament. He walked across the field to a buzz of excitement. A flock of Wrens had gathered near the hangar for a closer look. Improvisation was called for. Commander Dykes came over. 'Know the form, Olivier?'

He replied to the effect that it was a piece of cake to some of the crates he'd flown in the States. With a dignified climb into the cockpit, he revved up, throttled back, waved to the two men at the front-wheel chocks, and prepared to carry England's aerial challenge to the enemy. Like Henry V signalling the longbowmen at Agincourt, like Nelson leading his column of frigates into Trafalgar, Acting Sub-Lieutenant Olivier of Squadron 757 set his eyes towards the sky and gave his plane the gun. He failed to notice that the man on the left wheel had not yet pulled away his chock. The Blackburn Shark swung around into a 180-degree spin and crashed nose-to-nose into the plane on his left.

Dykes, a lawyer and the squadron's most experienced airman, winced at the legal complications. Two aircraft written off before the actor had even taken to the air! At least Richardson got off the ground. Such were the fortunes of war . . .

The C.O. bore the loss with stiff-upper-lip fortitude – and cancelled Larry's leave for a month. Such were the misfortunes of war.

Olivier had come into the service, as did so many from show business, with the expectation that somehow the unreality of the theatrical life-style would be exchanged for a more basic world in which a truer layer of self would be revealed. But he was soon to find among the 'real' people that the flesh reveals itself to be merely flesh, that the lean-jawed warriors who guard freedom's perimeters can be just as mean-minded, jealous, petty, vindictive, and human as any theatrical agent. Boredom, bull, and 'bumf' were becoming the texture of Larry's days, and he was growing increasingly dissatisfied with his role. Vivien, too, was showing the stress of restlessness and depression. She had ignored Selznick's demands to return to Hollywood for another film. She had also turned down Cedric Hardwicke's offer to play Shaw's *Caesar and Cleopatra* in New York. She wanted a play, but not that far away from Larry. She understood his frustration, as he understood hers.

A few days earlier, Larry had been in the Winchester post office. Recognising the actor, two teenage girls circled a few times. One had whispered loud enough to be heard from Elsinore's battlements: 'Oh, I'm ever so disappointed, aren't you, Mavis?' Larry perfectly imitated the flat Hampshire tones when he told the story on himself. Vivien knew that he was beginning to feel like an understudy for a warrior.

It was almost ludicrous. They had given up so much to do so little! Their careers were now stagnating in a Victorian cottage in a backwash of a war that neither needed them nor had use for their singular talents. They were left with nothing except the understanding of each other's needs to perform, create, exist; for only by acting do actors truly live. There was little that Larry could do for himself, but he could help Vivien. He suggested to his friend Hugh ('Binky') Beaumont that he put together a production of *The Doctor's Dilemma*, with Vivien in the role of Jennifer Dubedat. As managing director of H. M. Tennant, a leading English production company, Beaumont liked the idea and proposed a tour before opening at the Haymarket. Although Shaw's Jennifer wasn't a part Vivien relished, it was the only female role in the play, and would give her a chance to wear lovely Edwardian costumes. The character would be difficult, but very far from Scarlett.

Vivien seemed hesitant to accept, as it meant leaving Larry for the first time since their marriage. But he insisted it was the right thing for her to do.

One day, finding his brother officers looking glum, Olivier dispersed the gloom with a faultless imitation of the C.O. and the chaplain. He played all parts to perfection, recalls John Dykes.

'Skipper! Trouble on the tarmac! Spotted a nest of skylarks!'

'Good God! Er, sorry, Chaplain. Sticky business!'

'Dash it all, what'll we do?'

'Ticklish.'

'Can't just leave them hanging about. Wind slip could do them in.'

'Right! Got to think of something to save those birds and damned quick! Sorry, Chaplain.'

At which point the A.D.O., Lord Tennyson, butted in with a solution. 'If I had anything to do with it, I'd wring the little buggers' necks!'

'Good God!' breathed the chaplain. Then eyes to the sky, 'Sorry, sir!'

The actor left the mess in a better humour than he had found it.

On another occasion, Dykes recalls Olivier striding out across the field in padded flying suit and fur-lined boots, mounting into his open cockpit with soaring, wondrous voice ringing: 'Those friends thou hast, bind them to thyself with thongs of steel!' Then, spotting Dykes, he called, 'Johnny, old boy, lend me your flying helmet. And, by the way, took your photo the other day.'

Only a few days earlier Dyke's Lysander had landed in a ditch and gone over the vertical, leaving the intrepid Commander dangling head downward. Olivier, who happened to be flying over, photographed this bit of un-scheduled acrobatics.

After Vivien had left on tour, boredom and loneliness really set in. Larry faced no danger beyond the possibility of self-destruction, no death but from natural causes, no enemy but ennui.

One weekend he went on leave to visit Vivien in Edinburgh, where she was appearing with Cyril Cusack, her co-star. When he returned, with the scent of the theatre still in his nostrils, he was posted Officer of the Day.

An O.D. must be primed and ready to deal with any emergency, large or small. But since either type was virtually unknown at Worthy Down, the O.D. normally whiled away the dreary hours in his shirt sleeves playing cards in the mess. Olivier had just drawn an inside straight when he received an urgent call to the telephone. His ear was blasted by a crackling snarl. Hastily he returned to the mess, pulling on his tunic.

'The Fifth Sea Lord. He's here!'

'The who?' asked a cardplayer.

'God. In person,' announced Commander Dykes soberly. 'The Fifth Sea Lord is the biggest shot in the whole Fleet Air. Board of Admiralty.'

'He's looking for me,' Larry said.

'I'd rather face Goering's Luftwaffe single-handed,' Dykes allowed. 'And if he finds one button undone, you bloody will.'

The actor was frantically buttoning his tunic when he was called back to the phone: 'Officer of the Day!' This time a clipped, icy voice snapped through 'Fifth Sea Lord speaking! I'm making an unexpected inspection of the whole of the station!'

'Sirrrr!' gasped Acting Sub-Lieutenant Olivier, O.D.

'I don't know what sort of security you've got here, but I can tell you my car's driven right past the sentry, and the Guard Room seems in absolute disarray! What the hell the Officer of the Day's doing, I don't know. Playing cards with his tunic off, I'll wager.'

'Sir.'

'Are you the Officer of the Day?'

'Yes, sir,' came Larry's deflated reply.

The voice gusted up in fury. 'Well, what do you think you're about? We happen to be at war, although there's precious little hint of it here. You chaps are supposed to be guarding the skies over England. Report to the Guard Room immediately. And I want your C.O. down here as well!'

Larry pulled on an oilskin and was off across two hundred yards of blinding rain to the soggy sentry at the Guard Room door. 'Where's the Fifth Sea Lord?'

'There's no Fifth Sea Lord here, sir,' came the reply.

'No wonder he's upset. The biggest shot in the Admiralty and you don't even know he's in there!' The actor hastened in, came to ramrod attention, and snapped to salute. His hand froze. Behind the desk was Jack Bissell, the squadron clown.

'You son of a bitch!' Larry roared with laughter.

'You're not the only David Garrick in the squadron, old boy,' Bissell beamed. His cardplaying mates had all been in on the impractical joke. Boredom briefly vanished.

During the period that the Oliviers were at Worthy Down, and Vivien was not on tour, Roger Furse and his wife Maggie (the designers) came down for several weekends with them. Furse recalled a nonsense game they played, based on a fantasy 'art theatre' they would run after the war. Between shows, the audience were to join the cast in 'Old Englishy' country games. They all outdid themselves inventing these bucolic diversions, and Larry came up with an indescribable one called Honey-Belly-Flip-Cock. They would compile imaginary casts of actors and actresses who were bound to loathe each other. The theatre would flourish in a beautiful country house, complete with barn and farm buildings, which the Oliviers were seriously thinking of buying. There was a lovely sweep of lawn, forming a natural amphitheatre, where the audience would get piles from the wet grass. At the bottom of the lawn was a stream with reeds and marshy land beyond. Here Larry, dressed in rusty, ill-fitting armour, would recite 'La Belle Dame sans Merci' and Vivien, clothed in off-white flowing draperies, would ride up and down on an old white farm horse, moaning. This performance was only to be given on misty nights by the full moon. Tickets were to be so expensive as to guarantee an audience of no more than three – and if they looked as though they planned to stay the night they were to be treated to 'apple-pie' beds.

Of such madness does one survive ennui in war.

Furse (who became one of Olivier's staunchest friends and co-workers and remained so until his death in 1973) had first met Larry in May, 1934. He'd been invited to tea with Gladys Cooper. In her garden they had watched a slight young man battling with enormous courage and energy in a singles tennis game. And losing. Not surprising, since his opponent was 'Bunny' Austin, England's Davis Cup ace. After being thoroughly trounced, Larry had made everyone laugh by crawling off the court like a half-dead man towards a desert mirage.

It wasn't until 1938 that Furse and Olivier worked together, when Guthrie asked Furse to design the costumes for *Othello*. Furse tells of how Ralph Richardson and Larry, both dear friends, tried like hell to cast their wife and mistress respectively, Muriel Hewitt and Vivien, as Desdemona, and how 'Long Lil' Guthrie, 'with that small, atavistic, but smiling mouth, declined . . . This is where I saw the generosity of Larry. Though to anyone, and most particularly to him, Vivien would have been by far the more distinguished choice, once it was decided . . . he worked in real harmony and with generosity. Others didn't.

'I recall fitting Ralph's costumes. Ralph, bless his heart, was doing every kind of gymnastic until he managed to split his costume right down the back. Wardrobe were in tears, and I was fairly seething for them – and myself. But Larry, who had been there punctually for his fitting, smoothed everyone down, called all the girls "darling", praised their work and wanted to know all about the designs. Was it difficult to work in that thick felt (of which we were making the armour)? And why had I chosen Veronese as the basis of my designs?

'In the selection of prop weapons Larry was exacting.

Balance and ease were what guided him. He tried every sword and dagger in the large armoury of the Old Vic until he found what he wanted; then asked with an inquiring smile, "Is it the right period?" If I said it was not, he'd suggest altering the hilt, or else he would manage with the next best thing that would make *me* happy. Then for a beer at the adjoining pub.'

Olivier was realising increasingly that he would never get the chance to fly against the enemy. Vivien had been urging him to give it up. She had come down from London between performances at the Haymarket, where *The Doctor's Dilemma* had settled in for a run, to try once more to convince him to apply for a discharge. His post made him more of a scoutmaster than a pilot, and he had been reduced to amateur theatricals, recitations, patriotic broadcasts – all in aid of the war effort, and generally under the least favourable circumstances. He might as well be back where he belonged.

Coals glowed in the hearth, creating a warm refuge from the chill Hampshire afternoon. It was the spring of 1942 – and now the Yanks were coming!

'I've applied for the Walruses,' he told her suddenly. Her look was properly confused.

'Sounds a bit whiskery, puss. Some sort of disguise?'

'Small all-purpose amphibians. They're to be catapulted from battleships.' His hand described an eloquent movement. He had made this decision without even talking it over with her. But she had been otherwise occupied. He could see she was terrified and reassured her that Walruses were safer than a pony ride in an amusement park. Anyway, it could be months before they even read his application. It would be his last chance to do something useful, and there were no age limitations.

He promised that if this last effort of his was rejected, he would apply for a discharge. He was pleased to see that she was looking much better again. She was not so drawn and strained, her role of full-time officer's wife having been abandoned for the theatre.

G. B. Shaw had not seen Vivien's performance in his play since rehearsals. He always avoided his own plays once they opened. But the Hungarian producer Gabriel Pascal had, and he was planning to film Shaw's *Caesar and Cleopatra*. Vivien was longing for the part and knew that whomever Pascal chose would have to have Shaw's approval. She persuaded Beaumont to arrange a meeting with the Irish bard. Beaumont told her she would come as quite a surprise to the playwirght. Shaw had often said that actresses who coveted the teenage role of Cleopatra were generally giantesses over fifty. And she must, of course, be on her guard. Women always fell in love with him, red beard, bicycle, vegetables, and all – particularly actresses who coveted roles in his plays.

Some time around the end of the thirteen-month run of *Doctor's Dilemma*, the meeting finally took place at the playwright's Whitehall Court flat in London. Vivien showed remarkable genius of tact and charm by avoiding any mention of Cleopatra. As she was about to leave, he arrested her with his vivid blue eyes.

'You look like a Persian kitten. You know, what you ought to do is to play Cleopatra!'

'But would I be good enough?' she asked with her most Persian-kittenish innocence.

'You'd look wonderful. You don't *need* to be an actress. The part's foolproof!'

And so was Shaw. No one had made a fool of him. 'You are the Mrs Pat Campbell of the age!' he announced with honest admiration.

The Edwardian actress to whom he compared her had been known for her wit and shrewd stratagems in getting her own way with the wily playwright, whose parts she had so often adorned.

In January of 1943, Olivier, still awaiting the summons of the Walruses, was given permission to make a film at Denham, called *Demi-Paradise*, that was considered to be valuable pro-Russian propaganda. It was produced by

Filippo Del Giudice, a former enemy alien who had earlier been interned on the Isle of Man. Del Giudice had heard the actor's radio broadcast of *Henry V* from Manchester. It gave Del Giudice an exciting idea. Although nothing could be more audacious than attempting an epic film in a country sorely pressed by war, the Italian had already managed to produce Noël Coward's superb *In Which We Serve*. He was not deterred by such minor difficulties as raising money, finding able-bodied men for his film army, costumes, armour, horses, and locations. His dream was to bring *Henry V* to life on screen with Olivier, and he approached the actor at the right psychological moment. Walrus warfare had been abandoned by the Navy, untried.

To Vivien's relief, the actor encountered no problems in getting his release from the Fleet Air Arm. And she would play the role of the French princess, of course, Selznick willing. Selznick wasn't:

ABSOLUTELY UNDER NO CONDITIONS WILL YOU PERFORM MEDIOCRE PART IN HENRY V. YOU ARE STILL CONTRACTUALLY OBLIGATED TO SELZNICK. REMEMBER? SO STOP. DAVID.

A crushing blow, but nothing could be done. Olivier discovered his Katharine at the Mercury Theatre at Notting Hill Gate – playing the same role in which Larry had first seen Vivien in the West End, *The Mask of Virtue*. Renée Asherson (later the widow of actor Robert Donat) recalls: 'They sent me a telegram between them because I was playing her part.' Happily, Vivien's costumes (already made) would require little alteration.

As Larry was leaving the war effort, Vivien was plunging into it. She joined Entertainments National Service Association (ENSA), founded by Basil Dean, and went off to the Middle East to entertain troops. Selznick could not stop her from doing that.

Dallas Bower, co-producer of *Henry V*, took responsibility for getting the best possible actors and technicians out of the services. Larry had complete artistic control, though he'd never had anything to do with the production side, nor had he ever directed a film. Larry tried to get Terence Young to direct, then tried Carol Reed without success. Discovering that William Wyler was billeted at Claridge's as a United States Army Air Force major, he tried to lure in his associate of Goldwyn days. Though they had gone through some rough periods together, the actor's admiration for Wyler was unabated. He said later, 'Wyler taught me that films can do anything – all you have to do is find out how.' But his efforts to enlist an experienced director ended in failure – and out of this failure came the most important opportunity of his life.

Roger Furse recalled Larry's 'heart-searchings, and how he questioned me and the others as to whether he should take on the job of directing himself. He seemed to be as nervous and uncertain as a virgin. Then, when he had decided, I remember the tremendous vigour and confidence he exuded to all around him. Whether he really felt that confidence at the time, I don't know. I also remember the wonderful quality he always has of making you feel that you are possibly the most important adjunct to the set-up. No, that sounds as if he were a flatterer, which he is not. But he does give one a strong feeling of trust in your capabilities and therefore relaxation on his part.'

To film the Battle of Agincourt, Olivier was looking for a really poetic countryside . . . its green tranquillity to be raped by the hoofs of 30,000 French horses (150 would do). But where? France, of course, was out of the question. So was England. Dallas Bower came up with the park of an Irish estate near Dublin at Enniskerry. Its owner, Lord Powerscourt, was Commissioner of the Irish Boy Scouts and the grounds housed a permanent campsite. And Ireland was not in the war.

The unit left for Ireland at the end of May. No one can ever imagine the amount of organisation and preparation required for a film location unless he has been on one. There were hundreds of people to be fed and housed, as well as costumes, make-up. props. horses, dressing-rooms, and first aid to be seen to. Olivier himself commanded all from a caravan.

Furse recalled: 'Having scavenged Great Britain and Northern, not to speak of Southern, Ireland for stage armour, not necessarily of the right period, and having made all we could in papier-maché and the like, cartloads of Irish nuns as well as members of Institutes for the Blind were all busy knitting all the string we could buy up in the non-Nazi world into terrible chain-mail legs and arms – we were still on the *very* short side. In the mountains of County Wicklow a great long hut had been run up for Armoury and Wardrobe. Here Maggie and I, with our assistants, started the long, tedious business of fitting all the splendid young farmers' sons of Eire. We started with those doubling for actors who would play parts filmed later at Denham, and moved on down to those selected for looks, horsemanship, general intelligence, and size. as well as the size and looks of their nags. Two days later we had reached nadir – dressing only one side of each man. We'd try to get it into his dear potato-head that he should wear it like that if the camera appeared to be on his left, but that if it were on his right (not that he knew one from t'other) he should dismount and put it all on the other side. We were standing wearily at the door of the hut euphemistically known as the "conference tent" when Larry came over.

' "You are wonderful children," he said. "Now what about me?" At that moment we realised we hadn't reserved any armour for the star! We looked at each other and he looked at us. Then he roared with laughter and told us that in the morning an irate star actor would call on us to find out whether it was worthwhile going on with the film. Needless to say, in fact you perhaps noticed it, we did fit him up, and pretty well, too. What was so lovely about it all was the way he took it. I know of no, repeat *no*, other actor, let alone star-director, who would have taken it in quite that way.

'His physical courage was very obvious on that location,

particularly. Those of us who watched him illustrating on horseback what he wanted done and how, and with what fierce and abandoned spirit, had some very nervous moments. He'd told the men at the beginning that he'd never ask them to do anything that he wouldn't do himself. And he certainly didn't. There was a shot to be made of the mounted French knights riding into a wood towards camera. English foot soldiers were in the branches of the trees and they were to drop on to the horsemen. Not unnaturally, the rehearsal lacked heart and dash until Larry got up into a tree and demonstrated (with the co-operation of one of the most dashing horsemen and with a blood-curdling shout) just how it should be done. We all held our breath as he flung himself down on the horseman's back and stabbed repeatedly, finally bringing him off his horse. The boys took fire, and we shot a wonderful scene. It was only some days later when the rushes came back from processing in England that it was discovered that the camera had run out of film! Larry had only one rather inferior take. The one which was finally used.

'With typical restraint, though the negligence of a member of the camera crew had lost a sensational sequence, all Larry said to the cameraman was, "We can't afford to let this happen again."

'It was the same when he discovered that the whole splendid charge of the French cavalry had a long Techni-colour scratch right down the middle. "All right. We'll have to shoot it all over again. Roger, Maggie, can you refurbish the knights and their horses?" We did, though it was a bit difficult as the horses seemed to love eating the blind-tassels off each others' reins and trappings.

'It was about this time that dear Mr Rank got cold feet and wanted to call the whole thing off. This was where Larry's mental courage showed. Rank thought the whole thing was costing too much. I must say, there'd been great difficulties. The first production manager (someone from the BBC) had run mad in Dublin. He'd kept all the estimates of production with the piss pot under his bed and wouldn't let anyone, even Larry, see them. After he'd been carted off to a loony bin in a strait-jacket, there followed a series of production managers. One borrowed my own private horse one day and at a critical moment flashed past Larry at full gallop, elbows in the air, control of the quiet little mare completely lost. Larry shouted to him that if he couldn't control one horse he wasn't fit for the job of assembling two hundred-odd, and that he had better go back to England – on his horse! By this time the poor man was out of earshot and Rodger Ramsdell took over until the next victim appeared.'

But with Rank, Olivier was adamant and backed the embattled Del Giudice to the hilt.

One accident nearly took Olivier off the picture. He wanted a shot right in the middle of a mêlée of fighting knights, all hacking away at each other, very close to the camera. A small, rather ineffective barrier of stakes was run up in which he, camera, and crew, as well as Furse, were placed. The opposing knights were told to fight as near the camera as possible, being shoved and jostled closer by those on the outside. 'I remember with horror,' Furse continued, 'and the horror returns every time I see the film, noticing O'Donnell or McGee, or somesuch, wearing his helmet back-to-front, his shield bearing his arms upside down, and, because he was one of those who only had one armoured leg, exposing his quite modern riding breeches. However, that was a relatively small annoyance. As the boyos got thoroughly warmed up and the Irish blood and love of a fight took hold, the frail palisade gave way. A great caparisoned horse's arse finally bumped over the camera. Operator and crew jumped back as it heeled over. Not so our Larry boy. His enthusiastic eye was glued to the finder and he got the full weight and sharp corner of the big camera on his upper lip! The scar remains to this day. But he was very happy with the results of that day's shooting.

'There was a distinct difference between the horsemen and the infantrymen, who were mostly poor unemployed

Dubliners off the street corners. A rather touching incident occurred at the end of location shooting. Both horsemen and foot soldiers passed the helmet 'round in their respective camps in order to give Larry a present. The horsemen had a rather splendid hunting crop made with a silver band inscribed – all very correct. The dear foot boys got a good Irish bog-oak walking stick, also with a silver band, inscribed "To Mr L. O'livier". It showed they thought him a real Irishman, and it showed something more. Though we'd worked far closer to the élite horsemen, Larry had made the same warm impression on the less glamorous foot soldiers. In the following years when I've been working in Ireland, I've often been approached by ageing men who have said, "Weren't you, now, down in Wicklow when we fought that Mr O'Livier at the Battle of Agincourt – or was it Powerscourt, now?" It was, as the Navy say, a happy ship – and that is always due to the captain.'

While the rains of Ireland pelted Larry's caravan, Vivien sweltered in desert heat on her North African troop tour with Binky Beaumont's ENSA production of *Spring Party*. With her went Bea Lillie, Dorothy Dickson, and old friend, John Gielgud. Having travelled and performed for the last three exhausting months from Gibraltar to Egypt with sometimes as many as three shows a day, Vivien, looking somewhat emaciated, rested in a steaming Cairo hotel room. She re-read her most recent letter from Ireland:

. . . It is days since I have written to you, but things for the last three weeks have been getting so troublesome that what with not being able to hear anything from you I have really been so down in the mouth that I could write nothing but how anxious and perplexed I was . . . Anything I might have written would have been one long moan. But the day before yesterday Lady Powerscourt sent me over an old copy of *The Times* which reported your exciting doings on the 19th and my heart was so uplifted to know that at least

you were all right up to that time that already everything was much better and happier for me . . .*

He was referring to the report of Vivien's presentation to
His Majesty King George VI. The actress had met the
monarch on the terrace of Admiral Cunningham's villa in
Tunis, overlooking the Mediterranean. The King had
suggested that she add one of his favourite poems to her
repertoire of recitations: Alica Duer Miller's 'The White
Cliffs of Dover'.

She would never forget the vast spaces of desert crowded
with battle-worn troops, sometimes ten thousand, sur-
rounding the improvised stages under the stars. Vivien
had trouble making herself heard, but it hardly mattered
at all to the Desert Rats cheered by a glimpse of her rare
beauty in a long, flowing dress and picture hat. Her audiences included Generals Eisenhower, Spaatz, Doolittle, and
Montgomery. In a curious way she was happy – exhausted,
lonely for Larry, but somehow fulfilled by her contribution.

Vivien sent Larry a cable, and then a second, in case he
didn't get the first. On 28 June, he answered:

. . . Overjoyed to get your two cables today. AT LAST,
after more than three weeks with nothing. And so
you're in Cairo. How peculiar. Be careful of the
donkeys! I hear they're very forward. What joy . . . I
I sent you off a cable at once . . . I am so thrilled it's
been a lovely day. First hearing from you and second
we got the shot I was telling you about, so I won my
bets. FIRST TAKE! What a director! . . . I'm playing two
parts tomorrow, my own and the French mes-
senger . . .†

Olivier returned to England and Denham Studios to

*Felix Barker, The Oliviers.
† Felix Barker, The Oliviers.

complete the filming. His cast, on loan from His Majesty's Services, included Leo Genn as the Constable of France and Robert Newton as Pistol. Worries about Renée's accent had prompted him to pack her off to the French drama coach at RADA. 'I worked fearfully hard on that accent with Alice Gashet,' recalls Renée. The effort paid off. The love scenes became one of the triumphs of the film.

In the interests of economy as well as style, the actor had conceived the idea of letting the play begin in a reconstruction of Shakespeare's Globe Theatre, then expand into the full-scale settings of the film. In one of the final scenes, Henry takes the hand of his French princess, surrounded by courtiers who drape large cloaks over them. The camera was to move in close on the cloaks – then pull back revealing that they were now back on the Elizabethan stage, surrounded by a court of Shakespearian actors. The cloaks were therefore crucial. They must fill and hold the screen all on their own.

The two-day shooting sequence on the full court scene had begun. There were three or four hundred extras, as well as most of the principals, a large and expensive crowd. When the last costumed courtier made his way to the set, Roger Furse returned to the art department to collapse. Almost immediately the third assistant bounded in. Mr Olivier wanted Furse on the set. Pronto! Confident of a compliment on a job well done, Furse moved through production executives, cameramen, editors, continuity girls – all thronged around the chief. One glimpse of Olivier brought misgivings.

'Larry was wearing a rather anxious, strained expression, and at the same time trying to hide it. "My large cloak. And the Princess's, dear boy? I don't think you've ever even shown me a design of them." Indeed I hadn't! I had never thought of them since the first time they'd been discussed.

' "My God, sir, I'd forgotten all about them!"

'The crowd backed away from us in incredulous terror. Larry looked round at them a moment and I thought I could see laughter bubbling up inside him. However, he kept a straight but smiling face, saying quietly out of the side of it, "I can change the order of the shooting, but I can't hold this crowd after tomorrow afternoon. Try your best, boy. They must look marvellous. First shot tomorrow morning, then," he added in a louder voice with an encouraging slap on the shoulder.'

Furse selected two leaf and bird designs from a Book of Hours, and blew them up on brown paper. He sped to London with all the remaining clothes coupons and a wad of money, with which he bought yards and yards of white duchesse satin. He made it back to Wardrobe just in time to cut and stitch the material into two all-enveloping cloaks, defying the unions to work through the night painting thousands of birds and leaves and the arms of England and France on the centre backs. They were ready for that first shot in the morning. 'I shall never forget Larry's face when he saw them, nor the generous, grateful hug.'

Through all of this, Larry was cabling Vivien – sometimes in verse – to tell her how much he missed her. The ENSA tour was ending, but when they reached Gibraltar, Headquarters urged the company to extend the tour for a further three weeks. Vivien had been ill with a cough she couldn't seem to shake. She'd lost fifteen pounds, and although she was homesick for Larry, she wrote that she felt it her duty to stay on for at least a few more weeks to entertain smaller units and hospitals. The last letter she received from Larry before flying home mentioned that Gabriel Pascal was in Hollywood searching for a leading man to play Caesar to her Cleopatra.

Six days after the Normandy invasion, Pascal launched his film. The producer had shrewdly secured film rights to *all* of Shaw's properties by the audacious gesture of simply ringing the great man's doorbell.

It was late spring when Vivien returned. They found a delightful house in the country near Prestwick. Vivien filled it with friends on weekends. Friends were essential always, since they provided nonsense talk, and a wall against the world. There was a garden to potter in, and a vast tribe of cats – Tissy's ever-enlarging brood. And Larry had become practically medieval since *Henry*, even bringing his enormous horse, Blaunche, back from Ireland. Robert Helpmann, Stewart Granger, John Mills, or Noël Coward, down for the weekend, would watch him canter about. So did Claude Rains, who had arrived to play Caesar.

Larry and Vivien had never felt so happy. And their happiness was sparkling with expectation. Vivien was pregnant! She waved aside the doctor's concern that this new film might be too taxing on her frail health. She insisted to Larry and all that she had never felt stronger in her life. But Larry sensed, could see behind the fading tan, in the depths of those great eyes, the ghosts that he could never quite exorcise. Renée Asherson noted his worry.

Six weeks after the filming of *Caesar and Cleopatra* had begun, Vivien had a miscarriage and lost the child. The curtain dropped on the second act of the love scene. And the lives of the players were inevitably to be altered by the events of the play.

IO *Crown amid the thorns*

Cleopatra continued to materialise before the camera, a fragile resurrection of the effervescent kitten-queen who had troubled the dreams of a Caesar. But Vivien had allowed herself only a few days to recover from an experience most women would find devastating, and her state of mind showed through her performance, giving it deeper shadings, revealing new emotional depth never reached in any of her previous films. Pascal was emptying the pockets of his backers into the production to the tune of some five million dollars. But it was becoming unhappily clear that, despite some fine performances, the results would be less than a masterpiece.

As for the invisible presence behind every line, the sardonic Irish genius – not one word of his brainchild would he allow to be altered. That is, unless he changed it himself, as when his glittering eye fixed upon the film's well-moulded male star. Cleopatra had a line describing Caesar as 'thin and stringy'. 'You are hundreds of years old but you have a nice voice' was the Shavian substitute. Vivien quibbled, writing the author that she felt she could make the original line believable by the way she read it.

'I never change a line except for the better. Don't be an idiot,' came the acerbic postcard wrist-slap. G.B.S. added a final rebuke. She had failed to put her address on her letter!

The exchange brought her one of the few smiles in the coldest winter on record for many years. There were times when Larry came home from his new job as a director of the revived Old Vic to find her locked in an unaccountable fit of depression. Sometimes it ended in a wild flood of tears; and there were other times when an inexplicable metamorphosis turned his adoring wife into a venom-spitting Fury.

This was a creature Larry had never seen, never known. It was as though a coarse stranger had possessed her, put words into her mouth. When the seizure had passed, she remembered nothing, nor did she want to. But the questioning fear remained. Would it happen again? Would it be possible that her whole balance would be tipped into a darkness without end? The fear drove her on even more furiously towards fulfilling her talents, pushing herself to the limit of work and pleasure, storing every waking moment against the night that might fall. She refused to seek medical advice. She would be her own best doctor, with Larry's love as her shield, even against herself.

One weekend Larry drove her out into the frozen landscape of winterbound England through Aylesbury to Long Crendon, Buckinghamshire, about fifty miles from London.

'We shall probably hate it,' she prophesied.

Probably. But the idea of living in Notley Abbey, built in the time of Henry II, endowed by that same Henry V the actor had just portrayed, and closed by Henry VIII, was very appealing to Larry. Here was history to be lived in, not just read or performed.

Perhaps more than any couple except the Windsors, the Oliviers had become the most widely discussed lovers of their time. Newspapers and magazines were full of them – their careers, their deeds, their doings, their whims. Their photos adorned the media like flowers on a banquet board. The public hungered for some bright image to enliven the gloom of war-worn England. Even in America, they had become a byword for romance. For reality, there was always one's own life.

New York had the Lunts, but no theatrical couple existed to compete with England's new theatrical 'Royals'. And since Olivier had played Henry V, no ordinary house would do.

They headed their car through painted white gates up a drive lined with spidery black skeletons which the coming spring would explode back into trees. They drove over a little bridge spanning a frostbitten finger of the Thames. She brightened at the sight, for she always longed to be near water. Somehow its liquid flow gave her a pulsating sense of life. Out of the drive they crunched to a stop before the thickest oak door she'd ever seen. She could feel it even before it moaned open like a wall of wood. Mullioned windows in the grey stone retained the dignity of the old abbey through centuries of service as a farmhouse; the much-married Henry VIII had abolished its religious function when he cut the cord to Rome.

Vivien had the sort of mind that enabled her to stand in a bare room and envision it fully furnished. If she hadn't been an actress, she would have made an excellent interior decorator. Her taste – as everyone noted – was consistently impeccable.

Up the staircase they mounted to the central tower. Larry was in the process of falling in love. From an upper window, she surveyed the tangled wreck of the gardens, the burst water pipes wearing icy beards. Finally, back in the car he paused for a last look at the noble silhouette against the leaden sky.

'Well, that's it!' he said with finality.

'That's *not* it,' she countered with equal finality.

She was so dead against the idea that she recruited her decorator friend Sybil, Lady Colefax, Robert Helpmann, and David Niven to help her persuade Larry to abandon the madness of trying to make the abbey inhabitable.

The willingness of the armed forces to part with the services of its two most distinguished thespian warriors, Richardson and Olivier, must have been embarrassing. When the Governors of the Old Vic made formal application to the Admiralty, the reply had come back with 'an alacrity on the

part of My Lords of the Admiralty that was almost hurtful,'
as Olivier later observed. Perhaps the destruction of
friendly planes had not gone unrecorded – or that mythical
Fifth Sea Lord had materialised for the occasion. In all
events, the cause was worthy.

Since Olivier and Richardson had been away from the
stage for years, they were both grateful for this chance to
help resuscitate the Old Vic, which had operated only in
the provinces during the war. Along with John Burrell
(an ex-drama producer from the BBC), they took on the
Herculean task of bringing the Old Vic back to its former
glory. The building itself was a bombed-out shell, but they
would open at the New Theatre.

Larry had taken off his uniform for the last time, having
served three years and one month. He had been off the
London stage for six years when he signed his five-year
contract with the Old Vic in June of 1944. Richardson had
decided to open their first season in the title role of *Peer
Gynt*, with Larry as the Button Moulder. He was also to
play Sergius in *Arms and the Man*, and in *Uncle Vanya*. But
after all the great roles he had already played – Hamlet,
Macbeth, Henry V, Coriolanus – he must find something
arresting to follow Richardson's Peer Gynt. Something
he'd never played before.

Richard III? The reality in the twisted, mis-shapen
Prince of Evil murdering his way upwards to the throne.
Irresistible! Oh yes, Richard would be any actor's choice.

Yet the role definitely daunted Olivier. Not long before,
Donald Wolfit had played the part, and there would be the
inevitable question of comparison. Wolfit was a hard man
to follow – on stage, or in an exchange of anecdotes in the
members' bar of the Garrick Club (London's time-
honoured retreat founded in 1831 as a place 'where
gentlemen could mingle with actors').

The more Olivier considered it, the harder it was to set
Richard aside. The problem, as always, would be to bring
something new to the role. As Olivier later told Kenneth

Tynan in an interview,* 'One had Hitler over the way, one was playing it definitely as a paranoiac, so that there was a core of something to which the audience would later respond.'

The V-1 flying bombs were still soaring in over London when the company started rehearsals in an empty room of the National Gallery. They hoped the advancing Allies would capture the Nazi launching bases before opening night. And when they came back from Manchester to open the first production of *Peer Gynt* in London, the last flying bomb had in fact fallen. Richardson gave a brilliant performance in the lead role. And Olivier's modest Button Moulder was not lost on his fellow actors, critics, or audience.

Years later, Olivier was to recall to Tynan that while learning the role of Richard III for that Old Vic season, he could still hear Wolfit's voice in his mind's ear and see nothing but Wolfit in his mind's eye. 'I had heard imitations of old actors imitating Henry Irving ... That's why I took a rather narrow kind of vocal address ... Looks? I thought about the Big Bad Wolf, and I thought about Jed Harris, a director under whom I'd suffered *in extremis* in New York (*The Green Bay Tree*). The physiognomy of Disney's original Big Bad Wolf was said to have been founded upon Jed Harris – hence the nose ... And so with one or two extraneous externals I began to build up a character, a characterisation. I usually collect a lot of details, a lot of characteristics, and find a creature swimming about somewhere in the middle of them ... The actor who starts from the inside is more likely to find himself in the parts he plays than to find the parts in himself.'

But no matter how great the villain, no matter how unregenerate the rogue one was to play, Guthrie had always preached that an actor had to learn to love his character. Love? Well, understand, which is perhaps the best form of love. And thus Larry went into the problem of re-creating

* Ed. Hal Burton, *Great Acting*.

the role so many of the great actors had made great before him.

And, perhaps as never before, he was frightened.

The night before the opening, Vivien and he were locked into their suite at Claridge's with old friend Garson Kanin cuing him. Olivier was deeply concerned about his lapses of memory. At the dress rehearsal he'd gone up in his lines and had to lean on the prompter. Six years off the stage is too long for any actor. One forgets how to remember! They didn't stop until exhaustion set in at 4 a.m. For the first time, Larry was harbouring self-doubt and a fear of failure.

His make-up, as usual, was an intricate affair. It had taken hours of preparation, and had begun with sketches over his own photographs. He emerged with an enlarged lower lip, long slits of eyes, and a wart accenting the hollow cheek. His mouth was a sinister curve beneath an enormous nose which sniffed power like a wolf on the fold. Here was a man whose coffers were gleaming with purple and gold.

Olivier had opening-night jitters with a vengeance! Never before had he been so near nervous collapse. He phoned fellow actor John Mills and urged him to come backstage before the play. This was a surprising request, since most actors prefer to be alone during the preparatory process of merging one's identity into another personality.

When Mills arrived, Olivier violated another theatre ethic. He apologised for the performance he was about to give. He couldn't learn the lines! He'd be 'terrible! Terrible!' He asked Mills to pass on the dire warning to all who knew him. Expect the worst, and they wouldn't be disappointed. Mills tried to reassure him, and made a hasty retreat.

One person above all in that audience understood the terror, the tension that even the greatest of actors can suffer. Vivien held her breath. Larry materialised, a shadow moving out of shadow, his mis-shapen back almost turned to the audience, the light cutting sharply across his lupine nose.

'I went on to the stage frightened, heart beating, came on,

locked the door behind me, approached the footlights and started. I – I just simply went through it,' the actor recalled later.*

In the truly great performances there is something that every member of the audience can recognise in himself: cravings, longings, ambitions, self-justifications, even defeats. The stage is an enlargement of the visceral weaknesses – it's only a matter of degree. Olivier's Richard was a presentation of a complex nature stunted by his own appetites.

Bound by the spell of that forceful stage presence, Vivien knew instantly that what had not taken place during his rehearsals was now happening. Tonight the magic was there. More than experience, more than gift, more than talent – something extra filled the stage, something that made the familiar lines new, fresh, sudden. Was that part of why she loved him so much? Love without envy or jealousy – only admiration. She gave him the applause of her heart, for she knew how desperately he had searched himself to create the performance.

'His Richard gives to every speech a fire-new glint. His diction flexible and swift – often mill-race swift – is bred of a racing brain. If outwardly he is a limping panther, there is no lameness in his mind,' raved J. C. Trewin next morning in the *Observer*. James Agate, the dean of critics on the *Sunday Times*, cavilled: 'If I have a criticism it is that Mr Olivier takes the audience a little too much into his confidence . . . This Richard coheres from start to finish and is a complete presentation of the character as the actor sees it and his physical means permit . . . If this Richard is not Shakespeare's, it is very definitely Mr Olivier's, and I do not propose to forget its mounting verve and sustained excitement.'

Other comments were unequivocal: 'An outstanding occasion in the history of the English theatre.' 'A masterpiece!' 'The marriage of dramatic force . . . bravura and

* Ed. Hal Burton, *Great Acting*.

cold reason.' 'His Richard entitles him . . . to be enrolled in the company of the great!'

Great. Greater. Greatest. Merely words. The true measure of success is the degree of communion between actor and audience. Olivier and Vivien had read all the notices, stayed up until 3 a.m., and drunk a little too much. His next performance was the matinée the following day. He still felt underprepared, still worried about lines. But the moment he walked on stage he sensed something in the atmosphere. As he recalled it later: 'There is a phrase – the sweet smell of success – and I can only tell you . . . it just smells like Brighton and oyster bars and things like that . . . as I went on stage – the house was not even full – I felt this thing. I felt for the first time that the critics had approved, that the public had approved and they had created a kind of grapevine . . . I felt, if you like, what an actor must finally feel . . . a little power of hypnotism.'

Some time after the *Richard III* opening, drama critic Alan Dent, still in naval uniform, delivered a package to Olivier. It was long, slightly bulging at one end, and it came from John Gielgud.

Naturally, comparisons were being made in the press and the 'Green Rooms' between Gielgud and Olivier – for the former had long reigned as acknowledged 'greatest actor on the British stage'.

Olivier unwrapped the package. It contained the sword worn by Edmund Kean, that unrivalled eighteenth-century actor when he played Richard III, and later brandished by Henry Irving in the same role. Now on its blade was a new inscription: 'This sword given him by his mother Kate Terry Gielgud (daughter of Ellen Terry) 1938, is given to Laurence Olivier by his friend John Gielgud in appreciation of his performance of Richard III at the New Theatre 1944.'

On the last night of the second season of the Old Vic, enthusiasm reached such a peak that St Martin's Lane had to be closed off to traffic. Some three thousand fans wild with adulation pressed and struggled to the stage door. A great throbbing chant arose: 'We want Larry! We want Larry!' Olivier and Richardson finally emerged behind a bodyguard of stagehands. Buttons were torn from their clothes, people shook their hands, kissed their faces, clung to them until they were forced to mount to the roof of their taxi and try to manage a few coherent words of farewell.

Olivier's film of *Henry V* had opened in London in November of 1944 to great acclaim. The path of Larry's King Hal would be strewn with honours. Its American opening in 1946 gained him the New York Film Critics' Best Actor of the Year Award, closely followed by Hollywood's Oscar for his performance. By the spring of 1945, even before the American opening, the profits were beginning to roll in, and the actor finally persuaded Vivien that they must own Notley Abbey.

They told themselves the kind of things people always tell themselves when making a purchase of palpable prodigality – that they could afford it if they restored one room at a time, as money and permits allowed. So while Larry was busy with the Old Vic, Viv took charge of the builders and plans for the seventy-five-acre estate.

The purchase coincided with a lawsuit brought by David Selznick against his truant star. She was rehearsing *The Skin of Our Teeth*, Thornton Wilder's *avant-garde* comic allegory, at the Globe, when the legal thunderclap struck.

There had been no parts for Vivien in his current Old Vic season, a circumstance which seriously concerned Larry, since absence from work never agreed with her. They had both been searching for a suitable play for her when someone sent him a copy of the Broadway hit in which Tallulah Bankhead had scored an enormous personal success. They were both taken with the play, and it was decided that Larry would direct the production himself.

But Selznick was determined that his errant Scarlett would not undertake the folly of trying to follow Tallulah. His lawsuit was based upon the not unreasonable contention that a 'screen personality' (the designation 'actress' was rather pointedly omitted) is like a sensitive and exotic plant which must only be exposed with the utmost wisdom, care, and caution. A person investing in such a property must naturally wish to prevent her from entering into precarious 'adventures' without the investor's consent.

Vivien's ingenious defence held that Selznick's 'exotic plant' was, in fact, a married woman of thirty-one and subject to National Service regulations. The Minister of Labour, who had graciously exempted her from war work to appear in *Skin*, would, if Mr Selznick's injunction were successful, be forced to put Vivien to work in a munitions factory. Surely Mr Selznick would not wish his star to exchange the footlights for the factory?

Mr Justice Romer, hearing the case, found this argument irrefutable. In the interests of Selznick, he ruled against him. Miss Leigh would be allowed to perform in *The Skin of Our Teeth*.

When Olivier read the court decision to his cast at rehearsals, they cheered.

At the Edinburgh première, a perplexed audience applauded vigorously, without a clue as to what the play they were watching was all about. But it came as a welcome romp, wherein all laws of conventional theatre were tossed aside in favour of fun and frolic. The cast stepped in and out of character at will, even to protesting against their own roles. Vivien had never shown more verve and gift for comedy than as Sabina. The part gave her the scope to lose the Scarlett image once and for all, and Olivier's direction was superbly inventive.

But the London opening at the Phoenix Theatre seemed more like an obstacle course of errors. On 16 May 1945, just eight days after V-E Day, the nervous director watched his cast struggle on into the second act with every lighting cue late. Actors were performing in total darkness while the audience's attention was being directed to spotlit areas of empty stage, and it was hard enough to follow the play when you could see it!

As the third act began, Olivier scanned the aisle seats for

the critics. To his fury, he noted that James Agate had not returned from the bar. It was nearly ten minutes into the act – the ten vital minutes which made sense of the allegorical symbols of the play. Then he spotted the short, balding pundit of the *Sunday Times* drifting casually back down the aisle.

'You're late, blast you!' seethed the indignant director. His fist struck the critic hard across the shoulder. Agate's owl face lifted in stunned surprise in the darkened auditorium.

'Who the devil are you?'

'You know who I am, all right!' Without waiting for the amazed critic to recover, Olivier turned on his heel, barely managing to regain control as he resumed his own seat. Already he regretted the incident.

But Agate's review reflected his superb sense of priorities: '. . . owing to Mr Olivier's ingenious, inventive producing [read 'directing' for America] backed by some brilliantly co-ordinated teamwork, the play must be reckoned a complete success. Through it all, flittered and fluttered Miss Leigh's hired girl, Sabina, an enchanting piece of nonsense-cum-allure, half dabchick and half dragonfly. The best performance of this kind since Yvonne Printemps.'

The Oliviers had barely managed a few weekends together at Notley when the Old Vic was asked to bring their season to the troops. With Vivien's play off to a blazing start, Larry felt he could leave her, although she was looking thinner, more exhausted, and the cough persisted. But she insisted work was her cure, and so he joined the company on a tour of Antwerp, Ghent, Hamburg, and finally Paris, where the Old Vic appeared at the Comédie Française, the first foreign company to perform in the National Theatre of France.

Katharine Cornell was once asked by an aspiring actress to name the most important single attribute needed for a successful stage career. The great lady of the American theatre replied unhesitatingly: 'Good health.' And probably no artistic pursuit can be more physically taxing than touring a play, and playing a show every night, plus two and sometimes four matinées a week.

According to her close friend Alan Dent, 'Vivien had learned almost every aspect of her job except the art of husbanding her resources . . . She had never really acquired the gentle art of rest.' *Gone With the Wind* had drained Vivien's energy reserves. Before she had fully recharged them, she had plunged into the pressures of producer-backer-star of the ill-fated *Romeo and Juliet* tour. To keep up with Larry, who has seemed at times to possess the energy of five men, would be daunting even to a Russian lady gymnast. But Vivien tried. After *The Doctor's Dilemma*, the North African tour left her gaunt and coughing, but still chain-smoking. And she was beginning to lean rather too heavily on a glass of wine to unwind. Cleopatra's flimsy costumes against the worst of English winters hadn't helped. Finally, there had been the miscarriage – and the first signs of manic depression.

Larry had his hands full at the Old Vic with *Richard III* and a season that included *Uncle Vanya*, *Oedipus*, *Henry IV Parts 1 and 2*, and *The Critic*. Then, while he was on tour in Hamburg and she was in Liverpool with *Skin*, she became ill, seriously ill.

The news first eached him through a pilot friend in Hamburg – Anthony Bartley, who had seen her in London. He could only report that a doctor had taken X-rays and found some sort of patch on the lung. Olivier had written at once, begging for news. Her letter of explanation never reached him. But a second did – which made things sound even worse, since it began: 'Now that you know the worst . . .'

Since he didn't, he could only imagine it. The company moved on to a Paris crowded with uniforms, an electric spirit of victory in the air. Olivier was scarcely aware that his performance was making him the toast of Paris, his thoughts all on Vivien and getting back to her. Then he saw the Lunts, who had visited her in London. They assured him that tuberculosis was no longer the dread killer. Besides, she was still performing, so it couldn't be all that serious.

But it was. Larry returned in time to take Vivien to the hospital for observation.

On 21 August 1945, a London *Star* reporter noted: 'I received today a charming but entirely illegal smile from Miss Vivien Leigh. It was through the glass pane in the door of her flower-bedecked private ward in University College Hospital.

'Hovering near were a battery of nurses and sisters, ready to pounce with their "positively no visitors". Only one man besides the doctor can pass through that door. He is husband Laurence Olivier, and a sister told me, "Even he is allowed only a very short while each day." Miss Leigh, looking sweetly apologetic, is having to obey orders . . . She has a chest complaint that even her most optimistic friends expected . . . Her doctors ordered her to Switzerland but transport difficulties were too great . . .'

Whe she was released from the hospital two months later, the news media reported her whereabouts as 'somewhere in the country'. She had gone to Notley, where she had been ordered for six months of complete rest. The abbey she had been so hesitant to let Larry buy had now become a haven of rest, and she was learning to love it.

Vivien Leigh's miscarriages, manic-depression, and bouts of tuberculosis have always been thought of as separate illnesses. But they form a pattern of physical neglect. She mistook drive for energy, energy for strength, and certainly she gave the impression that however physically fragile she might be, her spirit was invincible. Even Noël Coward, who knew her so well, watched her several years later herding a group of exhausted friends through a Paris railway depot, issuing orders to porters as she went. 'She has a body like swan's down and the constitution of a GI on leave!' he observed.

Recovering her health at Notley, confined to her bed for four months, Vivien was, she supposed, becoming the best-read actress she knew: Dickens, Confucius, Montaigne, Balzac. Beyond the windows of her L-shaped room she could watch time slip by. Spring came to the Buckinghamshire valley, the chestnut and elms flourishing their banners of green, the silver poplars bowing beneath courtly clouds, pear trees parading their first bounty. And then at last she was allowed out to potter about the garden, and oversee the gardeners at their cleaning and pruning and planting. A frail Vivien sat in the frail sunlight, wrapped in a shawl or heavy sweater, writing her thoughtful answers to all the get-well messages. Beverly Nichols had called her 'sparkling as a diamond' when he reviewed her performance in *Skin*. Now her glow was more moonstone, deeper, softer, in tone.

Nine months at Notley, and she had fallen in love with it. This was no longer just Larry's historical backdrop with its frescoes of Notley's arms of hazelnut and lovers' knot. It was no longer just a weekend refuge from London. It was to be the cradle and hub for a very special and beautifully designed new life style.

What a setting for entertainment! The dining-room could seat twelve comfortably, and there were five guest rooms for weekenders. The walled garden would be conjured into a dwarf's forest of roses, all her favourite colours, but mainly white, of course. Their cows must be christened for the characters she had played: Cleopatra gently masticating her grassy cud, Titania fat with milk, Ophelia drinking at the river but not falling in. But no Scarlett! She wouldn't even punish a cow with that name. And like a Marie Antoinette creating bucolic elegance in her Petit Trianon, she dreamed of producing rustic revels for their privileged circle, and Larry, even the hard working Larry, must learn to love their county carnivals.

She had it all carefully planned. The weekends would begin after theatre Saturday nights. Everyone would rendezvous at Durham Cottage, Chelsea, for sandwiches and a drink to bolster them for the ninety-minute drive down to Thame. They would arrive at Notley after midnight, the abbey ablaze with lights, fires crackling in every hearth, flowers in every bowl arranged with Vivien's own unique touch. Each bedside table would hold some book of special interest to the particular guest. How she loved this detail of planning! She would select the menus for the four-course dinners, and choose the wines. Drinks in the library first, and the guests would be expected to dress, of course. Could one imagine making an entrance down that stately staircase without a long gown? Then games: charades and canasta. Servants would remain on duty day and night through the weekends. They wouldn't mind, since Larry and Vivien would almost never be there during the week.

Her plans for Notley must have sounded exhausting to Larry. But the important thing was to have her well again, and social planning seemed as necessary a step towards that objective as breathing. Friends were so special to her. They were her creed and she was ever considerate to the smallest detail, pampering them with gifts and thoughtfulness. They filled the waking moments, hedged her in against the growing fear of periodic nervous depressions.

An important difference was beginning to cleave the pattern of their marriage. She was the marksman of many targets; career shared importance with pleasure, and pleasure required the geography of personal relationships.

'It drove him mad because she was accepting invitations from everyone who was anyone of her practically endless court of friends and admirers,' recalls David Fairweather, by now their full-time press representative. 'Not that Olivier lacked friends. It was just that his dedication to work did not leave time for very much else.'

The morning was cold and drizzly for early May. A crowd of people huddled together at LaGuardia Airport, watching the overcast sky. Then a drone of motors brought a Pan American Constellation winging down, ten minutes late on its seventeen-hour flight from England.

The entire cast of the Old Vic Company filed out, having

arrived for their historic first visit to America. But for the waiting crowd there were only two people: Vivien and Larry. She came first, her dark hair tucked into a paisley snood, and wearing the same mink coat she had left New York in six years before. Behind her, the actor beamed broadly.

And then, the perfect stage effect, courtesy of nature: as though it had been switched on, the sun flashed out, spotlighting the Oliviers. Vivien insisted to the dazzled press that she'd only come along for the ride.

But Larry was glad she had come. He could keep an eye on her. Their suite at the St Regis was blooming with flowers from Helen Hayes's garden, gift tokens and presents piled high from friends and strangers. Garson Kanin and Ruth Gordon had hand-picked the suite. There were welcomes from the Lunts, George Cukor, Katharine Cornell. There would be late-night suppers at the Colony and the Stork, with menus that read like Roman orgies after the shortages of Britain.

Looking out across Fifth Avenue, she could only have thought how different this time was from that ill-fated *Romeo and Juliet*. Her illness was receding and she had put back some weight. With returning health came the need to return to work. But she wasn't ready yet.

While she was still at Notley, the doctor had forbidden cigarettes and alcohol. It seemed as though even a glass of wine at the wrong moment could trigger a manic mood, and the Notley rest period had not been free of them. These moody highs and lows could turn her into a stranger, and they came on like a devil of possession. They might last a few hours or half a day, during which she would spiral from strident over-exhilaration into the pit of depression. When all had passed and she had returned to her charming, loving self, she was unable to explain, remorseful, needing desperately to be forgiven, yet still unwilling to consult a doctor. Worshipping her as he did, Larry bore the anguish of the bad moments with incredible courage. But fears were beginning to erode his own health.

In a Broadway season that included Walter Huston, Maurice Evans, Raymond Massey, and the Lunts, the Old Vic Company played to 87,000 cheering theatre-goers, with another 30,000 turned away. The roles of Oedipus, Mr Puff in *The Critic*, Hotspur and Shallow in *Henry IV*, and Dr Astrov in *Uncle Vanya* would have seemed enough for any actor. But there was still Sunday, so Olivier filled that with broadcasts. It was a matter of simple economics. His salary of a hundred pounds a week just wouldn't stretch far enough to keep them living at the St Regis in the style their fans had become accustomed to expecting. Along with his worries about Vivien, Larry had given himself little or no rest, and his own mental condition was beginning to show signs of strain.

A horrifying recurrent dream of falling began to haunt his sleep. Sometimes it was a plane crash, sometimes he was on stage as Mr Puff. The fears were not without some justification. Olivier had contrived a typically acrobatic finale for Mr Puff. Astride a painted cloud, he was glimpsed by the audience being swept up into the flies to reappear clinging to the curtain as it descended. This Fairbanksian effect was, in fact, managed by climbing down an unseen rope. In London there had been several near accidents. But Olivier's dreams confused Puff's crash with a plummeting plane. He considered exchanging their flight plans for a return voyage to England by ship. And without mentioning it to Vivien, he began a countdown of Puff's remaining exits. Yet if one started pampering nightmares, there would be no end.

The heat of New York's June weighed on the air like a shroud, clinging to the skyscrapers. Soon the American tour would be over, and Puff's last thirty-foot descent would become history. On the last night, Larry swung down to the final curtain call without a scratch. Relief was so great that he executed two somersaults of sheer exuberance – and came out of his 'victory roll' with two torn tendons in his heel.

To some extent, the accident set Olivier's mind at rest.

His premonition was certainly fulfilled, and the fact that he could barely walk wouldn't now stop him from flying to Boston with Vivien the following day. Tufts College was presenting him with an honorary degree as 'the real interpreter of Shakespeare of our age'. The degree in hand, Larry and Vivien had barely an hour to catch the plane back to New York. He sent her on ahead to try to delay the plane's take-off while he put in a token appearance at the reception. But it would have taken a social Houdini to extricate himself swiftly from the academic circle of admirers. Only after many apologies and explanations could the actor hobble into a waiting limousine, still clutching cap and gown, and head for Logan Field.

At the airport, the authorities were sympathetic to Vivien's pleas. She boarded the plane and waited. But finally, the plane could not. The propellers whirled. From the plane's window she saw him hobbling out across the field, waving in gestures that had stopped the charge at Agincourt – but didn't stop the plane's inexorable rush down the runway.

They had promised each other never to fly separately! Now the nightmare became a distinct possibility. Tears burst from the actor's eyes. Was it possible he would never see Vivien again? A woman reporter took his arm and suggested a stiff drink.

'Just a cup of tea,' murmured the actor. Much to his surprise, he arrived safely in New York by the next plane.

The theatre's royal couple was cheered at the première at the City Center Theatre. Two days later, they took off for England. Impoverished royalty, they had exactly $17.46 left between them. But the money didn't matter. Much more important was the thought of a summer of rest, peace, and tranquillity ahead of them at Notley. Nightmares could be forgotten.

The New York *Herald Tribune* of 19 June 1946, told of their flight.

EIRE-BOUND PLANE CRASH-LANDS IN CONNECTICUT!
CONSTELLATION DROPS ONE MOTOR AND WING CATCHES
FIRE AFTER LEAVING LAGUARDIA FIELD; OLIVIER AND
WIFE ON CRAFT; EDEN CANCELLED TRIP.

... after leaving at 5 p.m. yesterday it crash-landed on
its belly an hour and ten minutes later in a small emergency
landing field at Willimantic, 25 miles east of Hartford ...
The plane developed engine trouble about 45 minutes
after leaving ...

Frederick Cook of the *Evening Standard* interviewed
Olivier by phone when they landed: 'We were up 15,000
feet thinking how wonderful it was to be homeward
bound, when suddenly the outer engine on the starboard
side caught fire. The crew immediately stopped the
engines while they made desperate efforts to put the fire
out ... Finally, the entire engine just fell off! By this time
Captain Miller was looking for a landing spot. There
was a sudden break in the cloud formation and we
found ourselves near a small airfield ... We were
coming down fast, about three hundred miles an hour,
when the pilot discovered he could not work the under-
carriage. He then made a crash landing. There was
scarcely a jolt and none of the passengers were thrown
forward. It was such a brilliant piece of work that every
passenger stood and cheered the pilot after the airplane
came to rest.'

Most of the rest of the Old Vic Company had returned
a few days earlier, and the former British Foreign
Minister Anthony Eden had cancelled his reservation
minutes before the take-off.

For Olivier, the nightmare had fulfilled itself and might
now be finally laid to rest. For Vivien, the nightmare lay
ahead.

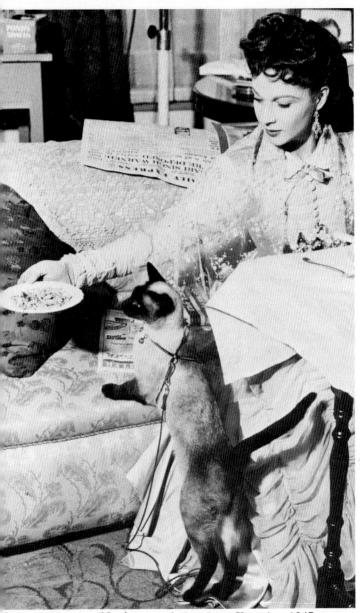

Vivien and her cat, 'New', on set during *Anna Karenina,* 1947.
London Films

Hamlet, about to land on Claudius. *Rank (Courtesy National Film Archives)*

The Oliviers' return from Australia in November, after his operation.

Filming *Elephant Walk* in Ceylon, 1953. Vivien with Peter Finch. *Paramount Pictures (courtesy Irving Asher)*

Finch with replacement Elizabeth Taylor in Hollywood. *Paramount Pictures (courtesy Irving Asher)*

Return to health, after holidaying in Rome, February 1953. *Copyrigh[t]
Keystone Press Agency Ltd*

The film of *The Prince and the Showgirl*, 1956: Marilyn's arrival in London – with glacial bridegroom Arthur Miller. *Warner Bros.*

Together in *21 Days*, 1939. *London Films*

II Trouble in paradise

'2 POLICEMEN GUARD OLIVIER FROM HIS WOMAN FANS,' proclaimed London headlines for 25 September 1946. 'Hundreds of shouting, singing women and girls packed the stage door entrance to the New Theatre, waiting for Laurence Olivier. Girls climbed on to a phone kiosk outside the theatre, stood on window ledges and builders' ladders. An inspector and a dozen police constables were summoned . . . As the supporting cast appeared the crowd booed, chanting, "Where is Laurence?" Police formed a shoulder-to-shoulder guard about him. The crowd beat in exasperation on the constables' shoulders with their fists trying to break through to their idol. Olivier's progress down the closed-in alley was brought to a snail's pace by the clapping waving, kiss-blowing women. The police half-carried, half-led the star through the pack, appealing for passage. A policeman stumbled and fell. In the instant Olivier disappeared under a sea of women! The police re-formed, dragged him to his feet and carried him the last thirty yards to his car.'

It could hardly be believed. This – for a classic King Lear in staid old London town? He seems to have stirred an emotional adulation generally accorded pop performers.

Olivier's third Old Vic season (as one-third of the triumphant management which included Richardson and Burrell) had opened with more solid enthusiasm from fans than all the critics. While critics conceded Lear to be one of the most daunting of Shakespeare's anti-heroes, the word 'ham' crept into at least one review. Beverley Baxter of the London *Evening Standard* suggested that Lear had 'floored Olivier almost as completely as though he were a British heavyweight'. Tynan called it a 'moderate Lear'.

Agate noted Lear s 'grim and unexpected humour . Humour was a quality Olivier could spade from the loam of any role. Agate went further: 'Olivier is a comedian by instinct and a tragedian by art.' But Olivier had a fair share of supporters in the press. J. C. Trewin, critic of the *Observer*, was not alone in hailing it 'the best Lear yet!'

Not quite all of Olivier's fans were adoring. When the Old Vic Company arrived in Paris to perform *Lear* at the Théatre de Champs-Elysées, the press noted that he was hiding his left hand in his overcoat pocket. The only explanation he would give was that he'd been attacked in London the previous night.

In fact, there had been a series of three assaults on the actor by a twenty-eight-year-old out-of-work teacher and would-be actor 'of no fixed address'. The man had written to Olivier and was rewarded with a small walk-on part at the Old Vic. Soon after, he was dismissed, and complained of persecution. He decided, he later admitted, 'to pester Mr Olivier'. One night as the Olivier Rolls drew up in front of Durham Cottage, the man sprang out from the bushes, seized Vivien in his arms, and attempted to kiss her. Olivier delivered a restraining left, and summoned the police, who were also assaulted by the man. In court, the molester claimed that he had deliberately committed the offence to bring the injustice of his treatment to the attention of the public. An example of a crank lunatic fringe against which most celebrities must protect themselves.

Olivier's Paris production was a resounding success in which a little-known actor named Alec Guinness was greatly admired in the role of the Fool.

Back in London, Vivien was less notably involved in the revival of *The Skin of Our Teeth* at the Piccadilly Theatre. All was warmth and quiet in her dressing room in the bowels of the theatre, so far beneath the freezing bustle of adjacent Piccadilly Circus. Her handsome Siamese cat, New (named for the Theatre), sported an elegant Parisian collar ornamented with tiny gilt bells, brought back by

Larry from France. The much-travelled New almost always accompanied Vivien on tours and had become perfectly used to settling down in strange hotel rooms or dressing-room armchairs. Now he blinked a blue eye at the sandy blonde Sabina wig as Vivien adjusted its elaborate, high-piled curls. Through one of the curls she stuck a red-handled toothbrush, an added eccentricity of the ice-age skivvy she was playing.

'I love wigs,' she purred at New. 'They're such fun.' In truth, she seldom appeared without one, as Stanley Hall, her wigmaker and great friend, confirms. The call bell rang and she was off.

The Oliviers' separate productions came as the climax of a glorious summer at Notley, which restored health but depleted bank accounts. The old need was gnawing – find a film! But, however costly, that summer was perhaps the happiest time they would ever share. The happiest, but not the quietest. For Vivien there was always the need of people.

Guests at Notley were generally drawn from a tight little coterie of theatrical people and a handful of socialite friends. Noël Coward was a constant visitor and inventive games master for the charades and other after-dinner diversions, and Larry could always produce robust humour for such occasions. Cecil Beaton recalled a charade miming a production Olivier was planning: the actor flailed his arms, emulating with a big *whoosh* a great curtain falling – a pillar "pffutting" down there ... He would illustrate ... by making prep-school sounds – of pops, bangs, and corks being drawn, of internal combustion explosions, farts, and all sorts of other coarse noises. The camera would "raspberry" down ... and then "raspberry" away at the end ... Larry is, heaven knows, serious about his career, but the project on hand is referred to only in ribald terms ... A great blob here (Bang! Bang Ho!) – a great cowpat there (Bunghol) ... Larry's imitations have about them something of the original clown or, at least, the essential entertainer ... the mummer, the ale-drinking Thespian –

not the rather overwhelmed and shy cipher with wrinkled forehead that goes out into society.'*

The actor loved nothing better than spending his Notley day pruning trees, dredging out the clogged river, or consulting with his brother on farming problems. Dickie, with his wife, Hester, now occupied a cottage on the estate and managed the dairy farm. George Cukor recalls an 'informal but elegant' visit to Notley when Larry had dammed up the river and everyone went swimming. Doug Fairbanks, Jr., recalls: 'There'd be fairly good tennis. Larry liked to keep fit. Never could get out until late Saturday night after the play (when they were performing in London). Weekends were really Sunday and Monday.'

Vivien seemed to regard sleep as a waste of precious life time. The parties often went on until four or five a.m. But no matter the hour, she would always inspect the arrangement of the breakfast trays in the butler's pantry before finally retiring. She had a superb cook and house-keeper, Val Pallin, with whom she planned the menus – always elaborate.

David Fairweather was at dinner one night when a very complicated and elaborate first course started the menu – *moules au beurre d'escargot*. Vivien looked less than pleased when the dish was served. Later, he learned the aftermath from Val. She had been summoned next morning to face a stern Vivien, seated at her dressing-table mirror.

'Absolutely disgraceful last night, Val!' the actress snapped. 'You're supposed to be a marvellous cook, yet you sent out the *moules* looking like the dog's dinner!'

Val's face fell, and Vivien, immediately sorry for her sharp words, added quickly, 'But of course they *tasted* delicious.'

At his first invitation to a Notley weekend, Ralph Richardson was on his best behaviour. That rocket episode at Durham Cottage may have been forgiven but it was not

* Anne Edwards, *Vivien Leigh: A Biography*.

forgotten. As the guests sat around the fire sipping liqueurs after dinner, Larry invited his old colleague to have a look at the extraordinary frescoes of the Notley arms in the loft. Together they mounted the great staircase, then climbed the ladder into the unused upper regions of the abbey. Richardson followed his host gingerly across a creaking section of old beams. Suddenly the boards gave way beneath his feet and he plunged from view through the floor.

Larry hurried down into the room below to find that his friend had made a three-point landing on the Olivier bed. There he lay in a downpour of dust and rubble, tarnished but unscathed. The two hastily swept up the debris as best they could, and made an entrance as though nothing had happened.

Vivien had warned Richardson on his arrival: 'It must be distinctly understood that you don't set foot outside the library.'

For 8 July 1947, Olivier had scratched in his diary: 'Buckingham Palace, 10.15.' Beneath this, he had drawn the picture of a sword. His visit to the Palace was made in Anthony Bushell's braid-trimmed morning coat, Ralph Richardson's black waistcoat, and Hamlet's blond hair (dyed for his current film). The purpose of his appearance before George VI was to receive a tap on the shoulder with the royal sword, and thus become a Knight Bachelor of the Empire. At forty, the new Sir Laurence had been cited in the King's Birthday Honours List 'for services to stage and film'. He was the youngest actor to be so honoured. Henry Irving had been the first, followed by only nineteen others in half a century. Richardson, five years Larry's senior, had been knighted on the January Honours List, thus beating his friend to the blade.

Elegantly simple in a black dress without jewellery, Vivien accompanied Larry to the Palace. She waited for him in the Grand Hall, and then, as the new Lady Olivier, she left on his arm to return to filming *Anna Karenina* at

Shepperton for Korda. It had seemed to the producer that Vivien would be ideal casting for Tolstoy's unhappy heroine, and it offered Vivien an important role while Olivier was busy with *Hamlet*.

But from the start of filming, she and Korda's French director, Julien Duvivier, did not get on. Her periods of depression had begun again the previous Christmas. Her attitude on the set seemed at times irascible, aloof, and isolated. Cecil Beaton, who was costuming the film, found her difficult even during a pre-production trip to Paris (where fine fabrics were beginning to be available again). There were flare-ups over trivialities like glove sizes. And when filming began, she was untypically difficult about admitting unannounced journalists. She even became short-tempered with a fellow actress. This was not quite the Vivien that everyone knew and adored.

Mrs Hartley began to accompany her daughter to the set, perhaps at the instigation of Larry. Her mother had brought Suzanne back from Canada during the summer, but Vivien seemed to have more time for her mother than her daughter at this period.

But there were still examples of her customary consideration for others. Character actress Madge Brindley needed to leave the set promptly at five p.m. for an important film test. Brindley had notified Duvivier, but when five o'clock came he showed no signs of freeing the slaves. To save Brindley's chance, Vivien folded her book of crossword puzzles and marched off the set, thereby cancelling further shooting and insuring that Madge got to her test in time.

More and more, the careers of Olivier and Leigh were drawing away from each other – not by wish or will, but by circumstance. In the tradition of David Garrick, the great eighteenth-century British actor-manager, Olivier liked to be on both sides of the curtain. It was inevitable that he should form his own company. Laurence Olivier Productions Ltd. mounted as its first production Garson Kanin's Broadway hit *Born Yesterday*. It opened the 1947 season at the Garrick Theatre, starring the American actress Yolande Donlan.

Too busy to direct the production himself, he and Vivien watched the dress rehearsal and were convinced it would be a flop. 'Come and sit with us in the dress circle, Feathers,' he said to David Fairweather. 'See what you think. You can't ever tell with a comedy.' And they couldn't tell. *Born Yesterday* got rave reviews and ran almost a year.

But Olivier wasn't able to launch his company into full-scale operations for another two years. He had turned all of his attention to a new Shakespeare film project close to his heart. Filippo Del Giudice had once again been the persuading influence. The flamboyant Italian had a capacity for raising money (a producer's most prodigious achievement) and he would, as always, give Olivier an artistically free hand.

Since Orson Welles had beat them to the post with a filmed *Macbeth* and was already considering *Othello* as his next venture, their choice fell on *Hamlet*.

But when pre-production conferences began, Vivien could not ignore the plain truth. Ill health had now aged her beyond any possible consideration of playing the youthful Ophelia. It was easy for them both to find the excuse that she had become too important a luminary to fill so minor a role. But as Larry began considering all the young, available beauties, all Vivien could do was look on, offer suggestions, while the production grew in every detail of planning. Thirty actresses were tested for Ophelia. Olivier chose Jean Simmons, a sparkling eighteen-year-old who looked not unlike the Vivien of Elsinore days.

Olivier also felt himself too old for the screen Hamlet – another reason to dye his hair blond. He told Anthony Bushell (assistant producer, and in charge of casting) to 'get the other people's ages right' and he would hope to give a 'half-decent performance' the audience would accept. As it turned out, Hamlet's mother was played by Eileen Herlie, who was thirteen years younger than her film son –

a fact she helped disguise with make-up.

Shakespeare's *Hamlet* uncut generally lasted about four hours. Olivier and Alan Dent, who worked with him on the screenplay, had decided to confine their film story within a two-and-a-half-hour frame.

'It's really not Hamlet,' explained Olivier of his heavily pruned blueprint. 'You might say it is a study, or essay on Hamlet.'

It had been Vivien's suggestion, since they were simplifying and tightening the plot, to dispense with Rosencrantz, Guildenstern, and Fortinbras. They also updated a few of Shakespeare's more archaic words, which insured for Olivier that his mythical 'Gertie' (somewhere in the back stalls) could follow the story.

Olivier chose to film his soliloquies in 'voice-over'. Such verbalised keys to conscience as 'To be or not to be' became more soul-searchingly self-analytical than the usual asides to the audience. The volume of delivery was reduced at times to a mere whisper, which intensified the thought process in a uniquely appropriate cinematic manner; it was Shakespeare translated to the screen in contemporary terms.

When shooting finally began in May of 1947, the set was closed to all visitors. This unusual practice, instead of antagonising, actually made people more curious. Desmond Dickinson, director of photography, recalled it as the most difficult film he had ever photographed. Shooting took place mainly on one large permanent set. Since they were photographing in black and white, they could use 'deep focus' camera technique, but they needed special lighting. The brooding mood of the play affected crew as well as cast. It was hard work and little horseplay.

Olivier had decided to play the Ghost himself. After months of testing, the proper spectre effect was achieved by smearing the lens of the camera with Vaseline, creating an appropriately fuzzy silhouette. And to get the proper 'hellish' noises to herald the Ghost's entrance, Olivier went to enormous trouble, making fourteen separate sound tracks. In addition he recalled an effect used in Paris on stage by Jean-Louis Barrault: a throbbing heartbeat. He wanted to incorporate that rhythmic, pulsing sound, bringing the camera in and out of focus in time with each beat. To his credit, he never borrowed from another artist without permission, and insisted on paying Barrault for the use of this idea.

In filmland, where aping and filching amount to a tradition, such examples of ethics have seldom been known.

Although six months of intensive filming produced few moments of levity, Olivier's sense of the comic wasn't totally absent. Roger Furse recalled 'During the rather tense shooting of Ophelia's mad scene, he suddenly called a halt. With a serious face he suggested an improvement on the shot. He proposed that we should suspend Ophelia by her ankles from a Kirby flying machine, so that when the camera (following the person of the King) discovers Ophelia, she is spinning like a top on her head for the King's line "How long hath she been thus?" '

A good director knows when to relieve the tension with laughter. Olivier had devoted considerable time and effort into coaxing a performance from Jean Simmons, whose great natural talent made up for her almost total lack of training.

Any production that called for effective athletic show-manship was likely to include an accident to Olivier. 'You know at times I despaired of ever getting through it alive. Bad luck dogged my footsteps for months,' Olivier later told *Screen Guide* interviewer Margaret Gardner. 'First I fell off a rostrum and injured my leg. Just when that was beginning to heal, a camera dolly rode over my foot, and after I had let out a yell of pain – with some justification, I believe – the cameraman got so flustered, he backtracked again over the same foot, and I ended up in bed for a week. (Two broken bones.) To complete my bad luck cycle, I was stabbed in a duelling scene.'

He did not mention a more personal loss. The *Daily Express* of the fourth of July reported that Olivier had lost two rings while filming. He had left them both in his dressing-room caravan. When he returned, they were gone. One bore a treasured cameo head of Henry Irving. The other, even more treasured, had his monogram in gold and was the first present he had ever received from Vivien.

The accident-prone performer had saved Hamlet's last and most dangerous leap for the final day of shooting. If he had to go to the hospital after it, production wouldn't be held up. Hamlet was to jump from the balcony, landing on Claudius with the cry 'Then, venom, to thy work!' Upon which he would plunge his prop blade against the padded body of the King. Basil Sydney, playing Claudius, was understandably reluctant to serve as a human trampoline. A strongman double, George Crawford, took his place robed as the perfidious potentate – with his back to the camera.

Olivier's graceful dive did not take into account the frailty of the flesh even in strongmen. Crawford was knocked unconscious and lost two teeth, thus joining the rank's of filmdom's unsung heroes. The publicity department kept the accident to themselves.

But Hamlet's gilded locks were another matter. 'I bleached my hair for this role,' he told Miss Gardner. 'Not that I saw Hamlet as a purely Nordic type, but I wanted people to forget it was Olivier they were seeing and only see Hamlet. It's been a mess, this hair business. After the picture was finished I had it dyed back again, and it is only just beginning to grow back on the forehead where I had it shaved to give me a higher forehead line. But I think it was worth the trouble. It's a good thing I'm not the romantic type. Otherwise, it would matter.'

To Rank's surprise, Olivier brought the film in on schedule and well within its £500,000 budget – an incredible feat for this masterpiece. Every day throughout his filming, the 'unromantic' actor took time off at noon to phone his wife, whose portrait miniature held the place of honour on his dressing-table. She, too, kept personal mementoes of him always close at hand.

Although the script cuts of *Hamlet* did not please all critics, the film received many awards, including five Oscars. Best of all, it played for over a year in New York – something no English film had done up to that time.

The stunt man hadn't been *Hamlet*'s only casualty. Filippo Del Giudice, that colourful Italian showman who had invested so much faith in Olivier and British classics, fell victim to changing times. Rank's tough-minded management considered Del Giudice extravagant. He was sacked before the film was released, thus depriving him of credit and profit. Never again was he able to pull a cinematic rabbit from his Borsolino; the audacious little producer retired to a Roman monastery, where he died forgotten.

David Fairweather recalls a London ball, after the filming. Among the guests at the Olivier table were John and Mary Mills. Mills had just completed filming his portrait of the intrepid explorer *Scott of the Antarctic*. Across the room Vivien spied Jean Simmons in a romantic tête-à-tête with the dashing actor Stewart Granger, who was still married to Elspeth March.

With astounding self-righteousness, Vivien pronounced the liaison 'absolutely bloody disgraceful!'

She nudged Mills next to her. 'Go on, Johnny. Do tell him what we think of him!' Mills was understandably reluctant to become involved, but rather than brave Vivien's wrath, he downed his champagne, rose from the table, and crossed over to Granger. There he could be seen chatting away. In a few minutes he returned and quietly resumed his seat without a word.

'Did you tell him?' Vivien demanded. Mills offered a lame smile and a limp excuse.

'Well, actually, Viv, there wasn't a chance. The opportunity didn't present itself.'

Vivien's eyebrows – a banner of disgust – flew up.

'Scott of the fucking Antarctic!'

At about this time another ghost returned to haunt Olivier, this one from his Hollywood past. Greta Garbo arrived in

London, trying desperately to persuade the new Sir Laurence to play Chopin to her George Sand. Perhaps it afforded him some small satisfaction that he was too busy to accept the offer from that one-time Queen Christina in sunglasses who had jilted him for John Gilbert. For ahead of the Oliviers lay twenty-four rehearsals for an Australian tour with the Old Vic Company. Their repertoire would include *Richard III*, *School for Scandal*, and *The Skin of Our Teeth*.

The Australian tour was launched with Vivien's favourite indoor sport, a party. Seventy guests crowded into tiny Durham Cottage, among them the John Millses. Last to leave at five in the morning were Danny Kaye and Roger Furse. The comedian offered a valuable last tip.

'If you prepare every speech you are asked to make, you'll have a nervous breakdown. If you make enough lousy speeches – lovely! They'll stop asking you to make any more.' This was clearly advice easier given than followed.

After only three hours' sleep, and with a tearful farewell to New, curled amid the party debris, they left for Liverpool Station, to board the *Corinthic*. 'Many sweet people seeing us off. Many sweet fans and many sweet flash bulbs . . . Masses of flowers on board, about 100 wires . . . dinner alone together in cabin. Vivien not eating much. Went for a walk by myself wearing duffle coat,' wrote Larry in his journal on 14 February.[*]

Once at sea, Vivien had set aside the charming bon-voyage smiles. Larry sensed the familiar signs that she might be sinking into another depression. On the seventeenth he noted 'Tonight at dinner at the Captain's table Vivien turned to me suddenly with an alarmingly wild look and said, "Tonight I should like to play dominoes".' His concern for her health was aggravated by his own. He had developed an agonising pain in his foot, but the ship's

---

* Felix Barker, *The Oliviers*.

doctor confirmed that it was not gout.

He needn't have worried about Vivien this time. The sea air seemed to revitalise her. She sparkled with charm and energy; she was considerate and gracious to all. Never before had she seemed so beautiful to Larry, and he was more in love with her than ever.

Rehearsals were launched in the ship's saloon. They were to appear together in all three productions: Vivien would play Lady Anne in *Richard III*, and Olivier would play Antrobus in *Skin*. The role of Lady Teazle fitted Vivien like a glove, and Larry had new ideas to inject in Sir Peter for *School for Scandal*. Hard work remained the lifeblood of their happiness.

The stopover at Cape Town brought a surprise. 'Happy hypocrite' Ivor Novello was beaming at them from the dock. As guests of honour at his touring production of *Perchance to Dream*, their entrance almost stole the show. Once again, Vivien was the person she pretended at times to hate – yet needed to be the Hollywood Star, recognised in any corner of the world, the target of attention. It seemed to feed her spirit: energy drawn from adulation.

15 March, their first day in Australia. Olivier's diary noted: 'Vivien quite all right.'

For their Perth opening (in a movie palace), the Oliviers dressed on stage, generously leaving the six dressing-rooms to their large cast. Vivien, energy high, even helped iron the costumes. It proved the pattern for the tour.

In Perth's hundred-degree heat, they began to comprehend what this tour would entail: days filled with personal appearances, lectures, receptions, interviews, and, last and almost least, their performances. Larry noted: Vivien 'makes the most damned awful fuss but I think she's beginning to like it; anyhow have tiny feeling she could not be discouraged even if that were necessary. "There are many advantages to being married," she told the delighted students, seizing the mike like Lamoret's duck, only even more bewitchingly . . .'

On the final night in Perth, the company brought down the house at the curtain call with a 'community sing' of 'Waltzing Matilda', only to discover they knew the words better than the Aussies.

In Adelaide, Olivier recorded that the opening night of *Skin* 'really went wonderfully. Vivien made a very good long speech . . .' He added less happily, 'I've wanted to play the part so often I hate to be disappointing myself in it. V. is wonderful. Better than ever.' But *Skin* was even more of a perplexity to the Australian press. 'To say that I was bored almost to tears would be putting it mildly,' groaned one candid reviewer.

Melbourne held less bruises for *Skin*, but hid a few brickbats in their personal interviews. 'Now that England is finished, Sir Laurence, what do you think about . . .' 'Tell me, Sir Laurence, about your *stoop*, was it a childhood accident?' So much for Richard III.

Anzac Day, 24 April, Canberra. A benefit performance before two thousand people: 'Vivien looked wonderful in pale lime green and a blood red rose at her waist. Halfway through she hesitated but went on with Sonnet 116. Then my turn – oh, it was really horrid. I left out a wodge but got through.'

The forty members of the Old Vic Company played, and followed their leaders, at a pace worthy of young Bonaparte's first Italian campaign – while the stars themselves filled their extra-curricular engagements, which even included reviewing a 'march-past' of the Royal Australian Navy. Melbourne, Sydney, Brisbane – they had chalked up six months of tour with scarcely a private moment. With Vivien in good health, they were blissfully happy.

Now it was Larry's turn. After recovering from his painful foot, he slipped a cartilage in his knee during the *Richard III* sword fight. It had happened in Sydney, and was followed by a slight thrombosis in the other leg. But Larry carried on, playing Richard for several nights on crutches. What acting it must have taken to cry, 'My kingdom for a horsel' and not get a laugh.

But the unkindest cut of all arrived by post. Lord Esher, Chairman of the Old Vic Governors, informed him that his services as a director would not be required when his contract expired. His co-directors were similarly served. Richardson's and Olivier's filmdom fame and knighthoods had not endeared them to all. Richardson was currently in Hollywood filming *The Heiress*, and the press had carelessly referred to the tour as 'Olivier's Old Vic Company'. Complaints were in the air that what had been 'a people's theatre' was now drawing white ties and evening gowns.

In August the company was in Sydney, where they encountered Peter Finch's Mercury Theatre company.

Peter Ingle-Finch (who was to become the first post-humous winner of a Hollywood Oscar) had been born in London in 1916, the illegitimate son of a Scotsman named Campbell. His tumbleweed childhood took him from France to India to Australia, where he was raised by cousins. In time he blew into show business as a straight man to a comic, drifted into radio, and then formed a portable-tent theatre company that toured Queensland and New South Wales. But the war cast him in the role of gunner in the Australian Army for a tour of North Africa. When the war was over, he returned to the boards – this time touring canteens and factories. It was at a glass-blowing factory in Sydney that the Oliviers first saw him perform. To their surprise, the factory workers were enjoying a lively production of Molière's *Le Malade Imaginaire*. The Oliviers were unexpectedly impressed by young Finch, so much so that Larry was prompted to say, 'I'll do all I can for you,' if and when Finch should come to London.

One of Finch's young student actors, Trader Faulkner, was among the lucky ones chosen by David Kentish, the Oliviers' marvellously efficient stage manager, to play a 'super'. The company was playing the Tivoli Theatre, which was equivalent to the London Palladium or New York's old Roxy in size. The young actors were ushered into Olivier's presence.

'He was a very elegant man in a brown herringbone suit, with buckles on the sides of his shoes,' Faulkner recalls. 'He looked as though he'd come straight out of Duke Street, St James. That suit had been worn, it wasn't *nouveau* tailored.' Olivier was tremendously popular in Australia, because he had the common touch, a genius for getting on with people and getting what he wanted from them. 'He was a very physically attractive man. I'm heterosexual, but I could see his enormous attraction for both men and women, a charismatic personality.

'Then Vivien came into the interview, beautiful, exquisite, but also capable of the common touch. They didn't look down on the Aussies as so many had foolishly done and the Aussies loved them.'

Faulkner asked Olivier for permission to watch all performances from backstage. 'I'm so keen, sir! Can I?'

'Yes, my dear boy,' Olivier said. 'As long as you don't get in the way of a light or in anybody's way coming on or off.'

'He put his hand on my shoulder,' Faulkner recalls. 'He had this marvellous avuncular charm. He wasn't a paternal man, he was an avuncular man. A great difference. Because an uncle doesn't usually tell you what you shouldn't do, but you know you can always go and ask him. This was his aura.'

During *Richard III*, Olivier understandably didn't want people near him. In his elaborate make-up as Richard, he impressed Faulkner as a bluebottle fly in colour, but like a scorpion underneath. When he walked about, there was something lethal in his movements. Even off-stage he gave the feeling that he wasn't a person to go too near. He created an illusion of physical danger.

When he played Antrobus in *Skin*, or Sir Peter Teazle in *School*, he would, as Faulkner observed, duck behind the scenery with Vivien, kissing. It was very touching to the young lad, whose eyes were 'out on stalks'. He worshipped the Oliviers because he saw a side of them the public didn't see. He recalls a night when the curtain was about to go up: 'It was *Richard III*, and their dressing-room door was locked. No one could get in. They banged on the door, and David Kentish was in a flaming row, and he said, "Oh, I know why you can't get him on stage. He's making love to Vivien."

'I thought, "How undisciplined for this great disciplined man of the theatre! But also, how human . . ." This terrible pull between his art and his passion, and for the moment his passion won. We Australian boys expected him to come out on all fours, but he didn't. He came out and gave a wonderful performance.'

New Zealand saw forty-four performances in less than six weeks. Larry's leg now caused him such agony that his understudy, Derrick Penley, took over for the last three performances. An operation was necessary, but there would be the chance to recuperate on that long voyage home. London would offer no time for hospitals.

Rain saturated Wellington's dreary dockside. Watching from the ship's rail in a soaked mackintosh, Vivien saw Larry carried from the ambulance. A young woman fan stepped out of the throng to hold her umbrella over the actor as his stretcher was placed in a canvas sling and hauled aboard. A strangely downbeat ending for a gloriously successful tour. It was not quite the exit either of them had foreseen. But they could remember entertaining more than 300,000 people – and having given 179 performances.

New Zealanders who saw her will never forget the heart-shaped white face alone at the rail in the downpour as the *Corinthic* nosed out to sea to bear its famous lovers across leaden waters home to England.

On that gloomy, sunless voyage one more blow was waiting. Word reached her that New, her beloved Siamese, had run under the wheels of a car and been killed.

She had read *A Streetcar Named Desire* in 1948 and had not been able to get it out of her mind. She knew that it was a sensational success on Broadway, but more importantly she knew that something in the haunted character of Blanche DuBois touched the hidden person within her own psyche, the animus of her being.

Irene Selznick, David O.'s ex-wife, had produced the Tennessee Williams play, and director Elia Kazan had guided it to success on Broadway, with Marlon Brando and Jessica Tandy in the leading roles. Binky Beaumont had the London production rights and was prepared to wait almost a year for the Oliviers, who were tied up with the Old Vic season through most of 1949.

Vivien had long wanted to perform the leading role in Sophocles' tragedy *Antigone*. The French playwright Jean Anouilh had recently written a modern version that had been performed in Paris. Because Vivien wanted to do it, Olivier decided to direct a production in London and play the role of the Chorus himself, in a dinner jacket. Vivien's health had continued to be excellent, and she had missed only a few performances because of a fall down the narrow winding staircase at Durham Cottage.

With *Antigone*, she reached a new level as a tragic actress, and the ghost of Scarlett was truly buried at last. Larry knew from her performance that she had found the emotional muscle to attack *Streetcar Named Desire*.

In preparation for the arduous project, they took a very private holiday together. Vivien's new Siamese cat, Boy, went with them. Boy had been a gift from Larry awaiting her at Durham Cottage on their return from Australia.

For Larry as director, *Streetcar* was an agonising task. The difficulty was inherent in its very success in America, for success tends to coat a theatrical piece in sanctity. In this case, both Irene Selznick and Kazan were so concerned about deviations from the holy writ of their Broadway hit that they gave Olivier their bible – Kazan's prompt script, which Larry felt obliged to follow. Irene had even sent over the original stage designs of Jo Mielziner. The effect was so inhibiting to Olivier's creativity that he insisted the credits note 'After the New York Production.' He would later describe it as the most painful undertaking of his career.

Bumble Dawson, the designer, and one of Vivien's closest personal friends, recalled Irene Selznick's tart comment when it was pointed out to her that she was dealing with the King and Queen of the theatre world. Louis B. Mayer's daughter reminded Dawson not inaccurately – 'But my father is an emperor!'

Vivien was less amenable to Irene's dictums. She felt her interpretation must be no carbon copy. She had not seen Jessica Tandy's Blanche on Broadway and so could feel total freedom. Her characterisation grew out of her understanding of that grey land of her own illness. Those close to her could see a change in her even before the play opened. She was tense, nervous, and touchy. They could also see that this would be perhaps her greatest role.

Vivien followed Tyrone Guthrie's advice of learning to love the character she was playing – love, in the sense of understanding. She learned her part from the outside in and the inside out, until it became a layer of herself that could live on its own upon a stage. Her Blanche was a victim, a dream-world escapist from the nightmare of reality.

Renée Asherson, who played Stella, was working with Olivier for the first time since *Henry V*. She recalls an eccentricity of Vivien's during rehearsals. 'Vivien always appeared in the same black jersey dress. She wore it as a kind of uniform so she wouldn't have to be thinking about what she would wear and could give her full concentration to the work at hand. She worked terrifically hard on the part. It was good because of what she brought to it, but 1 don't think it was very good for her. It was a tremendous strain. It drained her emotionally. Vivien had obviously worked with Larry in great detail before we even started rehearsals. It was much more difficult working (for me) with him when he was working with her. She absolutely needed his full support. Every minute. This, one felt very strongly . . . and Larry had a super-protective feeling over Vivien. But I did get on with her well. A kind of sympathy between her and me, although everyone said she was edgy, which she was.'

But however supported, Vivien showed a strong creative will of her own, not merely for her own part, but for the play. When Olivier decided that one of Renée's lines should be cut because it might offend a London audience, it was Vivien who insisted the line should remain. The cast could not refrain from speculating about who would win the point. Next day, Olivier decided that the line would remain.

Although she would not consider it when testing for *Cyrano*, Vivien now had her hair dyed an arresting blonde. On Notley weekends she restored her normal appearance with a dark wig – 'which in those days – not the days when everyone wore wigs – was rather sensational,' remembers Asherson, who was present at the weekend when Danny Kaye brought Larry a cheesecake. 'It ended up with Larry smashing the cheesecake into Danny's face in the great Mack Sennett custard pie tradition. Young Tarquin, who was spending the weekend, fell under the table with laughter.

'Tarquin obviously thought she was wonderful. He loved to play canasta with her and idolised her. She was sweet with everyone. I remember going into the village with her and she had one of the chauffeur's children on her knee. She was awfully good with children.'

But still not awfully good with Suzanne. The mother-daughter relationship had been breached by the war separation and would take years to restore.

As the hostess in a dark wig, she played with the children, wandered the rooms at Notley in the early-morning hours, arranged flowers, arranged seating at dinner, arranged games afterwards, all the while glittering, chatting and laughing in a throng of witty friends, like a queen in her court.

As the actress in blonde-bleached halo, pitting her

strength of will against the exhaustion of eight long months in *Streetcar*, she gave one of the great performances of modern times without missing one of them.

'It proves I am not the hothouse plant they think I am,' she said.

Bernard Braden, playing Mitch (with whom Blanche tries to form a relationship), sat beside her on stage through one of her long soliloquies. It was the sort of stage moment when, after two hundred performances, an actor can be numbed into non-reaction. Braden kept himself alert by concentrating on the line of her profile. Even beneath Blanche's heavy make-up, her sheer beauty could still give him a lump in the throat. 'It was incredible, absolutely incredible,' he told Gwen Robyns. He marvelled at Vivien's technical skill and her drive to continue working on the characterisation up to the very last day of those eight months.

In her dressing-room after each performance, it would always take a long period of decompression from the emotional depths of hysterical madness she had plumbed. Perhaps the essential difference between the London and the Broadway productions was Marlon Brando. As Stanley, he was the play's pivot. But in the London production, Vivien's Blanche was so riveting that dramatist Robert Sherwood affirmed that Blanche was what the play was all about. Although Uta Hagen and Jessica Tandy had both given fine performances in New York, audiences tended to think the play was all about Brando.

Vivien's opening-night gift to Larry had been a Georgian gold locket. In it, she had placed a lock of Blanche's blonde hair. His gift to her was a triumph. When the play's final curtain fell, the gallery erupted into wild enthusiasm. His eye on his high-strung star, Larry ordered the curtain down quickly, with the ritual command: 'The curtain! The Queen! The King!' But he refused to make a curtain speech himself, saying only, 'It's not my night. It belongs to my wife. It is hers alone.' Later, he caught *The Times* critic Harold Hobson and asked him to come back another night before final judgement, when Vivien would be less overwrought.

Perhaps because of its very revolutionary nature, *Streetcar* hit a few critical bumps. It could not avoid the disapproval of some reviewers and the shock of audiences as yet unaccustomed to such sordid vistas of human behaviour. One complained that he felt as if he 'had crawled through a garbage heap!' Kenneth Tynan said that it was a good illustration 'of the way in which a good play can be scarred by unsympathetic and clumsy direction.' In his judgement, Vivien was miscast. Kazan, who was to direct the screen version, didn't agree.

On the first day of May, Vivien announced that her doctors had advised her to leave *Streetcar* in June and take a long rest. 'I feel physically exhausted,' she said. 'The play has sapped all my energy. Doctors have watched me continuously since we started and they now have advised me to give up acting for the time being.' However, she denied there was anything seriously wrong with her health.

Meanwhile, Peter Finch had not forgotten Olivier's offer of a helping hand. Larry and Vivien had told him that he was somebody exploitable in the theatre, somebody with a contribution to make.

Now Finch seized the first opportunity to follow the Oliviers back to London. They had told him that if he could get himself over on one of the ship's return voyages from bringing migrants to Australia, they would put him under their aegis. Trader Faulkner went to see him off and found Peter in his pyjamas with Tamara Tchinarova, his dancer wife, ironing his shirts and getting him ready. Their baby, Anita, was playing on the floor.

Finch arrived in London to find Sir Laurence in the midst of planning a production of the James Bridie comedy *Daphne Laureola*, with Dame Edith Evans.

After his dismissal from the management of the Old Vic, Olivier had been even more determined to re-activate and expand his own production company. His success with

Born Yesterday two years earlier gave him the impetus to project a season of plays. He kept his promise to Finch by casting him opposite Evans as the humourless young Polish student in *Daphne Laureola*. Finch's London début was well received.

Finch, who soon found himself in the Olivier circle, was a curious mixture of sensitivity, erudition, and candour. Basically he was a loner, a maverick, a nomad who followed no rules of conduct but his own, tried to shun permanent ties and possessions. He could project a genuine sense of understanding and warmth through his wonderfully expressive eyes and voice. One co-worker referred to him as 'a wild man'. Another, as possessing 'a remarkably sensitive bisexual quality.'

Daphne Laureola ran for a year, vastly encouraging its producer to re-form his Laurence Olivier Productions Ltd. Included on its new board of directors were Roger Furse, Korda, and, 'by way of décor', Vivien. But the company's first need was for a theatre of its own.

From Gilbert Miller, the American producing wizard of Broadway and the West End, they acquired a four-year lease on London's St James's. Built in 1835, the theatre was a monument of gilt and red plush antiquity. For Olivier it held very personal, sentimental memories, for it was here that he had visited Sybil Thorndike backstage when, at seventeen, he had come to see Sir Gerald du Maurier about a job. And it was also here, during the run of *The Mask of Virtue*, that he had first seen Vivien.

The season was launched in January 1950, with Christopher Fry's *Venus Observed*, specially written for Olivier, who directed and performed the leading role. While it was an artistic triumph, the expensive production failed to show a profit.

It was the last time he would appear on stage for several years. In July he was to travel to Hollywood to star in *Carrie* opposite Jennifer Jones – now married to David O. Selznick. (Because of the matrimonial musical-chairs of show business, the actor would be sharing close-ups with the newest wife of the man whose ex-wife had produced Olivier's current wife's current play.)

Hollywood always beckoned more alluringly when pockets had been thinned by theatrical adventuring and personal extravagance. Greer Garson recalls Olivier's attitude about film-making when they worked together in *Pride and Prejudice*: 'I have to make some money now, so I'll make a picture.' But since *Henry V* and *Hamlet*, he had acquired a taste for film as an art medium.

There was a roaring farewell party for Vivien, who was to leave first to film *Streetcar*. Drinks flowed at Durham Cottage into the small hours, and when gloom descended on the assembled chums, David Fairweather recalls Larry striking a melodramatic pose with a toast to Viv. 'Farewell,' he cried. 'You to your streetcar – and I, to my stratocar!'

He wrote to a friend to the effect that his new production, Captain Carvallo, was opening at the St James's and he would plane out next day. It was a great and worried sadness to him that Vivien had to leave the week before.

Vivien broke her trip to California with a stop-over in Connecticut for discussions with 'Gadge' Kazan. She had first encountered him as an actor in the 1938 London production of *Golden Boy*, and it had been respect at first sight. But now, Gadge felt the need of 'de-Larrying' his new star. Too many of her comments were beginning with 'When Larry and I did *Streetcar* in London . . .' and the director knew that no matter how brilliant her stage performance, it would be necessary to bring it down for the camera's magnifying eye. But once they were rolling, he would discover that Vivien was a superb screen technician. She always preferred playing a role in films she had worked out first on stage.

Actors find it more difficult to sustain the growth and development of a characterisation when scenes are shot out of sequence. Vivien told a *New York Times* interviewer, 'From the actor's standpoint, filmwork calls for much more concentrated effort. On the stage, the audience contributes by telling you when you are building logically towards a move. In films you may have to start out with a big emotional scene first thing in the morning and perhaps keep doing it over and over all day. You have to learn to conserve your energy. If an actor can do that, I see no reason why, other things being equal, a given interpretation can't be as telling on the screen as on the stage.'

En route to Hollywood, Vivien made another stop, in Wisconsin to pay a short visit to the Lunts. She wanted to draw on the well of experience of her friend Lynn Fontanne. They discussed in depth Blanche's attitude towards marriage to a homosexual. Both actresses concluded that Blanche could have lived with such a discovery, but not with the guilt feeling brought on by his suicide.

Kazan wanted to ensure not only that his sensitive star was not too influenced by her own stage performance, but also that she wouldn't be exposed to the contagion of other actors. Wright King, playing the young newspaper collector in the film, as he had done on the stage, found himself chatting with the star, to his delight.

'She remarked what a lovely and delicate scene it was. I told her it always seemed to hold stage audiences, except on Saturday nights in Chicago.

' "What happened then?" asked Miss Leigh.

'Well, when the young collector is asked if he'd had a chocolate soda and he replied, "No, ma'am, cherry," the delicate scene turned into a farce.

'She didn't understand why the young collector's response should have been thought so funny. I was about to tie myself in a square knot, translating this bit of Americana slang into its English counterpart, when Kazan politely took me aside and inquired, "What are you two discussing?"

' "How this scene had played in Chicago," I told him.

' "That's not a good idea!" he said rather firmly, adding that such a discussion would dissipate the spontaneity of the relationship. With that, he bustled Miss Leigh off to her wig dresser and me to a make-up man." '

In the scene the characters were standing some eight to nine feet apart. On stage the floor was always clear, but on the film set big clusters of electrical coils and cables lay like boa constrictors between the two performers. Blanche had to cross this obstacle course twice. Wright King, new to movies, thought Kazan must plan some clever cutting to make her crosses look smooth.

'Nope! Without a word, from the first rehearsal through all takes, she sailed lightly over to me, seeming to float above the cables, never missing a step or a beat. Technique – and what a teacher!'

It had been ten years since the Oliviers had been in Hollywood. They had changed, but so had the place. One unwelcome squatter was *smog*! Now the yellow blanket that stung the eyes was laid out over the thirty-mile radius of Greater Los Angeles. A seething six-million-headed monster jammed the new asphalt ribbons above the land from which the oranges had vanished like virginity. The Queen of Angels was growing up – and her handmaiden Hollywood had lost all innocence.

But it had found a new competence. Olivier marvelled at the technical efficiency he encountered, and William Wyler (directing him for the first time since *Wuthering Heights*) marvelled at his new enthusiasm. Larry sat back in Ray Milland's dressing-room, generously lent him by the actor (complete with refrigerator, tape recorder, and fabulous record collection) and told Hedda: 'I wanted to make another picture because I haven't done one since *Hamlet*, and I wanted the challenge of playing an American. And I didn't want Vivien coming to Hollywood without me.'

Ten years before, they had lived here as secret lovers. Now they were Sir Laurence and Lady Olivier – sought-after pillars of social respectability and success. But both took care to caution their American cousins against using their titles in advertising. It just wasn't done in the British theatre.

And into Vivien's plush dressing-room at Warner's, guarded as usual by Sunny Alexander, came the press. Did the new 'Sir Olivier' – that is, mister – plan any more Shakespeare in the States?

Vivien's cagey reply: 'I don't know, but if he did, even *he* wouldn't say anything about it – because Orson Welles would try to do it first.'

Vivien was now thirty-seven. The press nipped two years off that, and commented that her waist was still twenty-three inches, the smallest in Hollywood. Vivien retorted they had already nipped a few inches off that back in Scarlett days, when they had measured it a wispy seventeen! But the most over-publicised – if briefest – encounter was the much awaited meeting between Brando and Vivien, which took place in Warner Brothers' Green Room.

The New York actor had arrived on his motorcycle, wearing an orange T-shirt, clean on this occasion. As a special concession, he wore slacks instead of jeans – and even shoes. *Photoplay* recorded: 'Director Elia Kazan introduced them. The mighty Marlon nudged the vivacious Vivien with his elbow and muttered, "Go ahead and eat".' With that he left, and slouched off to join their producer, Charles K. Feldman.

Brando and Leigh took a bit of time getting to know each other. At first mumble, the 'method' star found his British co-star affected, formal, and too cheerfully polite, in contrast to his own sometimes offensively rude style. But they came to admire each other enormously even though it was a bit like pairing a gazelle with a wild boar. Talent was the leveller. One day he amused her with a perfect imitation of Larry doing his Henry V. It was then that Viven realised that the mumble was removable.

Brando did not manage to steal the show from his fragile protagonist. It was she who won the Oscar.

Larry received almost equal press coverage.

Item: 'Charles Laughton ran into old friend Laurence Olivier at La Rue and exclaimed, "Larry Olivier!" Olivier answered, "Charles Laughton!" Muttered a bystander, "Name-droppers!" '

The press also recorded his chance meeting with Jean Simmons, now so indoctrinated into the local scene that she was attending a football game at the Coliseum.

Item: 'She was munching a hot dog when she heard a voice cry out, "Simmons!" An unkempt, bearded man in dark glasses approached. Only when he removed the glasses did she recognise Olivier, who has also become a football fan.' Hamlet reminiscing with Ophelia over dripping mustard.

28 July. One journalist regretted she would be 3000 miles away when Sylvia and Danny Kaye were entertaining for her favourite dream couple at a formal dinner dance in the Crystal room of the Beverly Hills Hotel on the 19th.

3 August. Hollywood *Reporter:* 'Invites were Western Unioned yesterday from the Danny Kayes for the shindig in honour of the Oliviers. If you think Danny got a reception in England, wait'll you see what Vivien and Larry get at this whopper!!!'

Item: 'Anyone who hasn't been invited is leaving town for fear of being considered a social leper!'

Vivien's love for partying had always been characterised by sincere affection for a host of genuine friends. Now she found herself hounded by friends and strangers alike, wanting to be included on her guest list. It was deeply upsetting to her, driving her to tears which were soothed away by Sunny in the Warners' dressing-room.

On the night, Vivien wore a low, square-cut, emerald-green gown with one large jewel surrounded by pearls suspended from a thin chain. Larry wore his *Carrie* moustache. Danny wore bright red-dyed hair for his current film. The guest list was spectacular: Baby and Bogie; Ginger Rogers and Greg Bautzer; Tony Martin and Cyd Charisse; the Colmans; the Bart Marshalls; Joan Caulfield and her husband, producer Frank Ross; Ann

Sheridan, up to her chin in a satin dinner suit; the distinguished Ezio Pinza, who clowned with his host; Van Johnson; Sonny Tufts; Lana Turner, pregnant, but dazzling in diamonds on the arm of Bob Topping. Also on the 'preggers' list: Mrs Pinza, Esther Williams, Cyd Charisse, and June Allyson. Louis B., looking smug in a tight dinner jacket, came with his new wife and danced non-stop from nine till two-thirty, and when he left he looked more fit than most who entered. Danny had spent over four thousand dollars to entertain some hundred and seventy guests. Montgomery Clift crashed – the only one on record.

Hedda and Louella, both officially 'out of town', recorded the event as though viewed from a satellite.

Item: 'Best combinations on the dance floor were Ginger Rogers and Danny Kaye, Greg Bautzer and Lana Turner, Roz Russell and Van Johnson, and Laurence Olivier with Lynn Baggett.'

Hedda noted from afar: 'Evelyn Keyes, who played V.L.'s sister in *G.W.T.W.*, didn't think the English star would remember her. She was about to reintroduce herself when Vivien said, "I'm sorry I had to slap you so hard". Evelyn recalled that they'd had to do the scene over seventeen times!'

23 August. The Hollywood *Reporter's* final obituary: 'People went into hiding rather than admit they weren't invited.' Radie was the only member of the press asked.

To make anyone who might have known forget she hadn't been where she wasn't, Hedda promptly threw a huge splash in honour of Tallulah. Betty Hutton 'dittoed'.

At this moment the Oliviers could be hailed as the world's most beautiful, successful, admired, even adored couple. But there is at all peaks a cutting wind. Like the wise Chinese man, Vivien should have looked towards the heavens and proclaimed, 'I am a poor thing, vulnerable, easily wounded; I am destructible.'

Vivien caught a bad cold the night after the party. Jack

12 *From bright Egypt to dark Ceylon*

'Why don't we go home on a slow freighter?' Vivien asked seriously. 'I think it would be worlds of fun.'

Which is precisely what they did, returning on the French Line freighter *Wyoming* – along with a boatload of Washington State apples. Both were excited by the prospect of gliding through the Panama Canal with, for once, unhurried ease. In Hollywood they had been too busy even to celebrate their tenth wedding anniversary properly. They had settled for a quiet, sentimental dinner, and the promise to make up for it on their twentieth anniversary – when they might have more time!

Once back in London, Olivier was to prepare two plays for the Festival of Britain. The first of these was to be Shaw's *Caesar and Cleopatra.* They needed one more play. But what?

As usual, Virginia and David Fairweather were in charge of publicity for the productions. 'I remember how the two Cleopatras came about in 1951,' David recalls. 'Roger Furse suggested as a joke that it would save money to have the two plays [it had by now been decided that Shakespeare's *Antony and Cleopatra* would go with Shaw's play] on one bill. This was ignored as beneath contempt. Then Larry took a second look, and before Viv knew where she was, protestingly, she was told she had to play both roles. She was in such a state she couldn't sleep at all the night before the company first got together. And I remember Larry a few days later, asking if I could get her photo in the *Evening News* to cheer her up.

'Though the "Dresden shepherdess" image persistently

clung, her Lady Macbeth, later on, was really superb and the best I ever saw.'

Whether she was a classical actress or not, the challenge inherent in the idea of alternating Shaw's Egyptian kitten with Shakespeare's *femme fatale* of the Nile was an enormous dish to set before the Queen of the theatre. But the King felt she was up to it, and so one of the most daring showmanship adventures in theatrical history was launched. They had often discussed *Antony and Cleopatra*, but Vivien felt she wouldn't be ready for it for at least five years. Now she yielded to Olivier's decision.

The two plays opened together in Manchester for Olivier's own company in January, 1951. The double bill, presented on alternate nights and sometimes as matinée and evening performances, turned out to be a stroke of genius. The plays counterpointed some of the sharpest prose in contemporary theatre against some of the most powerful poetry in the English language. Shaw's Caesar portrays senile sagacity, while Shakespeare's Antony reveals the frailty of a mighty warrior touched by the firefly of infatuation. Michael Benthall had been recruited to direct both productions, for Olivier felt he had enough on his plate producing, performing, and giving Vivien the support she had come to rely upon.

For the first time they were acting together in their very own theatre for their very own company. On opening night, 10 May, emperor and queen exchanged gifts; a gold link watch strap for Caesar, an eighteenth-century necklace of rubies and gold for Cleopatra. The following evening, her older Cleopatra met Antony.

Kenneth Tynan's review suggested that the actor had scaled down his Antony in a gallant, gentlemanly effort not to overshadow Vivien's performance. 'Miss Leigh's limitations have wider repercussions than those of most actresses. Sir Laurence with that curious chivalry . . . gives me the impression that he subdues his blow-lamp ebullience to match her . . . Antony climbs down and Cleopatra pats him on the head.' The critic had cast an unjustified reflection on Olivier's professionalism, since it was indeed against the author's intent for the character to be a man of titanic will. Shakespeare had carved his ageing Antony of jelly, deliberately made of him the 'strumpet's fool', the scarred mastiff led on a silken leash to his own destruction. Olivier searched out and found the nobility in Antony, the afterglow of greatness, although he was never totally happy in the part.

The actor was equally unhappy playing the elder states-man, for he found too many weaknesses in Shaw's play. He wanted to develop the romantic relationship between Cleo and the ageing Caesar, which Shaw had chosen to leave ambiguous. Vivien had vivid memories of Shaw's attitude towards any variation of interpretation. Although Shaw had died the year before, his caveats still haunted his plays. But she accepted to some extent the logic of Olivier's approach.

Her two Cleopatras were almost unanimously hailed as her best stage performances, the dissenter being Tynan. The Oliviers, at the height of their reputations, were the perfect mark for the ambitious and genuinely brilliant young critic. Later he not only won fame, but the admir-ation of his lofty victims. Tynan had indeed been rough on the plays, and particularly on Vivien.

Much later, Tynan recalled to actor Richard Huggett that he was rather surprised shortly after his review to receive an invitation to lunch with Vivien, which took place at the Ritz. She was absolutely charming, and gossiped and rattled on throughout the meal in a delightfully amusing and bitchy way. Clearly she was anxious to show that she bore him no ill will and wanted to make him a friend rather than keep him an enemy. Tynan enjoyed the meal very much. From then on, he found himself on the Olivier visiting list, and was eventually invited to Notley Abbey for a weekend.

In that weekend party was Vivien's mother, Gertrude. One evening after dinner, the subject of St Joan came up, a role that Vivien had always wanted to play.

'Did you know that I've got Sybil Thorndike's original suit of armour in the house?' Vivien asked.

The guests didn't, but everyone expressed keen interest to see it.

'I'll go and put it on.'

Gertrude tried to stop her with, 'Now then, Vivien, don't be silly. Behave yourself!'

'Well, how are you going to stop me?' her daughter demanded. 'I'm too old to be spanked.'

With that, she headed upstairs, taking Tynan with her to help. As Huggett reports it, Vivien undressed down to bra and panties, and Tynan, rather embarrassed, helped her into the saintly suit. The armour was far too large for her, since Thorndike was a much taller woman. She clanked back down to the party, Tynan in tow, and struck a pose in front of the fireplace.

Sword in hand, Vivien treated the guests to a stirring rendition of the famous 'Light your fires . . .' speech from the trial scene, indicating to the critic that she would have been rather good in the part.

After a round of applause from the party, Vivien did a metallic striptease, offering the armour to Tynan, who was persuaded to put it on. It was, of course, too small for him.

The two Cleopatras ran for four months in London. Before taking the productions to New York, the Oliviers hosted their English company and friends with a movable feast; a hired barge floated the party down the Thames to Richmond and back. It is alleged that Robert Helpmann (who played Apollodorus) landed in the river. If true, he must have jumped, since he was one of the most graceful and agile dancers of his day.

The ship to New York conveyed a strange cargo: twenty-five tons of scenery. a revolving stage, a queen's barge, a Sphinx, a lighthouse, along with the Oliviers and some members of the company.

Their old friend Gertrude Lawrence was loaning them her West Forty-fourth Street apartment. As always, Vivien

kept it filled with masses of flowers arranged with pains-
taking artistry, though the Lawrence bedroom, draped in
cloth of silver, was theatrical enough. Every morning Larry
took himself off to Pilate's Universal Gymnasium on
Eighth Avenue where he went through his usual highly-
disciplined workout. This was followed by a singing lesson
to increase his vocal strength. His voice must now fill a
sixteen-hundred-seat theatre, much larger than the candy-
box British houses.

'Our theatres are smaller with many more shelves . . .
It's difficult to take the audience into one's confidence. If
one can't drop one's voice, it makes for a limited form of
acting . . . In a big theatre if you make yourself heard by the
people in back, it's fairly grotesque for those in front,' he
observed in a magazine interview.*

Just before the first night, Vivien came down with what
she described as 'psychosomatic laryngitis'. 'I always get it
a few days before an opening,' she said. 'Just a nervous
condition which soon disappears.'

Vivien's weight was down to ninety-eight pounds. Few
people could have existed on her normal diet through the
run of a play. For the last six years she'd kept to a regime of
only yogurt during the day, and one meal – after the evening
performance.

Opening night at Billy Rose's Ziegfeld Theatre turned
stage history into legend. Gilbert Miller, the man from
whom Olivier had leased the St James's in London, chose
the Ziegfeld for the production.

Antony and Cleopatra was one of the most glittering
theatrical openings Broadway had seen in years. Seldom
had such an array of stars and celebrities decorated an
audience, including old friends like the Lunts and Danny
Kaye, the daughter of a President (Truman) and a Prime
Minister (Churchill), David Selznick (who had forgiven and
forgotten his lost law suit against Vivien), and the
diminutive showman Billy Rose.

* *New Yorker*, 22 March 1952.

For the Oliviers it was a peak, a summit of theatrical success; the great duet at its most celebrated hour of perfection. Few couples could have known such a night of career fulfilment – the more wonderful for being shared.

'There has never been an *Antony and Cleopatra* to compare with this in New York in the last quarter of a century,' declared the *New York Times*. And there had been two productions of the play in recent memory.

The two Cleopatras were presented in two special matinées given for actors. On each occasion the audience – mainly professionals, for scarcely an actor in New York would have missed it – gave their peers a standing ovation. The theatre rang with whistles, cheers, and bravos, and there were tears of envy in many an eye for London's gift to Broadway.

Paul Crosfield, who played a soldier in that New York production, commented, 'Olivier staged the current productions purely for the sake of Vivien Leigh. He wanted to give her the marvellous opportunity of two Cleopatras.'*

This was far from the total truth, yet the opinion was shared by many. While Vivien could not equal Olivier's stature as a stage actor, her drive to be worthy of him was not competitive, and his decision to present them as a stage duet was not self-effacing. It was the right thing to do at the right moment – sound business and valid artistry.

The costume designer for both productions, Audrey Cruddas, was tremendously impressed by Vivien's will power, and cited her stamina to stand for hours without a break, being fitted for costumes. She appeared to have an almost monastic singleness of purpose. 'For her, the play is the only thing that counts – the only topic of conversation – the only reason for existing.'

Actor Brian Bedford referred to this ascetic dedication, common to many actors. 'Rehearsing is a monk-like period for a serious actor. When Olivier and Vivien Leigh were married and acting together, they didn't have sex during

* *Life* magazine, 17 December 1951.

rehearsal times. They needed all the energy they could muster for the play. If one is conscientious, one can't be anything but celibate during rehearsals.'*

But even triumph can be debilitating, glory a depressive. As the New York season drew towards its close, Vivien began to find the pure exhaustion of playing Cleopatra in two ages and two guises more and more soul- and health-destroying. For the first time there were rumours that all was not loving between the theatre royals. Instances of snappishness were noted on the actress's part. One night when the audience did not respond with their usual ovation, those in earshot of a gracious, smiling, bowing Cleopatra could hear her cursing under her breath.

Others reported a new coolness on Olivier's part, a new aloofness in his bearing which detractors chose to attribute to his loftier station in life. He was quoted as saying, 'It is unfortunate that Vivien's and my conversations that should be normal conversations are all too frequently conferences about some business problem or some theatrical problem.'†

Before leaving for the States, Olivier had kept the St James's open by presenting, for the first time on the English stage, his most formidable Shakespearian film competitor, Orson Welles, in Welles's production of *Othello*. At Olivier's suggestion, Peter Finch, now well entrenched in the inner circle, was cast as Iago. It was, for the young Australian, an auspicious opportunity to share the stage with the mighty Welles – who took up quite a bit of it by himself.

The Fairweathers were, as usual, handling publicity for the production. Virginia Fairweather recalled how, on opening night, a few minutes after the curtain went up, a gargantuan figure, shrouded in a heavy black velvet cloak, materialised at the top of the stairs, advanced a few steps, looked down across the balustrade with some bewilderment, and in a most ringing resonant tone pronounced,

* *Los Angeles Times*, 12 December 1976.

† *New York Times Magazine*, 16 December 1951.

'Fuck!' With that, Welles vanished, bringing a murmur from the front stalls. They could not believe what they had seen and heard. 'Peter Finch was too nervous to do more than glance a trifle apprehensively towards the rostrum and hope for the best.'* Orson's direction of the play had kept his own movements even more of a mystery to himself than to the cast.

Olivier's comment on Welles's performance was that he had everything for the role except the breath. 'For Othello you need the breath, the lungs . . . you need the self-discipline and the rhythm. At the basis of everything is rhythm.'† Olivier would not be found similarly unprepared in 1964, when he performed *Othello*. The actor considered the role an abominable strain. 'It's said, rather jokingly, that the author said to Richard Burbage "Now I'm going to write a part that you really can't play," and it does seem almost impossible sometimes,' Olivier said later.

Olivier's interpretation was to be called stupendous and highly controversial. Welles's was fascinating, but not fully realised. The production, however, added an important rung for Peter Finch on his climb up the ladder.

While Vivien won her second Oscar in March of 1952 for *Streetcar*, no honours were being handed out for *Carrie*. Ironically, this venture, guided by one of Hollywood's greatest directors, William Wyler, based on a book by one of America's most important authors, Theodore Dreiser, with two brilliant stars heading its cast, turned out to be a flop. This only confirmed a perpetual truth of show business: you can put in all the right ingredients, and still bake a bad cake.

On the London theatrical front, the Olivier fortunes were scarcely faring better. His production company had dropped ten thousand pounds on an imported production of Gian Carlo Menotti's *The Consul*. Other near misses

* Virginia Fairweather, *Cry God for Larry!*

† Ed. Hal Burton, *Great Acting*.

included *The Top of the Ladder*, with John Mills; and protégé Peter Finch in *The Happy Time*, the company's twelfth production at the St James's.

By April of 1952 the Oliviers were feeling the cool breeze of financial reverses and were even beginning to talk about selling Notley Abbey. Their marital life was also under pressure. Vivien seemed to be slipping into more frequent bouts of illness, which were becoming increasingly difficult to cope with. For some time the actress had been experiencing amphetamine-like highs. She felt bursts of energy and wild enthusiasm, believed herself capable of accomplishing anything. This hyperactivity was not only uncontrollable, but brought a compulsion to live to the hilt, a self-indulgent drive towards irrational actions, like spending sprees, parties, plans undertaken in an un-assailable mood of euphoria and optimism.

But along with the highs went the irritability that made her snappish and impatient with any interference. She couldn't sleep through the night, and had begun to have shrieking temper outbursts for no reason. At such times her usually infallible judgement and understanding were dangerously impaired. And, as usual, when the mood had passed, all memory of her actions had passed with it. No one, Olivier included, had yet fully understood the nature of her illness.

Since the fourth century BC, medical literature has described one of the oldest known mental diseases, characterised by strange and inexplicable mood swings and fluctuations of an inner tide between what the ancients called 'glee' and 'melancholia'. The sufferer was seen to pass from a euphoric state into one of bleak sadness and sleeplessness.

These high and lows, so opposite in mental outlook, have one thing in common: both render the victim unable to function realistically within the framework of his or her world. The inner pendulum swings from one emotional extreme to the other, blinding the person to dangers and difficulties as well as good fortune. This inability to be aware of or to appraise these signals and situations is one of the most dangerous symptoms of the mood disorder described as manic-depression.

The pattern of the manic-depression often includes a compulsion to alcohol and spontaneous, promiscuous sexual adventuring. Conveniently, when the high has passed, the sufferer emerges from the tunnel of the disease without any recollection of actions and excesses. Then the pendulum swings. The victim sinks into a pit of acute depression, a listless black landscape of heart and mind where all is hopelessness and nothing of any worth.

Although Vivien's attacks were occurring more frequently, their duration was brief. Her doctors saw no reason why, after proper rest and treatment, she shouldn't continue normal career activities. The unpleasant appellation 'manic-depressive' had been kept from the press. 'Nervous breakdowns' were a convenient carry-all for a multitude of troubles. Nor was there much mention of the recurring lung condition, although the tuberculosis had returned to settle into a chronic state. Vivien was taking strong medication for both conditions, but stubbornly refused to give up drinking and smoking.

There were whispers around filmland that she might not be trustworthy to employ. There were also whispers about the marriage. Could it survive these troubled periods? A difficult fact of this illness for any mate to tolerate is the violent personality shifts, moods which must inevitably affect his own. And since there is little that a mate can do, the relationship generally aggravates his own sense of helplessness and guilt. The depressive quite often suffers from a persecution complex and can violently attack the nearest and dearest.

Rumours that Vivien had become a problem actress and financial risk did not deter Irving Asher, one of Hollywood's finest producers. He was an old friend of Laurence Olivier's, and a courageous gambler. Since the days when they made *Q Planes* together, he had kept in touch and, when Larry was knighted, had sent him a telegram:

'OBVIOUSLY THE KING HAS SEEN OUR PICTURE — THAT'S WHY HE HAS KNIGHTED YOU.'

Olivier promptly wired back: 'I'M SURE IT WAS BECAUSE THE KING DID *not* SEE THE PICTURE.'

Asher cabled again: 'HOW DO YOU ACCOUNT THEN FOR THE FACT THAT RICHARDSON WAS ALSO KNIGHTED?'

Irving, too, had first seen Vivien's early performance in *The Mask of Virtue*. At the time he was in charge of Warners' English office. He had tried to get Jack Warner to bring Vivien to the States and sign her up, even before Korda made his bid.

Irving recalls: 'Warner, with his usual fine judgement, didn't even want to see her. A dear, delightful man. I worked with him for nineteen years, God forbid. Vivien was beautiful, ethereal, just floated.'

When Olivier filmed *Hamlet*, he promised Irving tickets to the première. Asher couldn't understand why Olivier hadn't made the film in colour.

'I wouldn't ruin it by making it in colour,' Olivier told him. 'This picture requires black and white.'

When Irving saw the première, he couldn't wait to phone Larry and tell him that of course he had been right. 'That picture would have been terrible in colour. The black and white and the greys – the values were marvellous! The performance tremendous.'

In 1952, Asher had persuaded Doug Fairbanks, Jr., to part with the film rights to a book Fairbanks had bought to produce himself. Thus armed, he set up a production deal with Paramount to film *Elephant Walk*, and chose the veteran writer John Lee Mahin to work with him on the script.

Asher's experiences in planning *Elephant Walk* at Paramount typify a trend towards 'runaway production'. No longer would Hollywood accept its own axiom: 'A rock is a rock, a tree is a tree. Shoot it in Griffith Park!'

'The studio didn't want us to go to Ceylon,' recalls Asher. 'They would have preferred we shoot it in Griffith Park, or someplace. And I said, "Well, you deliver me

100 elephants in Griffith Park and we'll shoot it there. And also maybe 200 or 300 natives. Not only blacks, but I mean Indians, real Ceylonese. And don't think the public won't know the difference!"

'I talked them into letting me go to Ceylon to do a "reccy" [a film location reconnaissance], to see what certain sets would cost, and so on. I was stationed in Ceylon for several years in the Army and made some dear friends. One man, Etera Werra, was head of the Tourist Association. I told him I wanted the picture to be made there, and Werra said, "Give an interview and say that you're coming here to make this picture. Get it in the papers." The next day I had help coming from every captain of industry, the government, and so on. We built our sets there for about one-tenth of the cost with local labour. We started shipping the heavy equipment by boat: electrical, lights, generators, cameras, because it would take four months to get there from Hollywood.

'Then I went to London and shipped more from there. It all had to converge in Ceylon in time because of the monsoon season. If we had forgotten anything we were dead. It was like an Army manoeuvre. Every day I'd wake up and say – why didn't I stick to a nice love story on Stage 5?

'I got the director Bill Dieterle, the production manager, and general members of the crew, cameramen and wardrobe, make-up, and such of the cast as we had. We took a plane to London.'

The story called for an English leading man, and Olivier was Asher's first choice. He wanted the Oliviers to play in the film together, but Larry had too many other commitments. Vivien looked in perfect physical health, and was thrilled at the prospect of going to Ceylon. The schedule called for two to four weeks in Ceylon, and then filming the interiors in Hollywood. Vivien seemed troubled only by the dialogue in several scenes.

'I thought it was nit-picking,' Irving continued. 'She reminded me that I'd told her she could change anything, as long as she came to me and we agreed on it. She had an authoress friend, and wanting to start out on the best foot with Vivien, I offered to take her writer with us to Ceylon. "If there's something hard for you to say, we'll have her change it."

'Larry took me to a little art theatre in London to see Peter Finch in *The Straw Hat*. He was very high in his praise of Peter, and I didn't take that lightly. But I also saw that Finch gave a very fine performance and I went backstage and signed him for the picture. I didn't need a name, because I thought Vivien would carry us. We also had Dana Andrews and two or three other fair names. The project was so big I didn't think a name was that important.

'After I signed Pete, I telephoned the studio and told them what I'd done. They were sore as hell because I'd never seen him on the screen. I thought he was very handsome on the stage, but after I had signed him, I didn't sleep all night. Up close, his teeth were kind of protruding, and I worried that the studio might be right. He's not going to photograph! But then I thought if what Larry had said about him – that his acting was so great – was true, he'd overcome any physical defects. I believed he was one of Larry's very close friends when I signed him. I made a couple of photographic tests, and they came out better than expected.'

In London, they boarded the first commercial jet passenger plane – the Comet, which would fly to India in a quarter of the time it used to take. Vivien would not have been so elated about the trip had she known that on the following flight that very same plane was to crash. So did the next one after it. They finally grounded all of them. But although Asher had heard that his star was a nervous flier, she seemed exhilarated and happy as the Comet took off, winging powerfully above the mists and the winding Thames.

To introduce his company to Ceylon, the producer took them all sightseeing, and the sights were breathtaking.

Vivien was thrilled with this Garden of Eden where orchids festooned the trees.

For weeks Asher's native crews had been building a fantastic fake exterior front for the great plantation house. The interiors would be shot later, back at Paramount.

The story dealt with the son of a wealthy tea planter (Finch), whose father had built his plantation house right across the middle of the elephants' run to their watering hole.

Irving said, 'We advertised through every possible medium from town crier to local gossips. Elephants and their mahouts were soon appearing from as far as twenty-five miles away, lugging their own hay and working for pennies a day. "What would this elephant do if we put him near fire?" I would ask.

' "I don't know, sahib," the mahout would shrug. Nobody knew anything. But we found out. They ran crazy, and that was what we wanted. They ran amok! As soon as the builders had finished our fake plantation front, we set it on fire, and the elephants ran all over it. The natives just stood there and watched. They couldn't figure out why we'd built it, just to be destroyed. We went to all this trouble to build this beautiful thing, they all got money for it, and then we turned around and did *that* to it!'

But it wasn't only Asher's elephants who were running amok. The producer had been assured by Dana Andrews's agent that his drinking problem had been straightened out and the star was in perfect condition. But the jungle is corrosive. Andrews drank much of the time. Vivien's authoress was producing rewritten scenes which were weird and unusable. Asher brought them together for a discussion with Dieterle. The writer was silent, but Vivien lost all control and screamed at them. Asher had the impression that the writer had come along for a free ride and the irrational dialogue was being written by Vivien herself.

The actress couldn't seem to learn her lines, and then it became common knowledge that she and Finch were out almost all of every night, drinking. She seemed to want to embarrass her producer by flaunting the relationship in his face.

Now Finch had moved in with her, and she phoned the producer at one in the morning, demanding he come to her room. She complained about the script. 'How do you expect me to learn these lines, they're so fucking awful.'

'If you'd go to bed and get some rest, Vivien, you could learn them,' her worried producer urged, looking towards Finch for support. The actor didn't bat an eye.

The next day, Dieterle came to Asher's office. The producer had been trying to stay away from the set, so as not to upset the actors.

'I cannot photograph her, Irving,' the director complained.

'Why not? Does she look like hell this morning?'

'Worse. Come and see for yourself. I cannot tell you, because you will not believe.'

Asher went out on the set to find his star wearing an odd expression. To his horror, he saw that her wig was perched on the top of her head a good two inches above the hairline; her make-up began an inch below her natural hairline. No one had warned Asher that Vivien's mental problems were this serious.

'Vivien, dear, aren't you going to let the hairdresser fix your wig so we can get on with the shooting? You're keeping everyone waiting,' he said gently.

The actress's reply was frantic. 'God damn it, this is the way I'm going to wear it!'

Asher had a quiet word with Dieterle, instructing him to film all shots over the back of her head. He further ordered the director to start shooting complete process plates – just in case! It meant thousands of feet of background footage – either a prodigious waste of money or a life insurance policy for the film.

He had been reluctant to call Larry, but now with the situation out of control, he phoned the actor, trying to play it down: 'I think Vivien is ill. I'm trying to go as gently on her as I can, but I have to get a picture made. It's going to be rough on us – and her! I thought maybe you might talk to her, Larry. See if you can calm her down a bit. Yesterday she put on a tremendous display of temperament. She was on a horse and Dieterle was trying to get her to hear him. He yelled, and it scared the horse and it scared Vivien, and she screamed: "I won't work any longer if the director looks at me!" Well, Larry, a director has to look at you . . .'

Olivier's voice crackled over the long-distance phone. 'Do you think it's more than just the fact that she wants to play the star?'

' "Yes, Larry, I do. I definitely do! It's deep-seated – and I think it's serious," I told him,' Asher recalls. 'And he knew what I was talking about.

' "Irving, I think I'll hop on a plane and come down there," he told me.

' "You can't imagine how happy that would make me, Larry. You'd just take it off my shoulders a little bit!" '

The actor cleared four or five days between commitments and flew out at once. Asher had asked Larry if he could tell Vivien he was coming. He wanted to warn her, and Larry had agreed she should be told.

Asher had a discreet word with Finch, and saw that he was moved out of her quarters. He promised Vivien he would take her to the airport to meet her husband.

For the three days that Olivier visited her in Ceylon, Vivien pulled herself together with an almost superhuman effort. It appeared to all observers that she didn't want Larry to realise how ill she had been. And she was actress enough to succeed.

Fortified by Larry's visit, Vivien seemed able to continue, and they were ready to return to Hollywood. But the seventy-two-hour flight back brought on a pendulum swing to depression. Vivien moved into Spencer Tracy's small house on George Cukor's estate, which Tracy wasn't using at the moment.

As shooting began at Paramount, other actors joined the cast. One of them was Edward Ashley. He recalls one incident during the shooting of a banquet scene. The actors were seated around a long table. The character Vivien was playing had just arrived in Ceylon. Dieterle was shooting her in close-up. 'She did the take, and the director said, "Oh, beautiful, Vivien. Beautiful." And she replied, "You know, I've been thinking about this. If I could give this another dimension, I think it would add a great deal to the overall story."

' "What did you have in mind?" Dieterle asked.

' "I don't know if I can expain it to you, but I can show it to you. May I do another take?" Now Dieterle was happy with what she'd done, which was what was on paper. But he agreed. I watched. It was incredible, the nuances she brought into the portrait of this character. She brought a sense of foreboding, a sense of suspense. And this is where I must say she was a superb actress. Dieterle was thrilled.'

Ashley's comment on Peter Finch is revealing: 'I think he was running wild. Married to this ballet dancer. Used to spend a lot of time at Oblatz – a bar-restaurant across from the studio. If there were an opportunity [for a romance with the star], Peter would have taken it.

'In the drinking scenes, Vivien always insisted on real wine, because nobody would drink tea or anything like that since this was supposed to be Ceylon, and everybody was supposed to drink like crazy. There was an awful amount of alcohol consumed. I know when I lunched with her, I don't think it ended with one bottle . . . She was drinking, but I don't think she showed it. She knew wine. Good wine.'

But the producer couldn't fail to see that his star's condition was growing progressively worse. She looked ill, and was growing increasingly ill-tempered. She was heard to call Finch 'Larry' and when she forgot her own lines, began to quote Blanche's from *Streetcar*. Then, after a studio interview with Louella, she broke down in her dressing-room. Someone thought to call David Niven, the long-time loyal friend of the Oliviers. He calmed her hysteria, but his influence was only temporary. The alcohol was accelerating the manic condition.

As problems compounded, Asher was holding on to his own sanity. He recalls: 'During the madness at the studio, we also lost Dana Andrews for three days.' Asher sent one of the assistant directors out to find him. Andrews had just bought a brand-new Cadillac and the optimistic assistant told the troubled producer, 'Oh, he's probably just out driving that new car.' Three days later they found him. They took him to a steam bath to sober him up. He had lost the Cadillac and never could remember where he left it. He thought he had given it to someone to drive him.

Asher used to arrive at the studio at seven every morning because, as he said, 'I knew every day was dynamite.' One Saturday morning about a quarter to eight, Vivien sent for him. She walked him out to the parking lot, and pointed out to him that it was fairly empty.

'Where are all the big executives' cars?' she asked. 'If I have to work today, the fucking executives damn well better get their asses down here, too.'

He tried to calm her, explaining with some reason that it was only 8 a.m. and few executives came in on Saturday, and if they did, it was later.

The actress began to shout and scream so loudly that people were peering at them as he guided her back to her dressing-room to calm down. An hour later, she had become completely irrational, and Asher cancelled shooting for the day.

During the whole of the filming, everyone had tried to spare Vivien's feelings. Dieterle said to her, 'Vivien, dear, that is all we are going to shoot today. Go home.' No one told her why she was dismissed. Her driver took her home, and Asher phoned Sunny to be prepared for trouble; then he called a doctor to meet her at home.

The doctor's report was not encouraging. Vivien would require nurses around the clock. She was sedated and put to bed. Now all they could do was call off the shooting and wait. 'She is on the verge of a complete nervous breakdown,' the doctor had said. 'She must be kept very quiet.' And, of course, there would be no hope at all of her continuing with the picture. No one could tell how long her mental condition would last, and no one there seemed to have been aware that she was actually a manic-depressive.

The producer had a difficult decision to make. He didn't want to phone Olivier until he had a complete diagnosis. He had called Larry away from his work to come out to Ceylon, and he didn't want to do that again unless it was really necessary.

Then Vivien began to phone Asher at one or two in the morning from her bedroom. The night nurse let her do it, because she kept insisting that she had to talk to her producer. She would call and hold a most casual conversation. 'Hello, darling, it's Vivien. How are you, dear? It's a beautiful night and I'm going out and take a lovely swim in the pool . . . I'll talk to you tomorrow. Good night.' She would sound chatty and 'kind of normal' except that it wasn't her custom to call at 2 a.m. just to chat and say, 'Hello, darling.'

After several weeks of holding up production, Vivien invited Asher to come and see her. He checked with her doctor, and since he was told that a visit might do her some good, he went to the house.

She was standing at the head of the stairs in her dressing-gown. As though moving in reverse, thinking she was dressing for him, she took off the dressing-gown and descended the stairs, nude. Totally unaware of her appearance, she led him into the television-room and sat him down beside her.

'Shall we watch some television?' she asked. He got up, turned it on to a wavy-lined, unfocused picture. No sound. He started to adjust it but she stopped him.

'No, leave it. I want to watch it!'

He came back and sat beside her. For two hours they sat in silence watching the pattern. His heart was heavy but he didn't know what to do. Finally he got up.

'Vivien, I must go,' he told her, but she seemed oblivious to his departure. As he came out into the entry hall, Peter

Finch was just coming in. Asher burst into tears in Finch's arms.

Now there seemed little hope for the film. Y. Frank Freeman, head of the studio, was insisting they shelve it, but Asher held on. He asked Finch to stay in Hollywood for another two weeks, just in case of a miracle. But he added one proviso. If Finch wanted to remain on the picture, he must send for his wife immediately. Finch agreed.

Then came the doctors' decision: Vivien's condition wasn't improving. She should be sent back to England for long-term treatment. The producer paid a call on Danny Kaye.

'He was a close friend of both Larry's and Vivien's. But he didn't know much about her illness; we'd been keeping it secret,' Asher recalls. 'I told Danny the whole story and that I'd been very hesitant to call Larry. "Now I need your help. What do you suggest?"

' "We'll call him right now. From here!" ' Kaye advised. It was 6 a.m. in London when they got a call through. They finally reached Olivier in Ischia, where with the Garson Kanins he was taking a much-needed rest from his responsibilities of organising theatrical and film events for the Queen's Coronation to take place the coming summer.

On 10 March the press noted that Mrs Peter Finch had arrived from London via New York. Finch had been devastated by the film's shutdown. It was his first big chance in a picture.

Three days later, on the thirteenth, Olivier completed the difficult journey by boat, car, and plane. With him came good friend and agent Cecil Tennant. For Olivier, it was a terrible return to a scene he and Vivien had shared in happiness. It must have been one of the most difficult things he had ever had to face.

Through all these sad troubles, the Hollywood journalists, if not always fully-informed, dealt out cryptic tidbits. On the twelfth, Hedda noted that twenty-four

Academy Award-winning stars had given up three hours to be photographed with their Oscars. 'Only Oscar winner who refused to appear was two-time winner Vivien Leigh.' The secret of Vivien's illness was being well kept, and interpreted merely as temperament. But on the sixteenth the Hollywood *Reporter* observed, 'There's more to Vivien's indisposition than has been told.'

Another visitor to the ailing actress had emerged from the past. John Buckmaster (who had first introduced her to Olivier) was cited by the *Reporter* as 'giving Vivien Leigh Yogi treatments and spiritual advice until David Niven broke it up. Buckmaster's remedy included sleeping on the floor outside Lady Olivier's bedroom.'

Olivier lost no time in assuring himself that Vivien's best chance of recovery lay in England. Accompanied by Tennant, Niven, and two nurses, they had no difficulty with Vivien, who had been put under heavy sedation. Niven bade them a tearful farewell at Los Angeles Airport. But when the plane set down at Idlewild in New York, the drugs had worn off, and it was a very different scene. Vivien, white-faced and struggling against her own nightmare terrors, eyes swollen from weeping, face puffy with exhaustion, insisted upon walking down the steps. Strangely, it was Olivier who stumbled, and she who extended her arm to help him. Once off the plane, she held her head high for the photographers, but Larry quickly guided her to Danny Kaye's waiting limousine.

'We're taking her to friends until the London plane goes,' Kaye explained to the swarm of reporters.

The double-decked B.O.A.C. Monarch was waiting with only five minutes to take-off when Kaye's car returned. In the back seat Vivien was stretched across their laps, her head on her husband's knee. A steward laid a collapsible stretcher next to the car. He slipped it under the actress. Then came a terrible moment. Vivien resisted so wildly that the stretcher had to be removed. She slid down to the floor in a fit of weeping. Olivier, Kaye, and Tennant all tried pleading with her while the plane waited.

Then, finally, she straightened, took out her compact, applied some lipstick, and allowed them to conduct her aboard the plane.

Her arrival in London was, as the *Mirror* described it, 'one of her finest entrances'.

'For nineteen minutes the door of the airliner . . . stood open and empty like a stage setting, and like a first-night audience the crowd gathered and waited . . . apprehensive and silent. Inside three doctors tried to persuade Vivien to leave the plane – bundled in rugs and under close escort. They failed. The actress, still pale and dark-eyed, wanted to show England . . . she could still be gay, happy, and vivacious. She appeared suddenly at the doorway with an armful of red roses and a jaunty little sou'wester hat and a gay smile . . . In that first moment of surprise we could hardly believe she was ill at all, until we looked more closely at her careful make-up and the worried face of her husband. Someone shouted, "Welcome home, my lady!" and suddenly everybody cheered.'

Shivering slightly, Vivien whispered to Larry, 'We really are home, aren't we?' Throughout that terrible flight he had comforted her, held her sobbing in his arms for hours. He had persuaded her to eat, and held her hand all night while she slept.

'She'll be all right now,' Olivier told the waiting press, with a smile that must have demanded great courage.

Vivien was taken directly to Netherine Hospital, Coulsdon, Surrey, where she lay in a sun-filled ward. The doctors ordered no visitors, not even her husband. Understandably verging on collapse, Olivier was warned by his own physicians that he, too, needed a complete rest. He returned to Italy to finish his holiday.

The Hollywood *Reporter* buzzed: ' If you were supposed to be happily married and your wife became very ill, would you park her in a nursing home and go off to finish your "interrupted" vacation?' *Variety* was even more caustic: 'The Laurence Oliviers were about to call it off when the breakdown brought them together.' A conjecture no doubt born of *Variety*'s earlier note: 'Vivien Leigh and Peter Finch, her co-star and Larry Olivier's protégé, together at the Beachcomber.'

While Vivien was recovering health and strength in England behind a barrage of speculative rumours, six thousand miles away Irving Asher was struggling to salvage his fragmented fortunes. He had meetings with Y. Frank Freeman, who was trying to be sympathetic and helpful, but firm. 'We're going to scrap the picture, Irving. You can't go back to Ceylon. Can't start shooting all this over again!'

'But, Frank,' Asher pleaded, 'I've got the footage. All I need. And I've been eighteen hours a day in the cutting-room putting together every piece of film we've got. I've cut out all the close-ups of Vivien, trying to see where we could put someone else in. In long shots we've let her play the scene right up to where she turns around and you could recognise her. We can use all the long shots – and then cut to close shots – if we can find a girl of the same colouring and build. We've got to finish the picture. Otherwise we're in a million dollars and we'll see nothing out of it.'

'You mean, we're *out* a million dollars!' The office was blue with cigar smoke and anguish. Finally Freeman nodded his head. 'O.K., Irving. You get up a list of names for me.'

'That's what I've been trying to do, Frank. So far I haven't come up with anyone who'd be right for the story. Vivien was playing a bitch with tremendous charm, but big, like Scarlett.

'There *is* a girl, but she can't play a sharp-nosed bitch. We'd have to alter the part. She certainly isn't right for it, but she is the same build and colouring – there is a physical similarity we could match up with the film we've got. She's under contract to Metro. Her name's Elizabeth Taylor, and she's made nineteen pictures since she was a kid star, and she's just twenty-two.'

Freeman's swivel chair squeaked as he ruminated. 'How do you know she's available?'

'Because I have a spy at Metro, and he told me she's recently finished this thing called *Rhapsody* and they don't have anything lined up for her right now.'

'Listen, Irving.' The boss's voice lowered to an oracular whisper. 'If you put Taylor in that part and she comes downstairs and says "Come on up to bed" – and Finch tells her he wants to stay with the boys, the audience will think he's going to bed with Dana Andrews!'

'Frank, I know we'll have to rewrite.'

Irving recalls: 'The next thing I knew, Freeman was in hysterics because Metro was asking $100,000 for Elizabeth – which in those days he thought was the worst money he ever heard of. I got some figures together and was able to convince him that no matter what we paid Elizabeth, it was worth it. I showed him how it would work in the projection room, showed him the footage I'd shot. He's shrewd, smart. "Go ahead, Irving, you sign her," he said.'

The next day Asher saw Elizabeth for the first time. 'She came into my office. She'd take your breath away, so much more beautiful in person than on the screen. At twenty-two she was so beautiful I could hardly talk to her. Barely discuss the script. But we showed her the film, and explained that she'd have to wear clothes she might not like in order to match Vivien's.'

Asher assured her that they would rewrite the script to make it a girl she could play. It was tortuous shooting, trying to match the shots. And with the change of character, it became a different picture. Finch was fine, and Asher found him helpful. 'He was terribly anxious to get a picture under his belt. And he got on well with his new co-star, who knew everybody else's lines as well as her own.

'If Finch was emotionally upset by Vivien's departure, you didn't know it. He showed it at the start, of course, but when his wife and daughter came, he settled down. When we shot the fire scenes, the elephants [tuskers from a Sarasota circus] panicked, ran around knocking everything down, and Elizabeth worked right with them. She wasn't afraid. I was.'

Asher says, 'In the film today there are a lot of long shots of Vivien. When I ran the film, I used to groan when they came on, although nobody knew them but me, Dieterle, and the editor.' (Up to then, the only great star who had been unable to finish a film had been Jean Harlow. Metro used a double to complete *Saratoga* after Harlow's death.)

In the end, Paramount was financially generous to Vivien. She was reported to have collected $130,000 of her $200,000 fee for *Elephant Walk* – more than was paid to the actress who finally played the part.

While Vivien was in Netherine Hospital, thieves broke into Durham Cottage, stealing jewellery, furs, and even the Oscar she had won for *Streetcar*. But this, it seemed, wasn't enough. Ladder thieves also broke into Notley in June and stripped Vivien's bedroom of all her jewellery. Larry made an appeal through the press: 'There is one piece she treasures most. A ruby ring I gave her when I came back from Hollywood to join the Navy. It's a sentimental thing. If she could only have it back, I think she'd be satisfied.' He added, 'Everyone knows Vivien has been very ill, yet these men broke into her bedroom. They seem to be quite heartless.' Vivien's wedding ring was also among the missing objects.

Vivien's recovery took only four months, and plans to sell Notley (offered at £26,000) were now abandoned. The delicate actress needed it again as a haven of rest. Larry had postponed plans to produce Terence Rattigan's new play, *The Sleeping Prince*, until they could appear in it together as the prince and the showgirl.

In late August, after a holiday abroad, the Oliviers were ready to launch rehearsals for the Rattigan play. Vivien, back from the shadows, was ready to face the press again. But she confided to a friend, 'When they say I am well, I feel ghastly, and when they say I am unwell, I feel wonderful.'*

* Gwen Robyns, *Light of a Star.*

The Sleeping Prince was to open in Manchester and they were being publicised as 'the world's number one couple'. David Fairweather, again handling publicity, recalls that someone had arranged for them to appear at the Manchester Cotton Ball but neglected to inform the Oliviers.

'When told, Sir Laurence said, "Fuck the Cotton Ball! Somebody has slipped up, and it wasn't our side." When he was told it would cause a disaster since tickets had been sold for £5 each, he sighed, "Very well. We'll make an *acte de présence*," using a line from the play. They appeared, and drank champagne. He loathed publicity. Couldn't see any reason for it. She could.'

Vivien had also told the press: 'I did some hard thinking while I was ill. I just felt all washed up and never wanted to see a camera or stage again. But I stared myself in the face and mapped out a new way of living. I shall work hard, just as hard. But rest hard, too . . .' As for *Elephant Walk*, she beamed at a presswoman who had asked a loaded question, and said, 'You mustn't blame the elephants.' Then she added, with a wistful, faraway look, 'It was the heat of those overpowering afternoons.'

13 *End of a love scene*

14 July 1956. Bastille Day could hardly have produced a more explosive happening than Marilyn Monroe's arrival in London to film *The Prince and the Showgirl* with Laurence Olivier.

It was common knowledge in the inner circle that Terence Rattigan had written the stage play (*The Sleeping Prince*) for Vivien, to give her a light, uncomplicated vehicle after the strain of playing in *Streetcar*. It offered the ideal role in which to make a comeback from her *Elephant Walk* illness. And it was a success. She had performed marvellously as the showgirl to Larry's Carpathian prince. But filming the role would have been out of the question. Vivien was now forty-three. The sex-kitten showgirl needed a younger face for the camera's magnifying eye.

Marilyn Monroe brought to London twenty-seven pieces of luggage, her new husband, Arthur Miller, and a head full of ideas of her own – or at least of Lee Strasberg's. In November of 1954, Marilyn had walked out of her Hollywood contract and for some two years had been under the influence of the high priest of 'the method'.

'I want to be an artist, not a freak,' she had announced. (For 'artist', read actress. For 'freak', read sex symbol.) Strasberg and his wife, Paula, encouraged her in the belief that she had an immense creative potential and could become an actress of true theatrical worth. Cerebral playwright Arthur Miller fused ideally into her new self-portrait of the sexpot as dedicated artist.

The one attribute shared by the Magi of her new destiny was Marilyn's dependence on them, for her insecure nature required perpetually stronger crutches and deeper reassurances. As director of her newly-formed company,

Marilyn Monroe Productions, ex-photographer and close friend Milton Greene had acquired the screen rights to Rattigan's play. It was Marilyn's idea to film it with Sir Laurence playing his original role. Someone, probably Greene suggested that Olivier might also direct. As a noviciate in Strasberg's school of cognitive acting, Marilyn put the question to her guru. He thought the 'possibility' *might* be a good idea. Greene, taking it as gospel, cabled a firm offer to Olivier. Strasberg quibbled that he had only *thought* it might be a good idea. But since the cable had already been sent, they let it ride and the offer was accepted.

Actually, Strasberg had grave qualms, for his 'method' was diametrically opposed to Olivier's technique of working from the outside in. Marilyn had spent two years learning to develop her creative intuition from the inside out.

Olivier went to New York for consultations. At the airport he was stopped by a curious customs officer, who pawed through the Olivier luggage, his face hidden beneath the peak of his cap, muttering, 'What crummy laundry!' Sir Laurence was about to be offended when he inspected the inspector. It was Danny Kaye. But the bubble went out of the giggle at the horrendous press reception for him and Marilyn. Two hundred reporters and photographers stormed the Plaza Hotel Terrace Room, stampeding the stars against a wall. It was not only an occasion that merged what John Cottrell called 'the Knight and the Garter', but it was also the actress's first major press conference since leaving Hollywood. Little wonder that one spaghetti shoulder strap of Marilyn's slinky sheath gave way, and only a calculated clutch saved one of her most publicised assets from public display. The attention made Marilyn 'feel like something in a zoo, but I'm not sure whether I was a specimen or a spectator.'*

Olivier told the press that his new co-star was 'a brilliant

* Fred Lawrence Guiles, *Norma Jean*.

comedienne, which means to me she is a very fine actress . . . able to suggest one minute that she is the naughtiest little thing and the next minute that she is beautifully dumb and innocent.' He even allowed that she could play Shakespeare, although he didn't suggest which role. And he accepted the press uproar with astonishing good grace. This was a facet of Olivier's ambivalent quality – that he could, when required, dip gracefully into the fleshpots of filmdom after the glittering peaks of stage classicism. Such commercial athleticism could keep one from becoming typecast.

Both the Strasbergs and Miller accompanied Marilyn to London. Viven and Larry were there to greet them. It was scarcely less chaotic than the New York interview, with one important difference: for the first time Vivien, accustomed to being the star of such occasions, was not even carrying a spear. Graciously she stood aside, letting Marilyn have her day.

Although she had been left out of the film plans, Vivien was happily engaged in Noël Coward's new play, *South Sea Bubble*, an easy romp in which she played opposite the master himself. While lightweight even for Coward, the production was extremely successful, running for 276 performances. More important, her health seemed never better, as did her state of mind. Indeed, to the Oliviers' surprise and delight, she was pregnant again. Despite a history of miscarriage, the doctors had felt that this time all would go well, and optimistically allowed her to continue working.

The swarming press, anxious to hear the scarcely audible Monroe, pushed and nudged forwards into each other and, in passing, jolted Vivien. Marilyn seemed shy in the face of Lady Olivier, reflecting her natural awe of titles. Vivien enquired of Marilyn if this was the usual frenzy her press conferences brought on. Marilyn gasped back that this was tranquil compared to most. Olivier was called on to repeat most of Marilyn's *bons mots*, since no one could hear her above the din. Totally out of his element, Arthur Miller watched the proceedings with a glacial smile.

The Oliviers drove the Millers in their Rolls to an estate

at Egham near Windsor Park. The Oliviers still retained Notley, but had sold Durham Cottage, and rented a town house in Belgravia. With the expectation of the baby, the love scene was back in high gear.

But from the beginning of Olivier's working relationship with Marilyn, storm clouds hovered. The lightning rod was Paula Strasberg. Marilyn had brought Lee's wife along as her coach.* Joshua Logan, who had directed Marilyn in *Bus Stop*, had assured Olivier that Marilyn was difficult, but well worth the trouble. His advice was 'Load up the camera and put Marilyn in front of it, and keep Paula Strasberg . . . away from the set.'

Logan had also warned Olivier never to lose his temper, raise his voice, or unnerve the jittery star. It didn't take a week for the Knight and the Garter to start snapping. The director got off to a very bad start in one scene with a suggestion 'All right, Marilyn. Be sexy.' Marilyn headed for her dressing-room and the telephone. She got Lee Strasberg at his hotel, complaining bitterly, 'Lee, how do you become sexy? What do you do to be sexy?' Strasberg, too, was incensed at such irreverence for his protégée's artistry. Olivier was alarmed to discover that his star was totally without a sense of humour.

Olivier appealed to Miller for support when Marilyn began arriving on the set two, three, or four hours late, or failed to appear at all. Dame Sybil Thorndike, playing the Dowager Queen, said of Marilyn, 'She's the only one of us who knows how to act in front of a camera.' But that didn't stop the flattered Marilyn from keeping the elder actress waiting two hours on the set. Despite Logan's warning, the director's patience was not inviolate. 'Why

---

* The actress had always leaned heavily on coaches from her days at Twentieth Century-Fox when Natasha Lytess had been employed by the studio at Marilyn's request. Actress Barbara Hayden, also being coached by Lytess, recalled Monroe as a painfully shy, introverted blonde – with dark roots – who wore blue jeans and a satin shirt with spike heels long before such anti-dress became fashionable.

can't you get here on time, for fuck's sake?' he exclaimed one day.

'Oh, do you have that word in England, too?' murmured Marilyn.*

Worse, Olivier would be in the middle of explaining a scene when Monroe would turn on her heel and walk away to consult Paula. Every correction the director made brought Marilyn to Strasberg's wife for a private conference, while the entire cast and crew waited helplessly. Logan had suggested no antidote for such behaviour. Miller offered the excuse on his wife's behalf that she was merely distracted, while Olivier felt that Paula was driving him out of his 'squeaking mind.'

Marilyn was beginning to feel that Olivier's image of the showgirl was biased by Vivien's original performance. Without such directorial similes as telling her to 'feel like a kite in a high wind', or 'an artichoke about to be peeled', Marilyn had nothing to relate to.

Olivier waited until the film was half-completed before insisting that Paula Strasberg's presence was not required on the set. By this time the co-stars were barely on speaking terms. Larry had become 'Mister Sir'. Nothing he had experienced equalled the mental strain of this film.

But when the camera rolled, Marilyn Monroe, for all her neuroses and unprofessionalism, switched on like a bulb and the camera loved her.

Except for Olivier's problems with Marilyn, the Fates had not been too unkind of late. He and Vivien had been together for the Stratford season of 1955. They had appeared in *Twelfth Night*, *Macbeth*, and *Titus Andronicus*, taking comedy, tragedy, and horror in their stride.

Of Vivien's Lady Macbeth, critic Allan Pryce-Jones thought her portrayal had 'an icy serpentine quality, which made her the most dangerous Lady Macbeth' he had ever seen. Actor-author Richard Huggett recalls, 'She was a

* John Cottrell, *Laurence Olivier*.

much better actress than she was ever given credit for. Her Lady Macbeth was more than "just competent" as Kenneth Tynan said – although this was high praise coming from him. It had dignity, a vocal splendour, and an atmosphere of evil . . . enormously impressive to watch. Of course it was Olivier's evening. With the balance of the two parts, how could it be otherwise? Have you ever heard of a Lady Macbeth stealing the play from her husband?'

In the courtyard scene, they had played their dialogue in whispers, which built such tremendous tension that the knocking at the gate was a thunderclap in the ears of the audience.

Trader Faulkner, the young Australian actor they had met with Peter Finch in Sydney, had been invited to join the Stratford season, and found himself in political difficulties almost from the start. He was playing Sebastian in *Twelfth Night*. 'I was also hired to play one of the boys who's put in a pie in *Titus*. But at the opening rehearsal of *Macbeth*, in which I was to play Malcolm, the trouble started.' Glen Byam Shaw asked Trader to play Malcolm as a sybarite, a decadent Nero type. Trader objected that if he was to supersede Sir Laurence as monarch, he must make people believe that the sun was rising over what had been 'the sun of suns'. He wanted to show Malcolm's potential.

Olivier backed him. 'I've played it, and I know how difficult the role is. Glen I'm sorry, the boy's right!'

Trader said. 'Well, that was the end of me with Byam Shaw. My role in *Titus* was taken away, and I was made to carry a spear. I went to Vivien and asked, "Am I no good?"

' "No, darling," she said. "You stepped on Byam Shaw's toes." ' She considerately invited the young actor down to Notley for a weekend. The guests included Noël Coward, Ronald and Benita Colman, Danny Kaye, Marlene Dietrich, Marlon Brando, and Charlie Chaplin.

At the dinner table, Coward, who had seen *Macbeth*, suddenly called out across the centrepiece, 'Young man!

Trader from Australia! I think you are going to be a very considerable actor! And I very much admire what you've done with Malcolm.'

The entire table of celebrities suddenly beamed attention on the supporting player in their midst.

'I thought it had been spontaneous from Coward. But Vivien had engineered the whole thing,' Trader recalls.

In the two previous years, the Oliviers had had separate assignments. Vivien had squeezed in a film for Korda – *The Deep Blue Sea* with Kenneth More and Eric Portman, with a Rattigan screenplay from his own play, and charming Anatole Litvak directing. It was a tempting package, but the film was a disappointment, and Vivien turned in one of her least memorable performances.

During 1954 and 1955, Olivier had been more rewardingly occupied filming his magnificent *Richard III*, with Claire Bloom playing Lady Anne. The most impressive thing about his performance on the screen in this role was that it wasn't excessive. The make-up was so convincing that one could believe the nose on the bewitchingly malevolent Richard. From the moment he first turns full face into a camera shooting over the back of his head, and takes the audience into his confidence, one is almost rooting for him to win, despite the fate of the princes in the tower and John Gielgud's rattling good death scene. At his final cry for a horse, one would have eagerly supplied it, just to keep that fascinating figure on the screen.

But travelling back and forth between London and Stratford while supervising the final touches on the film had taken its toll on Olivier. The doctors prescribed twelve months away from the theatre and film studios, and for once he was tired enough to listen.

George Cukor had paid Larry and Vivien a visit at Stratford and recalls: 'The Oliviers gave a party after the opening. She was drinking something stronger than brandy – grappa. She was always funny when drunk. Viv loved wonderful food, but was never conscious of the mechanics of life. She was a romantic creature.'

With the passing years, Olivier was channelling most of his energies into his work. The parties that Vivien thrived on made him weary. Not that he was anti-social, but he liked his few friends in small doses, and he needed a full night's sleep. But Vivien's pregnancy gave reason to rejoice.

An heir to Notley – maybe a new town house large enough to hold the addition to the family. So much to be thought of! So much to share again. The bad times were washed away in a flood of expectation.

Should they choose yellow and white to decorate the nursery? Would Kathryn be a good name if the 'it' should be a she? And what man wouldn't cherish a daughter to comfort his old age, Vivien cheerfully confided to the national press. Indeed, their press relations were exceptionally cheery these days.

Vivien had been advised that with her pregnancy, she could remain in *South Sea Bubble* until the first week in August, which one would have thought was cutting it close, but the doctors saw no danger. Carry on she did, with parties, performances, and even a midnight charity benefit at the Palladium with Larry and John Mills, in a strenuous four-minute song-and-dance routine. She had spent thirty-five hours rehearsing, and the doctors not only approved, they were busily conjecturing on the possibility of Lady Olivier producing twins! Medical experts of the day agreed that the chances increased with mothers over forty.

On Saturday night, 13 August 1956, Vivien said goodbye to the cast of *South Sea Bubble* with a grand farewell party. Elizabeth Sellars would take over the role. The party was to launch the star into the rest the doctor had finally ordered. On Sunday, the actress was to go down to Notley, but that evening she began to feel sick. The doctors arrived too late.

'Vivien had lost her baby, and I do not think it is because she went on working too long. It is just bad, bad luck. Fate,' Olivier told David Lewin, the journalist. By another quirk of fate, that same day Dickie Olivier's wife, Hester, gave birth to a six-pound baby girl. Tactfully, she kept the news from her sister-in-law.

'We are bitterly disappointed and terribly upset,' Larry said. 'The main concern now is Vivien. The important thing is that she should make a complete recovery.' The saddened husband then dragged himself back to Pinewood to attend the caprices of Monroe.

Tragedy is such an easy word to cover an array of hurts, deep and shallow, present and future. And across the love scene now fell a lengthening shadow.

As soon as Vivien was well enough to travel, she accepted Rex Harrison's generous offer of his house at Portofino. He and Lilli Palmer moved out to stay with friends. Vivien was left alone to recover her health in the tranquil peace of southern Italy.

And to think about the future.

There was a new wave rolling across the English theatrical scene. It bore on its crest a tide of angry young men. Colin Wilson was opening windows of the mind with his brilliantly analytical book *The Outsider*, exploding ideas like a Marx manifesto. The theatre found its own Peter the Hermit in playwright John Osborne, who detonated a bomb under the Establishment with his first play, *Look Back in Anger*. This new venture into theatrical reality, while being a natural evolutionary step from America's 'method' and dubbed 'kitchen sink' by fascinated British critics, left traditionalists like Gielgud, Richardson, and Olivier in the wings.

But Sir Laurence was never one to rest on hardy laurels. His antenna was up. George Devine, his long-time friend, had formed the English Stage Company with playwright Ronald Duncan and Lord Harewood, the Queen's cousin, in 1956. Olivier had seen their production of Osborne's angry backward look. Seen it and hated it. But, accompanied by Arthur Miller, he had given it a second look and a rethink. He couldn't have chosen a more ideal companion than the American intellectual. Miller's opinion helped open the actor's eyes. He got in touch with Osborne. It wasn't long before the Royal Court Theatre in Sloane Square (as far out of the West End as one could get) found itself honoured by the presence of Sir Laurence playing Archie Rice, a ham-bone song-and-dance man in young Osborne's second play, *The Entertainer*.

More amazingly, the classic actor-director was allowing himself to be guided directorially by youthful Tony Richardson. Olivier had always been tremendously attracted to being a general entertainer and bridging the lines of demarcation in theatre. The busker was hidden deep in Hamlet. As he later told Robert Muller of the London *Daily Mail*, 'There's a morbid fascination in thinking what might have happened to me if I'd made good as a chorus boy. Because at one time I would have been glad to take a job in a concert party if it had been offered . . . There must have been something of Archie in me all along. It's what I might so easily have become . . . I've never had the opportunity to make people laugh as much as I would like. I'd like to make them die with laughter.'

Director William Gaskill said of Olivier's Archie: 'The heartless clown's mask is very much a part of Larry Olivier. I don't think he's cold and unemotional, but at the same time I think it's sentimental to expect him, because he is an outstanding actor, to be a man of great feeling and emotional depth. Not many actors are.'*

Olivier had said to Tynan, 'I think it's the most wonderful part that I've ever played.' The press agreed. 'Olivier is tremendous . . . Olivier has it all . . . the gurgling, leering, funny stories. The too hearty laugh that conceals the pang of shame . . . "Old Archie", he boasts, "is dead behind the eyes". Then he hears his soldier son has been killed. And the man's agony shows naked. Before your eyes you see how a body crumbles from within.' So wrote John Barber in the *Daily Express*.

Vivien had somehow missed the boat on the new wave

---

* Ed. Logan Gourlay, *Olivier*.

Larry was riding. There was no part for her in the play. She was too beautiful to play Archie's wife, the dowdy Phoebe, and too old to play his daughter. Fortunately she was sensible enough to discard someone's suggestion that she might play Phoebe in a rubber mask. She had worn one portraying the ageing Lady Hamilton years before. Brenda de Banzie took the role; Dorothy Tutin, who had appeared with Olivier in his film of *Beggar's Opera*, was chosen to portray Archie's daughter.

For Vivien it was an unhappy time. Never before had she felt so left out of Larry's work. As a spectator and sometimes unwelcome critic at his rehearsals, she felt a deep sense of exclusion. Now, for the first time, she found herself jealous of Larry's working with younger actresses. Before, she would never have listened to rumours. Now she did. On opening night, she greeted Miss Tutin backstage with 'Dottie! What a performance. Still the perennial virgin!'

The Entertainer enjoyed only a five-week run at the Royal Court, because the Oliviers were scheduled to tour their Stratford production of *Titus Andronicus* around Europe. By the time they were ready to launch the tour, Vivien's pendulum was swinging towards the danger zone of depression. There had been other disappointments. The film of *Macbeth* that they had planned so hopefully was still not financed, and another projected film, Terence Rattigan's *Separate Tables*, hadn't materialised.

Now Olivier could only hope that her health would stand the strenuous five-thousand-mile tour that included Paris, Venice, Belgrade, Zagreb, Vienna, and Warsaw. For her sake, he had arranged that the company, including some sixty actors, should travel by train. At least he could spare her the terrors of flying.

Things started off well enough in Paris. Vivien was even in a joking mood. In the first act, playing Titus's daughter Lavinia, she is raped, has her hands cut off and her tongue cut out, leaving her a mute with bandaged stumps for the rest of the play. 'I get so tired of having absolutely nothing to say and listening to Larry going on and on – that I'm thinking of getting a little wireless set to conceal in my draperies round my hand. Then I could listen to the radio programmes while I'm on stage.'

Paris, with its Grand Guignol tradition, should have felt right at home with Peter Brook's gory rendition of Shakespeare's crimson horror piece. But, according to John Cottrell, it caused Michèle Morgan to shriek, Jean Marais to bite his tongue, Françoise Rosay to consider vegetarianism, and Doug Fairbanks, Jr. to swallow his chewing gum.

'Why trundle this horror comic across Europe?' wondered one news story.

Larry celebrated his fiftieth birthday in Paris and Vivien was awarded the Knight's Cross of the Legion of Honour. Larry already had one, among his souvenirs.

And they opened in Venice. But what a different city from the one they had known as lovers so many years ago! Now it was sweltering, seething with tourists. An experience haunted by the memory of what they had been.

As the train bore them on through the blazing corridors of summer, close as a coffin, seething with temperaments, Vivien was slipping into her manic mood. Members of the company noted incidents.

One night in Zagreb, when for reasons of security the Oliviers were told to remain in their hotel, Vivien managed to slip out in a green silk gown and matching emeralds. For a whole night and day no one knew where she was, except her unnamed escort. Her return brought more trouble; when the breakfast tray arrived in their suite, it is alleged that she hurled the tray and contents out the window. Then on the train out of Zagreb, still in a hurling mood, she demanded money to buy chocolates and threw the change, twenty-five pounds' worth of dinars, out of the window. During a matinée in Belgrade, Vivien eyed Titus's wailing misery. Quite audibly she pronounced, 'You cunt!' The Belgrade audience no doubt took it as a line from Shakespeare.

By accident, Olivier, too, was guilty of a verbal in-
discretion. Bravely, he had memorised a curtain speech in
every necessary language. In Yugoslavia he brought down
the house with a mispronunciation. Instead of 'thank you,
all' – it came out 'Ladies and gentlemen, fuck you all'. The
audience was delighted.

Olivier's concern for his wife grew. By the time they had
reached Warsaw, she had been drinking heavily again,
smoking too much, and had been quite irrational with
other members of the company. In Warsaw a doctor was
called. The surprising thing was not that she was ill – which
everyone recognised – but that after hours of sobbing and
hysteria in what seemed the edge of a breakdown, she was
still able to pull herself together in time for the curtain and
face her audience as the First Lady of the theatre, which she
still was.

They returned with the play for a five-week London
season at the Stoll. Those around her, friends like Bumble
Dawson, had always formed a protective circle hiding
Vivien's bouts of illness. Now rumours of difficulty in the
marriage were becoming harder to suppress.

In a stunning grey-and-blue dress by Balmain, Vivien
Leigh seemed scarcely well cast as leader of a protest march.
Yet in July of 1957, such was her reaction to the news that
the St James's Theatre was on the demolition list. The Stoll,
where the Oliviers were currently playing *Titus*, was
similarly doomed. A zealous bureaucracy was finding it
expedient to dispense with 'obsolete Victorian play-
houses' in favour of shiny new office blocks.

The St James's had been *their* theatre. Larry and she had
seen it through too many productions in their effort
to keep British theatre alive and living in London. At the
moment, however, the actor had no time for crusades.
Bernard, the Oliviers' chauffeur, cruised behind the little
procession in the Bentley (licence plate VLO 1), like a
rowboat escorting a channel swimmer. Vivien was flanked
by ageing actress Athene Seyler and by Alan Dent, sand-

wiched into boards. They marched from Fleet Street to Westminster, Vivien ringing a large pub handbell, normally used to signal closing time. Now the bell rang to keep the St James's open.

'I was amazed at the lack of interest in our little demonstration,' she said. 'I have decided that if I want a quiet holiday and a rest, the thing to do is to walk up the Strand carrying a sandwich board.'

Vivien's next assault was more lofty. She had been invited to tea at the House of Lords by Lord Bessborough, and was seated afterwards in the spectators' gallery between him and Sir Brian Horrocks, Black Rod, guardian of the Lords' traditions. She rose dramatically and flouted a thousand years of Parliamentary protocol: 'My Lords, I want to protest about the St James's Theatre being demolished!'

Instantly, Black Rod touched her shoulder. 'I'm afraid you must leave, Lady Olivier.' They escorted her out.

She told a reporter, 'I did not go to the House of Lords with the intention of making a scene. But after Lord Blackford's speech [against retaining the St James's], I felt my temper rising, and I was suddenly on my feet. There was complete silence in the house when I said my piece. None of the Lords moved a muscle. In fact, it is what – if I had been on stage – I would describe as a *dead* audience!' She added, 'Larry knew nothing about it until a few minutes ago. He was most surprised.'

He was gracious enough to confide to the reporters, 'I think what my wife did was a very sweet and gallant thing.'

But as Vivien grew more and more passionately excited about the cause, defeats became less and less acceptable to her. 'If the St James's is pulled down I will leave England and act in other countries! I have paid enough money in taxes during my years on the stage. I can act in German, French, Italian, and maybe even Serbian.'

Statements like these were becoming deeply embarrassing to Olivier, as was her personal pursuit of property tycoons and financiers to save her beloved theatre. And she would not be stopped. She went on the air, then stormed out of the studio saying they'd cut her off too soon.

Even the cartoonists were beginning to make gibes at the Oliviers. And then came the final protest march. This time, Vivien announced, they would be 'frightfully well organised'. At least they were well attended. Three hundred actors and fans had gathered outside the St James's. She marched in a raincoat and hat, with a black patch over an infected eye. As she sailed into Trafalgar Square, the great Lord Nelson must have looked down with some sympathy. Someone in the crowd called out that he admired her but didn't agree with her views.

'Pipe down, then! You're a silly fool!' she snapped. Olivier, who had loyally attended this march, dropped an aside: 'I'm thinking of changing my name to Mr Pankhurst.' But he kept with her, and together they led the procession behind banner and band.

'My feet are killing me!' Vivien confessed in the most practical statement of the day. Sadly, the protest failed, and an edifice of glass and steel was erected on the site of the St James's. But inside the entrance can still be seen a plaque which bears the profiles of the theatre Royals who marched to save the theatre.

Yet something else besides a theatre was undergoing demolition. The love scene was crumbling.

Larry had confided to a friend, 'I go to these parties that Vivien gives in our home. All these people coming in to drink our wine and eat our food. It's go, go, go . . . I remember one night talking to some aristocrat and I literally had one eye propped open with a finger to keep awake.'

When does a love scene end? Not in a moment, but in a hundred thousand moments. Not with the single bang of the closing door, but in the long procession of events – the hurts, faults, and failures of the flesh.

With the close of *Titus* on 4 August came the need of a holiday from work – and from each other. Vivien would go to Italy with Leigh Holman and daughter Suzanne. This was not so strange. She and Leigh had always continued to see each other, and remained the best of friends. As one of Vivien's closest friends confided, Olivier also knew that whenever Vivien was with Leigh, she was on her best behaviour. Now he could only hope that this settling influence might halt the pendulum swing and bring back to him the Vivien he knew and loved. He was even grateful for anything that would bring a moment of quiet and peace to his life.

Larry made plans to take Tarquin to Scotland on a fishing trip. It was a rare opportunity for father and son to be able to talk to each other.

Another crusading lady, Jean Mann, a Labour MP from Coatbridge and Airdire in Lanarkshire, was publicly shocked in the House – and in print – on behalf 'of all young children'. Mrs Mann (who had five of her own) flayed 'an unnamed person in high place' for her holiday with an ex-husband. 'Ordinary wives may say, "Why should I stick on with that poultice of mine?"'

Curiously, the *News Chronicle* took the view that the MP seemed to have missed the point and owed Miss Leigh an apology: 'We do not regard such pillorying of a private citizen by an MP as desirable public conduct.'

The Honourable Mrs Mann remained recalcitrant. Vivien wondered why all the fuss, since she had often spent weekends with Suzanne in the company of Leigh. And when she returned, John Rolls noted in the *Mirror* that her journey back had been a sentimental one. She and Suzanne had stopped off at the places she and Olivier had known and loved. They had gone to the same hotels and restaurants, where she ordered the actor's favourite dishes: partridges cooked in cabbage at La Bonne Auberge; a fish dish smothered in powdered shrimp sauce at the Hôtel de la Côte-d'Or in Saulieu.

Despite speculation that the Oliviers were parting, when her plane landed from Paris, he was there to greet her with a hug and kiss. 'I am quite happy with things as they are,' Vivien announced. But how exactly were things? For the moment rumours had been scotched.

In December, Suzanne was married to Robin Farrington. Vivien flashed into the wedding scene on Larry's arm, wearing an eye-catching leopard-patterned silk coat. For the remainder of the event, Olivier leaned against a pillar, sipping champagne, aloof and apart.

'I want to stay in the background, as this is Suzanne's day. I don't want to spoil it for her. This is all very awkward.' He quickly added, 'It is only what people say that makes it so awkward.'

And they said a great deal more when Vivien drove off with Leigh, leaving him among the guests, calmly waving goodbye.

Whatever the rumours or denials, there was no doubt that the Oliviers were continuing separate ways with their careers. In the spring of 1958, Larry went into the Palace for an eight week revival of *The Entertainer*, before transferring to Broadway. Dorothy Tutin, who was otherwise engaged, had been replaced by a bright young talent, Joan Plowright, then twenty-seven. John Osborne later said of Miss Plowright that although Tony Richardson and George Devine thought 'she represented the new kind of actress, that she had reality and truth as opposed to the old Shaftesbury Avenue glitter, I didn't agree. But Olivier was obviously influenced by their opinion.'

Almost immediately gossip began. There had been trickles of gossip before concerning an actress who lived on a Chelsea houseboat. Vivien had dismissed it to a close friend with 'Well, darling, Larry is not used to having boiled eggs on a houseboat. I think I laughed him out of that one.'

But she wasn't laughing now, and he was off to New York with *The Entertainer* and Miss Plowright.

Again in fine physical and mental health, Vivien was to open in Giraudoux's *Duel of Angels* at the Apollo. She was ready to give Olivier any freedom he might wish as long as it didn't build an impenetrable barrier between them. She had no illusions about the suffering that her illness had caused him – and still might – or about the effect on him of her attachment to Peter Finch, which now, in her normal state, continued as a friendship. There had been no love lost between Larry and Peter after Ceylon. It had been a humiliating experience for Olivier, and Peter had betrayed his trust, as had she. But he had come to terms with the affair.

The Oliviers were still planning to film *Macbeth* together when he returned from New York. It gave her a hope that their work might yet bring their lives together.

She dined at the Ivy with Kenneth Passingham and told him, 'You know what I'd really like to do? Another tour like the Australian one.' That odyssey ten years before had been a sovereign processional in the syle of the old-time touring companies.

'Larry,' she continued, 'has done more for my career than any other single person. He is tremendous, dedicated, inspiring. There is no one else quite like him. And he is nearly always right about everything. I acknowledge him as a master. That's why I'm looking forward to *Macbeth*.'

But there would be no film of *Macbeth* for the Oliviers, and no return to working together.

Trader Faulkner had been invited down to Notley by Vivien on many occasions, often with his ballet-teacher mother, who had given the actress lessons in dance movement. Before the log fire in the evenings, memories would speed through Vivien's mind like film being run backwards in a moviola. The actress spoke of Finch, called him 'a gypsy'. 'He's unwashed, he's wild, but he's warm.' Then, as an afterthought, 'He paints beautifully.' He was every woman's dream: the pursuit of a Pan-like symbol, always free and unfettered, never to be possessed. 'It's the Virgin and the Gypsy – but I'm no virgin, and he's really no gypsy.' She laughed. Vivien understood Finch, and there had been no animosity when the gypsy moved his caravan to the next campsite.

One day she asked Trader if he believed in reincarnation.

'I don't know,' he replied.

'I think, Trader, you're an old soul!' she said.

He replied, no doubt, that he felt really antique.

'I'm an old soul, too.' Then she gave him a quizzical look and asked what he thought of Larry.

'Well, I don't think he's an old soul,' was the cautious reply.

'No!' she exclaimed. 'He's a brand-new soul!'

'Well, for the first time around, he hasn't done badly,' Trader told her. 'I reckon he'll go to the top of the soul class on the next incarnation.' At that moment Olivier walked in, and Trader had the impression that he had heard.

Another night, when the marriage was nearing its end, Trader and his mother were invited with Olivier's brother and sister. The actor was away on tour in *The Entertainer* with Joan Plowright. 'Here was Vivien, whose castle was literally falling about her ears, entertaining, and being so sweet to everybody. Finch was there, too. He'd left Tamara by that time, and when he saw my mother, a fleeting look of hatred crossed his face, because he'd seen someone from a past he didn't want to remember. Tamara had been a great friend of my mother's.'

Vivien confided that her marriage was doomed, 'because you cannot build a house on shifting sands – or,' she added, 'on the unhappiness of two other people. We were beautiful, we were ambitious, we lived for each other. It was a selfish seizure – and it has turned to dust.'

She said she thought their marriage never really deserved to be a success. 'You cannot fool yourself.' She had been brought up by nuns in a convent school, and they had taught her that.

'Because if you're fooling yourself, you're fooling God – and there's no way of doing that. But if you succeed in fooling yourself,' she continued, 'mental illness will come from it.' She called it a split – a lie in the body that festered like pus. She told Trader's mother that she had wanted more than anything to have a child because she felt it would bind her marriage. They had been so happy for such a long time. 'But it was a physical conflagration. We were drawn like magnets.'

She believed that a human being must operate on three planes. The physical and mental they had shared, but spiritually there was something sterile in their relationship. Something had gone wrong. They had each deserted partners, and now she realised what it must have been for them. 'If you desert somebody, you've got to live with it,' she told Trader.

Vivien's early training had always been in conflict with her life-style. Her Indian Army background had constrained her into a self-conscious cocoon of formality. Talent had freed her superficially, but deep inside the conflict remained. As an artist, she knew her shortcomings, and was prepared to work hard for everything she got. But life, love and friendships she had accepted as a gift to her beauty and charm. Yes, of course she had followed Larry's lead in the theatre. It was human to want to keep pace with this champion who could always go like the wind.

Olivier had a marvellous ability to present the right image at the right time. His timing in life had been perfect. Even in unsuccessful plays, he got good notices. Noël Coward had been an enormous influence in the early days. Once Olivier recalled to Trader how Coward had advised him to trim his nails, cut his hair, and had made him aware of how necessary it was to be groomed, to be what subsequently came to be known as 'a West End young man'.

The Entertainer marked the end of Olivier's 'boulevard playing'. With his Savile Row suits and buckled shoes, he was hardly a likely candidate to rub shoulders with the blue-jeaned 'working-class' actors, a breed unheard of before 1956. But it was on this ship that he sailed off to greater glories.

Sunday, 22 May 1960. Vivien Leigh, then playing in New York in *Duet of Angels*, issued a terse statement to the press that ended months of speculation: 'Lady Olivier wishes to say that Sir Laurence has asked for a divorce in order to marry Miss Joan Plowright. She will naturally do whatever he wishes.' The statement also ended Vivien's last hope that the love scene could be revived.

For some time they had been a continent apart. In 1958, she had opened *Duet of Angels* in London. He had been in New York with *The Entertainer*. In 1959, he played *Coriolanus* at Stratford; she went into Noël Coward's *Look After Lulu*, which warmed up in London and sped to New York. He was busy filming *The Entertainer* and then went to Hollywood for *Spartacus*. Vivien returned to New York for *Duet of Angels*.

It was there the news had reached her of Olivier's wish to make their separation final. They had put Notley up for sale. At the same time he was appearing in *Rhinoceros* in London with Miss Plowright.

At that time the legal ritual of divorce still required the admission of adultery. Miss Plowright's husband, actor Roger Gage, named Olivier in obtaining a decree nisi. (Olivier and Miss Plowright were absent, being on stage in New York.) The same day, 2 December 1960, Vivien was granted her divorce, naming Miss Plowright. She also admitted into evidence two instances of adultery with an unnamed person, one in Ceylon, one in London.

She left the court with actor friend Jack Merivale, her co-star in *Duet of Angels*. He would remain with Vivien to the end of her days. They drove off from the law courts, down the Strand in her pearl-grey Rolls, to the flat in Eaton Square.

But something of the old Vivien was much alive. She wanted to plan a party for a few friends in the Eaton Square flat, she told Jack Merivale. They would make it a sort of *après*-divorce party. And then go away to somewhere far. Somewhere she had not been before with anyone else. Montego Bay, Jamaica? Why not?

Notley was now sold. She had even paid it a kind of masochistic visit. The new owner had proudly shown off a bulldozer pushing up the rose gardens to make way for a swimming pool. It was all so different now – the trees Larry had loved to prune, the cloisters where they'd walked before dinner. Love scene ended.

New plans. New projects. New relationships. And old close friends now held even more closely. Bumble Dawson, Bobbie Helpmann, the Millses, the Colmans, Cukor, Doug and Mary Lee Fairbanks, Lady Metcalf, Stanley Hall, and all the flood of people who brought gaiety to her new little cottage at Tickerage Mill.

For Vivien there would be other roles: *The Roman Spring of Mrs Stone. Ship of Fools*, another Australian tour – this time with Merivale. *Tovarich, La Contessa*. Chekhov's *Ivanov*, with Merivale, was her last play.

In early July of 1967, Doug and Mary Lee Fairbanks visited her in her London flat. She had been ordered to bed. She was ill with tuberculosis, but she had not been told how serious it was. Tests were being made. The Fairbankses found her propped up, surrounded by flowers from well-wishers, reading a play script she had been rehearsing with Michael Redgrave – Edward Albee's *A Delicate Balance*. They were planning to open in August.

'She looked pale, drawn,' recalls Doug. 'But one had seen her look that way before, and seen her recover before from things like that. We found her in awfully good heart, busy trimming and cutting flowers in bed, and making fun of the doctors who were insisting she be kept in bed while their tests were completed. She was gay, interesting; talked about everything under the sun; was funny as well as serious. She wasn't supposed to smoke, but she did. She wasn't supposed to drink, but she did.'

Jack Merivale, a gentle, sensitive soul, remained her loyal companion. She had told him once, 'Oh, why couldn't I have something clean and decent, like cancer?' For she never could remember what had occurred during a manic period. The first thing she'd say when she came out of it was 'Is there anyone I should apologise to?'

'Imagine the courage of that creature! She faced that all the time, and still kept up with everything. As far as the public knew, marvellous, glamorous, exciting, fulfilled,' Jack recalls. 'I wasn't busy being a genius, and I went into it with my eyes pretty well open. But the thing was, she was irresistible!

'In a "high" she could be vile, really hit where it hurt. You wouldn't recognise her and she would say the cruellest things she could find to say. And would find them, too! Her targets were those closest to her, as though she wanted them out of her way.'

After the Australian tour with Jack, they had stayed together at Tickerage Mill where Vivien went through a bad manic period. 'Difficult, but not impossible, so that one couldn't force ECT [shock treatment] on her. She was sitting over by the fire. I was sitting in a chair beside her,' Jack recalls. 'Gertrude was there, too. Suddenly I looked across, and I don't know how to explain this, but she had rejoined us. She hadn't really been with us for all these weeks going on months, and suddenly this little face cleared, and I looked at her and said, "Hello!" And he said, "Hello", and it happened just like that and she was all right. To me, a miracle had happened, and happened as I was looking at her. Her mother didn't notice.

' "By heaven!" I said, "I'm going to church on Sunday!"

' "What?" Gertrude asked – because I never went to church, and she always did.

' "Because a miracle just happened," I said.'

Ten days before she died, Vivien had been feeling well enough to accept an invitation from Trader Faulkner to come to dinner. Trader had just been married.

'To meet your new wife? Of course!' she had said on the telephone. 'May I bring my man?' She gave Trader no hint that she was ill.

259

She arrived with Jack in a little Mini-Minor, wearing 'a rather pathetic red and black checked coat' – the same one she had worn to court seven years earlier. Trader's bride served artichokes stuffed with minced meat. 'It was undercooked and dreadful, but Vivien ate every bite,' Trader recalls. 'She got it down somehow, and, gracious to the end, told my wife, "What a beautiful dinner!" I didn't realise she'd pulled herself out of a sickbed to come! Or what a friend I had until quite a while after she died. I was too immature.'

On Friday night, 7 July, Jack came back from Guildford, where he'd been playing in the theatre. It was about 11 p.m. 'She was alseep with her pussycat on the pillow beside her, so I went into the kitchen and made myself something to eat. It couldn't have been more than fifteen minutes; I went back into the bedroom and she was lying on the floor, between her bed and the bathroom. She was warm and not breathing. I tried "mouth-to-mouth" but it wasn't any good. So I lifted her back on the bed and rang the doctor. I also rang Bumble Dawson and several close friends. I said, "I think she's dead". Bumble came, stayed the night, slept on the sofa.'

Olivier had been in the hospital when Jack reached him. He got himself discharged immediately and came and stayed all day with Jack.

'There wasn't anything that was going to save her, so it was really much better that she should make a nice exit,' Jack said.

'The thing that really caused the fun with her was her enormous zest for living. She had the most exquisite taste and the quickest eye that I've ever seen. She could be driving herself at ninety miles an hour – she used to drive that Rolls of hers very fast indeed -- and she would miss not a thing that was going on. She would say, "Did you see that marvellous doorway?" and I would have seen nothing at all. Her eyes took in fifty times what mine did. Victor Steele told a story of when he was driving back from Notley with her and Larry. Vivien saw a tree she didn't recognise on a hill, and shouted suddenly: "Larry, turn left!" They turned up sidetracks and got near enough. She got out of the car. She used to carry a little knife. She cut off a twig and sent it to the Royal Horticultural Society to find out what it was. Within two weeks she had one growing at Notley. She always pursued things to their end.

'She had a double-exposure picture of Larry that she had taken. She always kept it with her. And she had one of Alex Korda she'd taken on his boat, the *Elsewhere*, double-exposed with him in his garden. She said, "You can say what you like about bad photography and double exposures, but this is Alex in two places I know he loved to be, and I like it.'

In a sense Vivien was always in two places. Bumble once asked her what it felt like to be in one of her highs. She said that life was absolutely racing past and that you had to move as fast as you could to catch up with it. Vivien was more than a star, she was a comet. And, like a comet, she burned herself out.

For Olivier life would bring a marriage of domestic tranquillity, more children, and a career that changed with the times. No man could ask greater fulfilment than what lay ahead. Honours, work, happiness. Lord Olivier, the greatest actor of our century, would go on creating magic for his audiences.

Selected bibliography

Arnold, Elliott. 'Life and Laurence Olivier.' *New York World-Telegram*, 17 June 1939.

Barker, Felix. *The Oliviers*. London: Hamish Hamilton, 1953. Philadelphia: Lippincott, 1953.

Behlmer, Rudy, ed. *Memo from David O. Selznick*. London: Macmillan London, 1972. New York: Viking Press, 1972.

Bester, Alfred. 'Sir Larry.' *Holiday*, February 1960.

Burton, Hal, ed. *Great Acting*. London: BBC, 1967. New York: Hill & Wang, 1968

Busch, Noel F. 'Laurence and Vivien.' *Life*, May 1940.

Camp, Dan. 'He Won't Be Licked.' *Motion Picture*, January 1941.

Castle, Charles, *Noel*. London: W. H. Allen, 1972. New York: Doubleday, 1973.

Cocroft, Thoda. *Great Names and How They Are Made*. London, Chicago: Dartnell Press, 1943.

Colman, Juliet Benita. *Ronald Colman: A Very Private Person*. London: W. H. Allen, 1975. New York: Morrow 1975.

Connell, Brian. *Knight Errant: A Biography of Douglas Fairbanks, Jr*. London: Hodder & Stoughton, 1955. New York: Doubleday, 1955.

Conrad, Earl. *Billy Rose: Manhattan Primitive*. New York: World Publishing, 1968.

Cottrell, John. *Laurence Olivier*. London: Weidenfeld & Nicolson, 1975.

Creighton, Kyle. 'Hollywood Doesn't Count.' *Collier's*, 10 June 1939.

Darlington, W. A. *Laurence Olivier*. London: Morgan Grampian Books, 1968. Cranbury, N. J.: Barnes, 1969.

Dean, Basil. *Basil Dean. Seven Ages*. London: Hutchinson, 1970.

Dent, Alan. *Vivien Leigh: A Bouquet*. London: Hamish Hamilton, 1969. New York: International Publications, 1971.

Dietz, Howard. 'Gone With the Wind.' *Variety*, 1 August 1939.

Easton, Carol. *The Search for Sam Goldwyn*. New York: Morrow, 1976.

Edwards, Anne. *Vivine Leigh: A Biography*. London: W. H. Allen, 1977. New York: Simon & Schuster, 1977.

Fairbanks, Douglas Jr., and Schickel, Richard. *The Fairbanks Album*. London: Secker & Warburg, 1975. Boston: New York Graphic Society, 1976.

Fairweather, Virginia. *Cry God for Larry: An Intimate Memoir of Sir Laurence Olivier*. London: Calder & Boyars, 1969. Published in the USA as *Olivier: An Informal Portrait*. New York: Coward-McCann, 1969.

Flamini, Roland. *Scarlett, Rhett, and a Cast of Thousands*. New York: Macmillan, 1975. London: André Deutsch, 1976.

Furse, Roger. Unpublished notes to David Fairweather.

Gardner, Margaret. 'Sir Larry – Hush-Hush Hamlet.' *Screen Guide*, April 1948.

Gourlay, Logan, ed. *Olivier*. London: Weidenfeld & Nicolson, 1973. New York: Stein & Day, 1974.

Guiles, Fred Lawrence. *Norma Jean: The Life of Marilyn Monroe*. London: W. H. Allen, 1969. New York: McGraw-Hill, 1969.

Guthrie, Tyrone. *A Life in the Theatre*. New York: McGraw-Hill, 1959. London: Hamish Hamilton, 1960, 1972.

Halliwell, Leslie. *The Filmgoer's Companion* (3rd rev. ed.). New York: Hill & Wang, 1970. London: Granada Publishing, 1972.

Harris, Radie. *Radie's World: The Memoirs of Radie Harris.* London: W. H. Allen, 1975. New York: Putnam's, 1975.

Harris, Radie. 'Star-Crossed Lovers.' *Photoplay*, October 1940.

Harris, Warren G. *Gable and Lombard.* New York: Simon & Schuster, 1974. London: Cassell, 1976.

Kanin, Garson. *Hollywood.* New York: Viking Press, 1974.

Kanin, Garson. *Tracy and Hepburn.* London: Angus & Robertson, 1971. New York: Viking Press, 1971.

Kulik, Karol. *Alexander Korda: The Man Who Could Work Miracles.* London: W. H. Allen, 1975. New Rochelle, N.Y.: Arlington House, 1976.

Lambert, Gavin. *G.W.T.W.: The Making of Gone With the Wind.* Boston. Atlantic, Little, Brown, 1973.

Lanchester, Elsa. *Charles Laughton and I.* London: Faber & Faber, 1938. New York: Harcourt, Brace, 1938.

Lasky, Jesse L. *I Blow My Own Horn.* New York: Doubleday, 1957.

Leigh, Vivien. 'Larry and I.' *Sunday Dispatch*, 2 March, 1958.

Le Roy, Mervyn. *Mervyn Le Roy: Take One.* London: W. H. Allen, 1974. New York: Hawthorn Books, 1974.

Lewin, David. 'Vivien Tells.' *Daily Express*, 16 August, 1960.

Niven, David. *Bring on the Empty Horses.* London: Hamish Hamilton, 1975. New York: Putnam's, 1975.

Niven, David. *The Moon's a Balloon.* London: Hamish Hamilton, 1971. New York: Putnam's, 1972.

Parsons, Louella. *New York Journal – American*, 15 September 1938.

Robyns, Gwen. *Light of a Star: The Career of Vivien Leigh*. London: Leslie Frewin, 1968. Cranbury, N.J.: Barnes, 1970.

Tabori, Paul. *Alexander Korda*. London: Oldbourne, 1959. New York: Heinman, 1959.

Thomas, Bob. *Selznick*. New York: Simon & Schuster, 1969. London: W. H. Allen, 1971.

Trewin, J. C. *Robert Donat*. London: Heinemann, 1968.

Turner, K. H. 'Wind Rides Atlanta.' *Motion Picture Herald*, 16 December 1939.

Whitehall, Richard. 'Personality of the Month: Peter Finch.' *Motion Picture Almanac*, September 1960.

Wilcox, Grace. 'Sunny Looks at Scarlett.' *Screen & Radio Weekly*, 22 February, 1940.

Zierold, Norman. *Garbo*. New York: Stein & Day, 1969. London: W. H. Allen, 1970

Zierold, Norman. *The Hollywood Tycoons*. London: Hamish Hamilton, 1969. Published in the USA as *The Moguls*. New York: Coward-McCann, 1969.

Index

BARBARA CARTLAND

Her romantic novels are loved by millions. The refreshing purity of the characters, the beautifully romantic settings, the continuing theme of unfaltering love – these are the ingredients that make Barbara Cartland's recipe for love stories so appealing. And they're all there in her enthralling masterpieces THE THIEF OF LOVE and SWEET ENCHANTRESS.

THE THIEF OF LOVE

When petite, shy Alloa Derange happens upon an intruder trying to steal a priceless family heirloom, her quiet life is put into a turmoil. Alloa knows it is her duty to expose the stranger for the thief he is, but her heart tells her something completely different . . .

ROMANCE   0 7221 2274 8   75p

SWEET ENCHANTRESS

A serene voyage aboard a yacht adrift on a balmy ocean suddenly turns into a nightmare for Zania Manford – what is the yacht's real destination? Why do all the passengers seem frightened? And who is the sinister, yet charming, Chuck Turner?

ROMANCE   0 7221 2276 4   75p

And don't miss Barbara Cartland's other romantic bestsellers
THE PRICE IS LOVE
A KISS OF SILK

TREAT YOURSELF TO A LITTLE ROMANCE

STAR SIGNS FOR LOVERS

BY ROBERT WORTH

THE PERFECT GUIDE TO FINDING THE PERFECT PARTNER!

There's nothing else quite like it! Robert Worth's STAR SIGNS FOR LOVERS is the only fast, intimate and easy-to-use guide to the Venus and Mars signs that rule love, romance and passion. In its fascinating pages you will find the vital key to successful relationships – in fact, a moment or two is all it takes to look up the month, day and year of birth of any potential partner in order for you to obtain a clear and accurate reading of their romantic potential!

If you want to meet the man or woman of your dreams – rather than just go on dreaming about them – Robert Worth's STAR SIGNS FOR LOVERS is the ultimate astrological handbook for you!

COSMOLOGY   0 7221 9243 6   £1.50

**Give them
the pleasure of choosing**

Book Tokens can be bought
and exchanged at most
bookshops.

A SELECTION OF BESTSELLERS FROM SPHERE

FICTION
RICH	Graham Masterton	£1.95	☐
SUMMER'S END	Danielle Steel	£1.25	☐
SNOW FALCON	Craig Thomas	£1.50	☐
ARENA	Norman Bogner	£1.75	☐
WIFEY	Judy Blume	£1.00	☐

FILM AND TV TIE-INS
THE EMPIRE STRIKES BACK	Donald F. Glut	£1.00	☐
HUSSY	Rosemary Kingsland	£1.00	☐
SATURN 3	Steve Gallagher	95p	☐
GOODBYE DARLING	James Mitchell	95p	☐
DAWN OF THE DEAD (filmed as ZOMBIES)	George Romero & Suzannah Sparrow	85p	☐

NON-FICTION
LOVE SCENE	Jesse Lasky and Pat Silver	£1.50	☐
TRUE BRITT	Britt Ekland	£1.25	☐
PIERCING THE REICH	Joseph Persico	£1.75	☐
THE NEW SOVIET PSYCHIC DISCOVERIES	Henry Gris & William Dick	£1.50	☐
STAR SIGNS FOR LOVERS	Robert Worth	£1.50	☐

All Sphere books are available at your local bookshop or newsagent, or can be ordered directly from the publisher. Just tick the titles you want and fill in the form below.

Name _____

Address _____

Write to Sphere Books, Cash Sales Department, P.O. Box 11, Falmouth, Cornwall TR10 9EN
Please enclose cheque or postal order to the value of the cover price plus:
UK: 30p for the first book, 15p for the second and 12p per copy for each additional book ordered to a maximum charge of £1.29
OVERSEAS: 50p for the first book and 15p for each additional book.
BFPO & EIRE: 30p for the first book, 15p for the second book plus 12p per copy for the next 7 books, thereafter 6p per book.

Sphere Books reserve the right to show new retail prices on covers which may differ from those previously advertised in the text or elsewhere, and to increase postal rates in accordance with the PO.